PERSISTENT PERMEABILITY?

The International Political Economy of New Regionalisms Series

The International Political Economy of New Regionalisms Series presents innovative analyses of a range of novel regional relations and institutions. Going beyond established, formal, interstate economic organizations, this essential series provides informed interdisciplinary and international research and debate about myriad heterogeneous intermediate level interactions.

Reflective of its cosmopolitan and creative orientation, this series is developed by an international editorial team of established and emerging scholars in both the South and North. It reinforces ongoing networks of analysts in both academia and think-tanks as well as international agencies concerned with micro-, meso- and macro-level regionalisms.

Recent Titles in the Series

Reforging the Weakest Link: Global Political
Economy and Post-Soviet Change in Russia, Ukraine and Belarus
Edited by Neil Robinson

The New Political Economy of United States-Caribbean Relations:
The Apparel Industry and the Politics of NAFTA Parity
Tony Heron

The Political Economy of Interregional Relations: ASEAN and the EU
Alfredo C. Robles, Jr.

Globalization and Antiglobalization: Dynamics of Change in the
New World Order
Edited by Henry Veltmeyer

Persistent Permeability?

Regionalism, Localism, and Globalization in the Middle East

Edited by

BASSEL F. SALLOUKH
American University of Sharjah

REX BRYNEN
McGill University

ASHGATE

Published by
Ashgate Publishing Limited
Gower House
Croft Road
Aldershot
Hants GU11 3HR
England

Ashgate Publishing Company
Suite 420
101 Cherry Street
Burlington, VT 05401-4405
USA

Ashgate website: http://www.ashgate.com

British Library Cataloguing in Publication Data
Persistent permeability? : regionalism, localism, and
    globalization in the Middle East. - (The international
    political economy of new regionalisms series)
    1. Middle East - Foreign relations
    I. Salloukh, Bassel F. II. Brynen, Rex
    327.5'6

Library of Congress Cataloging-in-Publication Data
Persistent permeability? : regionalism, localism, and globalization in the Middle East /
    [edited by] Bassel F. Salloukh [and] Rex Brynen.
        p. cm. -- (International political economy of new regionalisms series)
        Includes bibliographical references and index.
        ISBN 0-7546-3662-3
        1. Middle East--Foreign relations. 2. Regionalism--Middle East. 3. National state. 4.
    Globalization. 5. Middle East--Economic integration. I. Salloukh, Bassel F. II. Brynen,
    Rex. III. Series.

    DS63.18.P467 2004
    956.05--dc22   2004048251

ISBN 0 7546 3662 3

Printed and bound by Athenaeum Press, Ltd.,
Gateshead, Tyne & Wear.

Contents

List of Figures   *vii*
List of Tables   *viii*
Contributors   *ix*
Foreword   *xi*
Preface   *xiii*

1   Pondering Permeability: Some Introductory Explorations
     Bassel F. Salloukh and Rex Brynen   1

2   Theory and System in Understanding Middle East International
     Politics: Rereading Paul Noble's 'The Arab System:
     Pressures, Constraints, and Opportunities'
     F. Gregory Gause, III   15

3   Systemic Factors Do Matter, But...
     Reflections on the Uses and Limitations of Systemic Analysis
     Paul Noble   29

4   Between Conflict and Cooperation:
     Accommodation in the Post-Cold War Middle East
     James Devine   65

5   Regime Autonomy and Regional Foreign Policy Choices
     in the Middle East: A Theoretical Exploration
     Bassel F. Salloukh   81

6   Regional Dynamics of Refugee Flows: The Case of Iran
     Asya El-Meehy   105

7   Permeability Revisited: Reflections on the Regional
     Repercussions of the al-Aqsa *Intifada*
     Rex Brynen   125

8   Globalization of a Torn State:
     Turkey from the Middle East to European Integration
     Ersel Aydinli   149

9   American Hegemony and the Changing Terrain of
         Middle East International Politics
         Michael C. Hudson   163

Index   *181*

List of Figures

3.1   International Systems: A Framework of Analysis/Explanation   33

4.1   Framework of Analysis   78

7.1   Frequency of Following News About Palestine   128

7.2   Personal Importance of Palestine Issue   129

7.3   Internet Usage in Arab Countries   138

7.4   Are Differences Among Arabs Greater or Smaller?   140

7.5   Accounting for Differences with US Policy   143

List of Tables

3.1   Regional Intrusive System Structures: Politico-Military Sphere   37

3.2   Regional Intrusive System Structures: Economic Sphere   38

3.3   Arab World/Middle East: Satellite TV Communication Links (2001)   45

3.4   Developing World (regions): Trade Links (2000)   53

3.5   Developing World (regions): Investment Links (2000-01)   54

3.6   Developing World (regions): Travel Links (1997)   55

3.7   Developing World (regions): Cyber-communication Links (2000-01)   56

7.1   Communications Connectivity   136

Contributors

Ersel Aydinli is Assistant Professor of International Relations at Bilkent University. His research concentrates on international relations theory and the modernizing world, globalization and security, and Turkish foreign and security policies. Some of his publications have appeared in *International Studies Perspectives*, *Current History*, and *Security Dialogue*. He is currently preparing a co-edited volume with James Rosenau on globalization and security.

Rex Brynen (co-editor) is Professor of Political Science and Chair of the Middle East Studies Program at McGill University, and a director of the Interuniversity Consortium for Arab and Middle Eastern Studies (Montréal). He previously served as President of the Canadian Middle East Studies Association and the Canadian Council of Area Studies Learned Societies. Brynen is author of the books *A Very Political Economy: Peacebuilding and Foreign Aid in the West Bank and Gaza* and *Sanctuary and Survival: The PLO in Lebanon*. He is also editor or co-editor of *Echoes of the Intifada*, *The Many Faces of National Security in the Arab World*, and the two-volume series *Political Liberalization and Democratization in the Arab World*.

James Devine is a doctoral candidate and sessional lecturer at McGill University and a research fellow at the Interuniversity Consortium for Arab and Middle Eastern Studies. His research focuses on Iranian foreign policy and the dynamics of regional rapprochement.

Asya El-Meehy is a doctoral candidate at the University of Toronto, and a research fellow at the Interuniversity Consortium for Arab and Middle Eastern Studies. Her research focuses on both regional (especially Iranian) refugee policy, as well as Egyptian political economy.

F. Gregory Gause, III is Associate Professor of Political Science at the University of Vermont. He is the author of a number of articles and two books, *Oil Monarchies: Domestic and Security Challenges in the Arab Gulf States*, and *Saudi-Yemeni Relations: Domestic Structures and Foreign Influence*.

Michael C. Hudson is the Seif Ghobash Professor of Arab Studies and Professor of International Relations at Georgetown University, and a past-president of the Middle East Studies Association. Hudson has edited and contributed to numerous books, including *Middle East Dilemma: The Politics and Economics of Arab Integration*, *The Palestinians: New Directions*, and *Alternative Approaches to the Arab-Israeli Conflict*. His other works include *The Precarious Republic: Political*

Modernization in Lebanon, Arab Politics: The Search for Legitimacy, and numerous articles appearing in *Middle East Journal, Comparative Politics*, and other scholarly journals.

Bahgat Korany is Professor of Political Science at the American University in Cairo and l'Université de Montréal, and a director of the Interuniversity Consortium for Arab and Middle Eastern Studies (Montréal). His authored and edited books include *The Foreign Policies of Arab States, How Foreign Policy Decisions are Made in the Third World, Régimes Politiques Arabes, The Many Faces of National Security in the Arab World*, and the two-volume series *Political Liberalization and Democratization in the Arab World*.

Paul Noble is recently retired from the Department of Political Science at McGill University, and is a director of the Interuniversity Consortium for Arab and Middle Eastern Studies (Montréal). He is also co-editor of *The Many Faces of National Security in the Arab World*, and the two-volume series *Political Liberalization and Democratization in the Arab World*.

Bassel F. Salloukh (co-editor) is Assistant Professor of Political Science at the American University of Sharjah, and senior research fellow at the Interuniversity Consortium for Arab and Middle Eastern Studies. He is co-author of the forthcoming book *Mapping the Political Landscape*, has published a number of articles on Arab politics, and is preparing a book manuscript on state-society relations and foreign policy choices in Syria and Jordan.

Foreword

Bahgat Korany

As the editors note, this book is in large part dedicated to our colleague Paul Noble. For a long time, the analysis of Middle East international relations—as that of other parts of the Third World—was confused with comments on current affairs. When this emerging field finally attempted to integrate itself into social science analysis, it was much more akin to traditional 'area studies' approaches than to the rigorous building and testing of main concepts undertaken in international relations theorizing.

From the outset of his work on the Middle East regional system in his Ph.D. thesis at McGill University in the early 1970s, Paul Noble aimed at joining international relations theorizing and Middle East data in a happy marriage. This he accomplished elegantly. Though naturally preferring some international relations approaches over others, he did not exclude any without giving its school an extremely fair hearing. Thus when he focused on the favorite 'parts', he was aware of the overall 'whole.' Moreover, Paul Noble maintained his heroic attempt to be aware of what was taking place on the ground in the region itself, paying attention even to the minutest but—as it turned out—significant details. He was also capable of putting his solid knowledge into accessible form through frequent media appearances and interventions.

Briefly, since the early 1970s, Paul Noble managed to put the Middle East as a region—and not only a single country—at the center of Canadian academic concerns. When we started institutionalizing our collaboration in the early 1980s with the first edition of *The Foreign Policies of Arab States*,[1] there was a felt need to combine the macro/systemic approaches and the micro/actor-level ones. His chapter on the Arab regional system in both editions became indeed *more* than just one of the chapters of the book; it became a pillar of this early research project and an essential element of its success. In retrospect, this initial success in bridging different levels of analysis and approaches paved the way for a more basic bridging, one which became the distinct trade of what some scholars have labeled the 'Montréal school' of Arab studies. This major bridging is between international relations and comparative politics, an antidote of their otherwise conventional separation. Though initially wary of our slipping into 'trendy' analysis, and rightly concerned about over-stretching our limited resources, Paul Noble let himself be convinced and contributed to the success of the second bridging. I still remember vividly our lengthy discussions in the early 1990s, then joined by Rex Brynen, about the concept of national security and the necessity of emphasizing non-military and developmental domestic threats. Rather than continuing eternally the debate between the 'old' and 'new' threats, Paul Noble's argument finally convinced us to emphasize *The Many Faces of National Security in the Arab World.*[2] It was such a commitment to high academic standards, but also readiness to accept new positions, that helped our research group to increasingly integrate bright graduates, now active faculty members and scholars in their own right: the Salloukhs, the Tehamis, the Dizbonis, the Moores, the Zahars, and many others.

I remember my first meeting with Paul Noble back in the middle 1970s. I had heard about him from common friends, notably Boutros Boutros-Ghali and Ali E.H. Dessouki (a McGill graduate and now Egypt's Minister of Youth). Fresh from my graduate studies from the UK and Geneva, my image of North American scholarship was at that time dominated by the 'publish or perish' conventional wisdom. But as a new North American faculty member, I was also concerned about over-rushing research and thus sliping into a trap of 'publish *and* perish.'

All along, Paul Noble embodied a different wisdom. He published only when he felt he had something important to say. This 'something' was rethought and rewritten almost continuously until he was, literally, pressured to 'let go' and send it to print. The result is a dense text with no waste of words and where the reader is fully rewarded for his efforts. Like his personal life, Paul Noble's work is what I like to call 'ethical scholarship,' where the reader is never short-changed. Let us take this example of his differentiation of the Arab system from other regional systems, one developed long before the coming of the 'buzzwords' of globalization and civil society, or Arab CNNs like the Dubai or *al-Jazira* channels:

> .... the Arab system resembled a set of interconnected organisms separated only by porous membranes or, alternatively, a large-scale domestic system divided into compartments of varying degrees of permeability. This gave rise to a transnational political process encompassing not only governments but also groups as well as individuals across the system.[3]

No wonder this chapter was one of the most quoted on the subject.

Paul Noble retired from formal teaching, but, as his chapter in this volume demonstrates admirably, he has a publishing agenda. He will obviously continue to benefit his discipline and colleagues in showing how to synthesize international relation theory and Middle East 'facts.'

Notes

[1] Bahgat Korany and Ali E. Hillal Dessouki, eds., *The Foreign Policies of Arab States*, 2nd ed. (Boulder: Westview Press, 1991).

[2] Korany, Paul Noble, and Rex Brynen, eds., *The Many Faces of National Security in the Arab World* (London: Macmillan, 1993).

[3] Paul Noble, 'The Arab System: Pressures, Constraints and Opportunities,' in Korany and Dessouki, eds., *The Foreign Policies of Arab States*, p. 57.

Preface

This volume has its immediate origins in a workshop concerning 'The International Relations of the Middle East: Approaches and Perspectives,' organized by the Interuniversity Consortium for Arab and Middle Eastern Studies (Montréal) in June 2002. In that meeting, the changing permeability and security dynamics of the regional system emerged as a key focus of discussions. The subsequent war in Iraq highlighted the salience of these issues, and the contributions to this volume were all updated before publication to address the repercussions and reverberations of that conflict.

This volume also has another set of origins in the work and career of Paul Noble. Paul played a central role in the establishment and direction of McGill University's Middle East studies program, and also served with distinction as chair of the Department of Political Science. He was a co-founder of the Interuniversity Consortium for Arab and Middle Eastern Studies <http://www.mcgill.ca/icames>. Along with another esteemed colleague, Bahgat Korany, Paul is a cornerstone of the so-called 'Montréal school' of Middle East foreign policy and international relations theorizing, with its rich emphasis on the interrelationship between regional dynamics, external forces, and the imperatives of local politics. His work on the Arab regional system is seminal.

Many contributors to this volume have had the benefit of Paul's contributions as a teacher, and all have found their work enriched by his insight as an academic colleague. We've also been lucky to count him as a friend, and we're pleased to dedicate this book to him.

Several others deserve thanks for helping make this project possible: series editor Tim Shaw, the helpful staff at Ashgate, the contributors, and especially our research assistants Crystal Procyshen and Alan Hamson. Crystal and Alan showed skill and dedication in turning raw chapters into polished, camera-ready copy. Finally, we owe a special debt of gratitude to our wives, Alex and Hala, for their persistent support and constant encouragement.

Rex Brynen, Montréal
Bassel F. Salloukh, Beirut

Chapter 1

Pondering Permeability:
Some Introductory Explorations

Bassel F. Salloukh and Rex Brynen

For more than two decades, scholars of domestic and international politics have pondered the changing 'permeability' of Middle Eastern states to transnational political influences. Historically, several sets of factors—the legacies of the Ottoman Empire and European colonialism, patterns of state formation, the religio-cultural identity of Islam, and the ethno-linguistic connections among Arab states—all created a situation in the Middle East[1] whereby ideologies, events, and political movements reverberated across borders to an extent not seen in other parts of the developing world. Peculiar political economies—of petroleum, aid, and migrant labour—reinforced this. In the 1950s and 1960s, pan-Arabism shaped politics in much of the region. Since the 1970s, Islamist sentiment has been a powerful transnational political influence.

On the other hand, there has also been considerable consolidation of Middle Eastern states, through a varying combination of institution-building, authoritarian repression, and petroleum-fuelled neopatrimonialism. State-centric and local loyalties have become more powerful over time, partially insulating states and societies from the siren calls of regional politics.

Finally, new factors have increasingly complicated this picture. Civil society and popular calls for more representative politics have made themselves heard in many authoritarian Middle Eastern regimes. Economic crises and structural adjustment have rendered old economic bargains obsolete, and created pressures for economic and political reorientation. New information and communication technologies—the internet, and especially direct broadcast satellite television—have created new regional fora for relatively uncensored information, civil society networking, and coalition building. The pressures of globalization, here as elsewhere in the developing world, have become acute. And the region finds itself profoundly affected by complex conflicts with local, regional, and global dimensions: the continuing Arab-Israeli conflict, the post-11 September 2001 so-called 'war on terrorism,' and the US-led military interventions in Afghanistan and Iraq.

Such questions of local and regional identity, regime and regional security dynamics, globalization, and the changing character of the regional system lie at the heart of this book. Despite differences in approach and subject matter, every chapter addresses an essential set of questions: how can we best understand the regional system? How have its dynamics altered? What are the (local, regional, global) forces for change?

Defining the Region

What is the Middle East? The first two chapters in this volume, by Paul Noble and Gregory Gause, together offer a theoretical dialogue on how best scholars might conceptualize the boundaries and properties of the regional system. In an earlier formulation, Noble charted a distinct course from contemporaries who were drawing attention to the existence of a 'penetrated' Middle Eastern 'subordinate' system with peculiar indigenous characteristics and a distinctive approach to international politics.[2] Instead, he opted for a narrower conceptualisation, and focused on the Arab state system per se. He argued that since its inception the Arab system has been characterised by a number of special features giving 'rise to relations between Arab states which were qualitatively different from those in other regional systems.'[3] Moreover, the presence of a high degree of cultural, linguistic, and religious homogeneity, and the intensity of the myriad material, societal, and political links among the member states engendered a situation where 'the political systems of Arab states have been closely interconnected and permeable.'[4]

Gause's chapter in this volume is a critical appreciation of Noble's original framework. He raises problems with Noble's definition of membership in the regional system, and offers his Middle East regional system as an alternative to Noble's Arab state system to explain high levels of regional conflict. Gause's causality is parsimonious. He explains regional conflict in terms of two independent variables, namely challenges to Westphalian sovereignty, and regional multipolarity. Moreover, Gause suggests that any attempt to understand systemic approaches to Middle East international politics must include an appreciation of two dynamics: the relationship between the regional system and the global system, and the impact of regional economic interdependence on regional political outcomes.

Noble's contribution in this volume accepts many of the comments made in Gause's chapter. He advances a multidimensional, multilevel systemic framework of analysis, one that includes the dominant major power system, the regional system, and sub-regional systems. He makes a strong case for the ability of system-level variables to explain both systemic outcomes as well as patterns of foreign policy choices at the unit level. However the latter entails the use of positional characteristics as intervening variables. The chapter best captures the extent to which the regional system has changed in the past decade. Unlike the earlier formulation in 'The Arab System: Opportunities, Constraints, and Pressures,' the significant regional system today is Middle Eastern, composed of Egypt, the Arab states of southwest Asia, plus Israel, Iran, and Turkey. This is not without cause, however. Both the range and scope of the involvement of these perimeter powers in the region has grown substantially since the late 1970s, in the process transforming its security dynamics. Nor is the Middle East system monolithic. Rather, it is composed of overlapping and interrelated sub-regional systems, such as the Arab-Israeli, the inter-Arab, and the Gulf sub-regional systems. Nevertheless, it is the region-wide interactions, rather than the sub-regional ones, that increasingly set the tone of regional security. The result is what Noble labels a 'growing regionalization of interaction' among the member states of the Middle East regional system, amounting to a 'genuine region-wide security complex' characterized by increasing military, politico-diplomatic, and transnational political linkages.

Think Locally, Act Globally? The Domestic Politics of Regional Foreign Policy

As is evident in the arguments of both Noble and Gause, there is and has long been a fundamental connection between domestic politics and regional foreign policies in the Middle East. The chapters by James Devine, Asya El-Meehy, and Bassel F. Salloukh cast more light on these connections.

James Devine, examining the ups and downs of Saudi-Iranian accommodation, highlights the complex array of domestic, regional, and global factors that shape relations between the two countries. His analysis points to the extent to which these various elements are both dynamic, in need of constant balancing, and how they sometimes result in major policy contradictions. In the end, he suggests, these contradictions (and indeed, Iranian foreign policy more generally) can best be understood from the perspective of domestic regime security.

Taking a very different case study and approach, El-Meehy's findings, concerning the determinants of Iranian refugee policy, also speak to the domestic/regional connection. They are an example of the non-military and transnational 'insecurity dilemmas' facing many states in the Middle East.[5] Explanations of Iranian asylum policy, El-Meehy's study suggests, are only partly explained by reference to global refugee norms and regimes or regional security challenges. Certainly, she notes, there were elements of both security concern and domestic political and economic grievance associated with the influx of Afghan and Azeri refugees. However, the different treatment of these groups (and changes in Iranian refugee policy over time) are also strongly affected by changes in state capacities, the nature of those capacities, and the bureaucratic-institutional context within which they are exercised.

Salloukh reviews a range of theoretical approaches to state behaviour—idiosyncratic-perceptual, realist/neorealist, domestic politics, and constructivism—and finds them all lacking in some important respects. What Middle East international relations theorizing requires, he argues, is greater attention to regime autonomy, and the political, social, and institutional configurations of state-society relations. In cases (such as Syria) where effective state corporatism results in strong regime autonomy, foreign policy and alignment choices most closely adhere to realist predictions. By contrast, regimes with different internal configurations and lesser autonomy from societal interests (such as Jordan) find themselves more driven to use foreign policy for domestic political purposes, such as securing aid, legitimizing regimes, neutralizing opposition, or seeking external allies against domestic threats. In this latter case, regime security calculations play a cardinal role in foreign policy decision-making, a theme also explored by Rex Brynen in his chapter.

Permeability: Thinking about Regional Transnationalism

As El-Meehy notes, her focus on refugee flows addresses one aspect of the permeability of state borders in the region that has received relatively little attention. Much more attention has been devoted to political transnationalism, and the regional flow of ideas and political movements.

This permeability, best exemplified by the spill-over effects of transnational appeals (such as pan-Islamic and pan-Arab ideologies) across state borders, has been a persistent characteristic of the Arab state system since its inception in the early twentieth century.[6] In this respect, the question of Palestine has been the Arabs' uncontested transnational *cause célèbre*. It managed to unite Arab societies across geographical borders, but at the same time divided post-independence *anciens* regimes from their increasingly mobilized and politicized constituencies. The shift from civilian to military regimes in many Arab states was but one consequence of this permeability; another was the 'Arab Cold War,' a contest between purportedly secular-revolutionary and conservative regimes, anchored in domestic exigencies and the quest for regional hegemony, but camouflaged by ideology.[7] This permeability dominated the Arab state system from the middle 1950s to 1967, an era which also witnessed 'the climax of Arabism.'[8] Its undisputed hero was Jamal 'Abdel Nasser, who embodied the idea of a socialist (read social equality), secular, and neutralist Arab nationalism, and resistance to decades of colonial domination. The permeability of the Arab state system allowed Nasser to slip through politically-porous borders and manipulate the domestic politics of other Arab states to advance Cairo's regional agenda. In this respect, as Albert Hourani has noted, 'the main function of Arabism was as a weapon in conflicts between Arab states and a pretext for the interference of one state in the affairs of others.'[9]

The 1967 *naksa* (setback), the death of Nasser in September 1970, and Egypt's decision to chart a unilateral course in its negotiations with Israel opened the way for the subregional fragmentation of the Arab state system and 'the return of geography' to Arab politics.[10] This trend continued through the 1970s and 1980s, punctured by a number of intra-Arab disputes that hardened the logic of state, rather than pan-Arab, interests.[11] In tandem, the process of state formation led to greater consolidation of the territorial state, a deepening of the sense of national sovereignty, and a concomitant decline in regional transnational permeability.[12]

The Iraqi invasion of Kuwait in August 1990 (and its system-wide reverberations) bore proof both of the ongoing permeability of the Arab state system, of the consolidation of this system and the concomitant ability of most regimes to dampen, contain, or control the domestic repercussions of transnationalism.[13]

Yet as Brynen argues in his chapter, the long-term decline of the permeability of Arab politics to transnational political influences has now halted. The question of Palestine remains *the* Arab cause *par excellence*, but is being currently used to highlight a set of domestic grievances shared across the Arab states, including those of the Gulf, hitherto considered immune from political pressures. These grievances are rooted in the political constraints imposed by authoritarian regimes, declining rentier revenues, and consequent demands for greater accountability and participation in public policy by a range of secular and religious groups. He suggests that new information and communication technologies have become central to the maintenance of regional permeability. Arabic satellite channels beamed the terrorist attacks of 11 September 2001, the US war against Afghanistan, Usama bin Ladin's declarations, the US invasion of Iraq, and Saddam's speeches into every nook and cranny of the Arab world. These new vehicles of permeability have created added headaches for Arab regimes trying to manage a host of domestic and external challenges. Their response has often been in the form of foreign policy choices fine-tuned to shield them from their angry publics: hence the loud support voiced by Arab regimes for the Palestinians, and the announcement on 29 April 2003 that US military forces will be withdrawing from Saudi Arabia.[14]

Brynen also argues that the Arab state system is less permeable today than it was in the 1950s and 1960s, but remains more susceptible to transnational currents than other regional systems. We may also add that the fodder for this permeability is also changing. In addition to Palestine, Iraq has emerged as another rallying cry for angry Arab publics. The US invasion and subsequent occupation of Iraq reverberated throughout the Arab world, and is bound to fuel systemic permeability for some time to come. Moreover, the terrorist attacks of 11 September 2001, and the consequent reactions to the US war on terrorism, suggest that whereas in the 1950s and 1960s systemic permeability was predominantly channelled through secular Arab nationalism, today both the discourse and networks of permeability are mainly religious. This amounts to a duel threat to existing regimes. On the one hand, it forces them to clamp down against those constituencies, such as militant clerics and their supporters, who may have been tolerated or encouraged by regime policies, and were once deployed as part of its legitimation strategy. The Saudi clampdown against local terrorist groups, even in sensitive Mecca and Medina, the firing of seven hundred Imams from their Mosques, the banning of some one thousand five hundred others from delivering prayer sermons, and Crown Prince Abdullah's 14 August 2003 declaration that Saudis are now fighting 'their decisive battle' against terrorism, suggest a belated regime realization of the depth of the danger posed by this new form of militant permeability.[15] On the other hand, the new transnational religious networks are mobile, heterogeneous, border-blind, and consequently lethal. Al-Qa'ida is a perfect example of this new form of organizational permeability: its discourse is readily permeable, its cells are globalized, and its permutations are localized, whether in the form of 'Usbat al-Ansar (Lebanon), Harakat Ansar al-Islam (Iraqi Kurdistan), al-Jama'a al-Islamiyya (Indonesia), Abu Sayyaf (Philippines), or other local groups. Protracted conflicts with transnational reverberations, whether in Palestine, Kashmir, or Afghanistan, served to mobilize and inspire these groups, and provided them the sanctuary of organizational autonomy.[16] In contrast, then, to the regionalized permeability from above of past decades, the new permeability is from below, but also globalized. Such is the contrast between the permeability of a Nasser and a bin Ladin.

Gauging Globalization

The impact of the international system on the regional dynamics of the Middle East is addressed by many of the contributors to this volume. Noble, for example, highlights a broad range of global systemic factors, and most notably the emergence of a quasi-unipolar distribution of global political-military power in the post-Cold War era, coupled with a more complex pattern of global economic power relations, including intensified globalization. Devine notes the extent to which the post-Cold War primacy of the United States in the region has shaped bilateral relations between Saudi Arabia and Iran. Brynen explores the connectedness of the Middle East to the broader information revolution, and also links attitudes in the region to the regional foreign policies of the United States.

 While the geostrategic effects of power distribution and alliance behaviour are addressed readily by realist and neorealist approaches to international relations theorizing, 'globalization' is a more difficult process to capture and explain. Part of the reason is a certain ambiguity in the term itself: does it refer to growing economic interconnectedness (through trade, capital mobility, and direct foreign investment), greater political-cultural interconnectedness (through communications, migration, and cultural exports), or the global flow of ideas and norms? All three are often seen as part of the picture, although each has rather different dynamics, complex and even contradictory linkages to each other, and political effects.

 Herein, the fullest examination of the impact of globalization is offered by Ersel Aydinli. Aydinli focuses on Turkey, and in particular pressures for political reform and greater economic/political cooperation with Europe (largely through the goal of eventual membership in the European Union). In Turkey, he notes, politics has often assumed the form of a pendulum: on one side, the pull of democratization; on the other a security discourse that emphasizes internal and external threats and the consequent need to maintain order. Moreover, there is a second significant dimension to all this: while globalization pulls Turkey toward Europe and the West, its history and geography also leave it firmly anchored in the

Middle East. As US-Turkish tensions over the war in Iraq showed, these contending pressures can pose a severe challenge to Turkish policymakers.

Another impact of globalization on regional security dynamics has been felt in the explosion of anti-American sentiments, and in terrorist attacks against US regional allies and interests. As Brynen reminds us in his chapter, these sentiments and attacks are a reaction to US regional policies. They are also angry responses to the projection of American economic, military, social, and political power by dispossessed peoples who have not experienced the political, social, and economic benefits of globalization.[17] The US 'war on terrorism' is bound to harden these sentiments in the future, particularly as Washington downgrades its concern for human rights in pursuit of victory in its global war.[18] Washington's defence against these pressures has so far materialized in the form of calls for educational and social reforms across the region, as well as improvement in governance standards through the support of civil society organizations.[19] It has also sought to increase the region's economic interconnectedness with the global economy, namely through a free trade Middle Eastern zone linking the regional economy with that of the US.[20] While the former initiative may propel regimes to crack down against radical clerics and their supporters, and the latter may encourage private investment in local economies, neither holds much promise for movement toward the kind of 'democratic gradualism' that the region needs.[21] After all, only the emergence of genuinely strong, representative, and participatory institutions can alleviate the socio-economic and political conditions that fostered the emergence of terrorist groups in the first place.

After Iraq

'We are currently living through a crisis phase and should look earnestly and sincerely at the working of the Arab system in the future,' laments 'Amr Mousa, Secretary General of the League of Arab States, on the failure of the Arab state system to cope with its systemic crises.[22] Indeed, the Iraq War has produced a plethora of voices bemoaning the demise of the Arab state system, and calling for a new system, one more responsive to the political, economic, and cultural challenges facing the region and its peoples.[23]

The abject failure of the Arab state system to manage its own crises in the past decade or so best illustrates the need to refocus attention on the Middle East regional system. The 1990-91 Gulf War, the Madrid Peace Process, and the Oslo Accords exposed deep fissures between the Arab states. The US intervention in Iraq serves as another reminder of the paralysis of the Arab state system and its institutions. Arab summit meetings have degenerated into arenas for mutual, and sometimes public, recrimination among Arab head of states, as the real-time squabble during the 1 March 2003 Arab summit between Saudi Crown Prince Abdullah and Mu'ammar al-Qadafi demonstrated.[24] Indeed, the Sharm el-Shaykh summit failed to even elicit an Arab veto on any kind of support for the impending US war against Iraq. Rather, the summit's final communiqué declared that the

Arab states refused to 'participate... in any military action that targets the security, safety and unity of Iraq's territory and [that] of any Arab state.'[25] The summit had thus diplomatically deferred the decision on supporting the invasion—logistically or otherwise—to the respective member states.

The US invasion also exposed the futility of the League of Arab States as an institution capable of mobilizing collective Arab action. Both the League and its Secretary-General came under sharp criticism on the morrow of the invasion. Some voices went so far as to call for the disbandment of the League, while others demanded a belated reform of the League and its voting procedures, particularly toward dropping from the League's Charter the unanimity condition on decision-taking vis-à-vis crucial topics.[26] Still others are suspicious of current calls to reform the League, viewing them as nothing less than a camouflaged attempt to remake what in essence is an Arab institution into a Middle East regional institution, one that will come to include non-Arab states, namely Israel, and that could set the pace for a new type of collective regional effort while serving the interests of its international patron, the US.[27] If anything, this dissonance suggests the lack of a clear view among Arab states as to what truly constitutes collective Arab national interests, a concept that the US invasion of Iraq has perhaps torpedoed for a very long time to come.

The transformation of the regional system can be viewed from other angles as well. Ever since it re-entered the Arab order in the late 1980s, Egypt has used either its own political weight, or its alliance with Syria and Saudi Arabia, to provide a semblance of leadership to the Arab system. This leadership role was manifested in Egypt's participation in the US-led coalition during the 1990-91 Gulf War, its support of the Madrid peace process launched after that war, its ability to defuse the Syrian-Turkish crisis of the summer of 1998, and its continued use of its 'good offices' to break the deadlock between Israel and the Palestinian political leaderships. However Egypt's erratic behaviour in the period leading up to the US invasion of Iraq exposed Cairo's inability to provide this leadership role anymore. Rather, Egypt was sandwiched between two competing Arab poles: a Kuwaiti-led, pro-American pole, and a Syrian-led, pro-Iraqi (people) pole.[28] Consequently, Cairo was left searching for a new regional role, and apprehensive lest a rejuvenated pro-American Iraq divest it of the regional role it once played.[29] Nor were Cairo's troubles all regional. Husni Mubarak's speech on the eve of the war, in which he refused to denounce the American position but rather blamed Iraq for the escalation of the crisis, exposed the wide rift separating the Egyptian regime from most Egyptians, a rift reproduced in many Arab capitals.[30]

The US invasion of Iraq also underscored the intimate role played by the perimeter powers in the affairs of the Arab core, and the connection between the local, the regional, and the global in the Middle East state system. Turkey's behaviour during the crisis and the subsequent war best reflects these dynamics. Ankara was promised substantial sums of US aid in exchange for granting US forces access to northern Iraq through Turkish territories, and its interests in Iraqi Kurdistan and the Kirkuk oil fields are long-standing. However the Islamist government of Recep Tayyip Erdogan deferred to a Parliamentary vote that rejected the use of Turkish territories by American forces, and refused to ask Parliament for a new vote despite American pressures. Ankara's position was shaped by a number of overlapping local, regional, and global pressures: the Turkish public, but especially its powerful Islamist component, was strongly opposed to the war against Iraq. Furthermore, avoiding an open identification with the US invasion brought Ankara closer to the EU position on the war, and hopefully one step closer to its long-desired membership in this union. But Ankara's international obligations to the US could not be ignored, and subsequently the government decided to open NATO's bases in the country to US forces. In return, Ankara received American assurances against accepting the emergence of an independent Kurdistan in northern Iraq, and against the permanent deployment of Kurdish forces in oil-rich Kirkuk. In the final analysis, Turkey emerged from the war at least with the minimum of its regional and international interests intact.[31] Given America's growing worries in occupied Iraq and Washington's desire for a Turkish helping hand, an Iraq under US control is bound to increase Turkey's involvement in regional security.

Turkey's modest gains in Iraq contrast starkly with Syria and Iran's losses. Immediately after the fall of Baghdad on 9 April 2003, both countries found themselves in the eye of the American storm. They were accused of smuggling weapons to Iraq, harbouring terrorists, supporting Hizbullah, developing unconventional weapons, and providing sanctuary to former members of the Iraqi leadership and to Iraqi scientists.[32] Syria's response has been both diplomatic and practical. It refused to recognize the US-installed Iraqi Governing Council, pledged to help the United Nations end the occupation of Iraq,[33] but at the same time assisted Lebanese Army units in a surgical operation in the Beqa' against an international network of drug dealers and money launderers, signalling to Washington its determination to fight organized crime and terrorist networks.[34] That Syria used a local operation to send an international message suggests the extent to which the local, regional, and global have overlapped in the Middle East. Syria's recent opening towards Turkey, consecrated in the first trip of a Syrian prime minister to Ankara in the past seventeen years, also underscores the increasingly transnational politics of the region. Despite their disagreements on water rights and Ankara's military cooperation with Israel, Syria and Turkey converge on the need to thwart the emergence of an independent Kurdistan in northern Iraq, an objective also shared by Iran.[35]

The US invasion of Iraq left Iran in a difficult bind. While the fall of Saddam's regime neutralized a long-standing threat to Tehran, neither the current power vacuum nor a strong Iraqi regime in the future, allied to the US, are preferences on Iran's menu of security choices. Indeed, the American occupation of Iraq has left Iran encircled on all sides. Washington has also escalated its language regarding Tehran's nuclear project, accusing it of preparing to produce fissile materials for nuclear weapons.[36] Iranian support for some Shi'a groups in Iraq is one bargaining asset in Tehran's hand; its support of Hizbullah and Islamic Jihad is another. Moreover, Tehran is detaining a number of high-ranking al-Qa'ida operatives, including Sa'd bin Ladin, Usama's son, and Sulayman Abu

Ghayth whom Washington wants transferred and tried in the US. In exchange, Tehran wants the US to hand over the senior leadership of Mojahedin-e Khalq.[37] All of these assets will prove essential and negotiable as Tehran tries to escape the American jugular and protect its regional security interests, especially in the Gulf sub-regional system.

Of the three non-Arab powers, Israel has emerged with the strongest regional position after the Iraq War. Nevertheless, the dynamics of the Palestinian-Israeli conflict remain relatively unaffected by developments in the Gulf, despite the pre-war predictions of some in Washington. A vicious circle of violence has become firmly entrenched, in which attack begets attack. The violence ill-disposes the Israeli public to make any political concessions to the Palestinians, while Israeli Prime Minister Ariel Sharon favours continued settlement activity and permanent Israeli control of much of the West Bank—policies that are clearly antithetical to peaceful resolution of the conflict. On the Palestinian side, the experience of occupation, economic crisis, and a hard-line Israeli government undercuts support for negotiations and strengthens militants. Support for Palestinian reform, internal and external, is bedevilled by power struggles within the Palestinian movement. While the war in Iraq may have (belatedly) increased US engagement in Arab-Israeli peace-making, the unravelling of the 'roadmap to peace' by the (US-EU-UN-Russian) 'Quartet' showed how ineffective this engagement was.

Looking Ahead

What does the future hold for the region? In the concluding chapter in this volume, Michael C. Hudson highlights and summarizes the many changes and forces for change at work in the region. In doing so, he emphasizes changing communal identities amid globalization, and new information and communication technologies in the cultural domain; liberal economic globalization and dependency in the economic domain; the proliferation of non-state actors in the structural domain; and the challenges of terrorism in the power domain. He also points to the key role of American policy. A new American assertiveness has had powerful if uncertain effects on the region, as the war in Iraq has shown. The importance of US policy as a variable in regional and domestic politics in the Middle East, in turn, points to the need to understand the domestic political, ideological, strategic, and other factors that shape American foreign policy. 'Middle East international relations in the twenty-first century will not be adequately explained by paradigmatic chauvinism,' Hudson stresses, 'rather, disciplinary eclecticism offers a more promising path.'

Of course, given such dynamism, prediction seems difficult—and even perilous—at the present juncture. Nevertheless, the contributions to this volume collectively suggest a variety of mounting contradictions: authoritarian states and inefficient economies confronted by the forces of globalization and by the exigencies of domestic reforms; foreign policies driven by both *realpolitik* and the complex dynamics of domestic politics; a consolidated state system set against a regional permeability now sustained by rapidly evolving information and communications technologies; American unipolarity set against its local (sometimes militant, and often Islamist) opponents; and, finally, a contemporary American neoconservative democratic discourse at odds with Washington's political legacy in the region.

We do not believe that either the removal of Saddam Hussein or the magic of free trade and economic liberalization will transform the Middle East in the manner that some (especially in Washington) have hoped. In fact, the linkages will prove complex and even contradictory: a smooth transition to something resembling democracy in Baghdad would strengthen regional calls for reform, but the (far more likely) result of a messy partial transition, schisms, factionalism, instability, occupation, and violence may well strengthen non-democratic forces hostile to a globalizing world. Radical Islamists, capitalizing on the wave of anti-Americanism sweeping through the region, may benefit in the short run; their liberal counterparts, now on the defensive, have the harder battle to fight, but the more decisive one in the long run. Women may pay a particularly heavy price as their rights are further restricted by the ascendant power of religious social conservatism. Market reforms may pluralize domestic economic power to a degree, but at the cost of marginalizing some social groups (and hence creating fertile grounds for a backlash).

But even if regime change in Iraq and economic liberalization are not magic bullets, we also believe that there is no going back: the forces for change in the region can no longer be contained. To be sure, however, these forces will express themselves in variable ways, and with varying consequences. As a result, some countries will adapt (Turkey seems the prime candidate in this regard); others will reform, but selectively, hesitantly, sporadically, and with the goal of preserving the essentials of the current system (most of the authoritarian regimes of the Arab world); and in some, the forces of conservatism and change will confront each other with uncertain but historic consequence (Iran). How these dynamics will unfold—and at what price for the stability of regimes and the region—are the major questions shaping the domestic, regional, and international politics of the Middle East in the near future.

Notes

[1] As will be seen in this volume, there is considerable debate as to the contours and dynamics of the regional system. In general, however, this volume defines the Middle East as comprising Egypt and the eastern Arab world, Israel, Turkey, and Iran—with North Africa sometimes also included.

[2] See L. Carl Brown, *International Politics and the Middle East: Old Rules, Dangerous Games* (Princeton: Princeton University Press, 1984), pp. 5-6 and 18; and Leonard Binder, 'The Middle East as a Subordinate International System,' *World Politics* vol. 10, no. 3 (April 1958), pp. 408-429.

[3] Paul C. Noble, 'The Arab System: Opportunities, Constraints, and Pressures,' in Bahgat Korany and Ali E. Hillal Dessouki, eds., *The Foreign Policies of Arab States: The Challenge of Change*, 2nd ed. (Boulder: Westview Press, 1991), p. 55.

[4] Noble, 'The Arab System,' p. 57.

[5] See Brian L. Job, ed., *The Insecurity Dilemma* (Boulder: Lynne Rienner Publishers, 1992).

[6] See Rex Brynen, 'Palestine and the Arab State System: Permeability, State Consolidation and the *Intifada*,' *Canadian Journal of Political Science* vol. 24, no. 3 (September 1991), pp. 595-621; Michael Barnett, 'Institutions, Roles, and Disorder: The Case of the Arab States System,' *International Studies Quarterly* vol. 37, no. 3 (September 1993), pp. 279 and 283; Barnett, 'Regional Security after the Gulf War,' *Political Science Quarterly* vol. 111, no. 4 (Winter 1996-97), p. 600; and F. Gregory Gause, III, 'Sovereignty, Statecraft and Stability in the Middle East,' *Journal of International Affairs* vol. 45, no. 2 (Winter 1992), pp. 441-469.

[7] See Malcolm Kerr, *The Arab Cold War: Gamal 'Abd al-Nasir and His Rivals, 1958-1970*, 3rd ed. (New York: Oxford University Press, 1971); and the analysis in Samir Seikaly, Ramzi Baalbaki, and Peter Dodd, eds., *Arabic and Islamic Studies in Memory of Malcolm H. Kerr* (Beirut: American University of Beirut, 1991), p. xxvii.

[8] See Albert Hourani, *A History of the Arab Peoples* (New York: Warner Books, 1992), Ch. 24.

[9] Hourani, *A History of the Arab Peoples*, p. 455.

[10] See Ghassan Salamé, 'Inter-Arab Politics: The Return of Geography,' in William B. Quandt, ed., *The Middle East: Ten Years after Camp David* (Washington, DC: The Brookings Institute, 1988), pp. 319-353.

[11] These included King Hussein's war against the Palestinian commandos in Jordan in 1970-71, Syria's entry into Lebanon in 1976, the Camp David Accords of 1978, the struggle between Syria and Iraq over Jordan, and Syria's alliance with Iran against Iraq from 1980-88.

[12] See, for example, the contributions in Adeed Dawisha and I. William Zartman, eds., *Beyond Coercion: The Durability of the Arab State* (London: Croom Helm, 1988) and in Ghassan Salamé, ed., *The Foundations of the Arab State* (London: Croom Helm, 1987). See also Roger Owen, *State, Power and Politics in the Making of the Modern Middle East* (London: Routledge, 1992), pp. 32-80 and 197-222. A qualifier is in order, however. Albert Hourani makes the important observation that as Arab regimes were moving further apart, Arab societies were experiencing greater interdependence. This was largely due to the mass education policies of the 1950s and 1960s, and the Arabization programs in North Africa. Oil wealth in the Gulf states also attracted Arab workers from the poorer Arab countries. This movement of individuals, and mass education in Arabic, strengthened the consciousness of the existence of a common culture shared by the speakers of Arabic. It did not increase the desire for a closer union between the Arab states, however. See Hourani, *A History of the Arab Peoples*, pp. 423-426.

[13] For a discussion of this, see Rex Brynen and Paul Noble, 'The Gulf Crisis and the Arab State System: A New Regional Order?' *Arab Studies Quarterly* vol. 13, no. 1-2 (Winter-Spring 1991), pp. 130-135.

[14] See Patrick E. Tyler, 'US Exit Is No Sure Cure for Saudi Royals' Troubles,' *New York Times*, 30 April 2003.

[15] See 'Tahqiqat Su'udiyya Tabhath 'An Fak Lugz fi Naql al-'Irhabiyeen Ma'rakatahum ila al-Mudun al-Muqadasa,' *Asharq Al-Awsat*, 18 June 2003. The figures are from *as-Safir*, 16 August 2003. Abdullah's comments were made in a speech to citizens and to security forces, in which he declared that 'whoever harbors a terrorist is a terrorist ... and whoever sympathizes with a terrorist is a terrorist ... and will receive their just ... penalty.' The text of the speech is reproduced in *Al Riyadh*, 15 August 2003.

[16] See Stephen M. Walt, 'Beyond bin Laden: Reshaping US Foreign Policy,' *International Security* vol. 26, no. 3 (Winter 2001-02), pp. 56-78.

[17] For a discussion see Audrey Kurth Cronin, 'Behind the Curve: Globalization and International Terrorism,' *International Security* vol. 27, no. 3 (Winter 2002-03), pp. 38 and 45.

[18] Stephen Walt advises the US government to do so in Walt, 'Beyond bin Laden,' p. 66.

[19] US Department of State, 'Powell Launches Middle East Partnership Initiative (12 December 2002),' US Department of State, 8 August 2003 <http://usinfo.state.gov/regional/nea/text/1212pwl.htm>.

[20] See, for example, US support for the World Economic Forum held at the Dead Sea in June 2003, US Department of State, 'World Economic Forum,' US Department of State, 8 August 2003 <http://usinfo.state.gov/regional/nea/summit/0613uswef.htm>. For a critical assessment, see Pete Moore, 'The Newest Jordan: Free Trade, Peace and an Ace in the Hole,' 26 June 2003, *Middle East Report Online*, 8 August 2003 <http://www.merip.org/mero/mero062603.html>.

[21] See Daniel Brumberg, 'The Trap of Liberalized Autocracy,' *Journal of Democracy*, vol. 13, no. 4 (October 2002), p. 67.

[22] See 'Amr Musa's comments quoted in *al-Hayat*, 2 April 2003.

[23] See, for example: Talal Salman, 'al-Nizam al-'Arabi – al-Nihayat,' *as-Safir*, 7 March 2003; Hasan Nafi'a, 'al-Nizam al-'Arabi 'Inda Muftaraq Turuq,' *al-Hayat*, 24 March 2003; and Faysal 'Aloush, 'Al-Jami'a Uwla Dahaya al-Harb 'ala al-'Iraq,' *al-Hayat*, 16 May 2003.

[24] The 2002 Arab summit in Beirut was another occasion when so-called brotherly Arab states confronted each other. This time the clash was between the Lebanese and Palestinian delegations.

[25] See the text of the communiqué in *al-Hayat*, 2 March 2003. For details on the summit, see the coverage in *al-Hayat*, 2 March 2003 and *as-Safir*, 3 March 2003.

[26] For a discussion of these views see 'Aloush, 'Al-Jami'a Uwla Dahaya al-Harb 'ala al-'Iraq;' Muhammad al-Rumayhi, 'Al-Hiwar al-Harej…al-Jami'a al-'Arabiyya wa-l-Muhal al-Dayyiqa,' *al-Hayat*, 25 June 2003; and Sameh Rashed, 'Mushkilat Jami'at al-Duwal al-'Arabiyya A'maq min Ikhtizaliha fi Shakhs al-Ameen al-'Am,' *al-Hayat*, 16 May 2003.

[27] See Jamil Matar, 'Jay Garner…in the Arab Summit!' *al-Hayat*, 23 April 2003.

[28] See Hasan Nafi'a, 'Misr wa Azmat al-Khaleej al-Thalitha: Ma'dilat al-Bahth 'An Dawr Da'i',' *al-Hayat*, 4 April 2003. The Syrian regime made a distinction between its condemnation of the US invasion of Iraq and its support for the Iraqi people rather than the Iraqi regime.

[29] See Wahid 'Abdel Majid, 'Dawr Misr Murashah lil-Taraju' ma lam Yahduth al-'Islah,' *al-Hayat*, 26 March 2003.

[30] See Nafi'a, 'Misr wa Azmat al-Khaleej al-Thalitha.'

[31] See Nivine 'Abdel Min'em Mas'ad, 'Turkiyya wa Iran…Hisabat al-Ribh wa-l-Khisara Ba'd Intiha' al-Harb 'Ala-l-'Iraq,' *al-Hayat*, 8 May 2003.

[32] See Walid Shuqayr, 'Mataleb Washington al-Muliha Tata'alaq bi 'al-Dawr al-'Iraqi' li-Suriyya,' *al-Hayat*, 20 April 2003; and Steven R. Weisman, 'US Still Critical of Iran Despite Al Qaeda Arrests,' *New York Times*, 28 May 2003.

[33] See Bashar al-Asad's comments in *as-Safir*, 17 July 2003.

[34] See Imad Marmal, 'Al-Qossa al-Kamila lil-'Amaliyya al-Amniyya fi al-Biqa',' *as-Safir*, 10 June 2003.

[35] See Ibrahim Humaydi, 'Tanseeq Suri-Turki li-Sawn Wihdat al-'Iraq wa-l-Qiyyam Bidawr fi I'adat al-I'mar,' *al-Hayat*, 31 July 2003.

[36] See the comments by Ari Fleischer, quoted in Weisman, 'US Still Critical of Iran Despite Al Qaeda Arrests.'

[37] See Salim Nassar, 'Thalatha Ightalu al-Sayyed Muhammad Baqer al-Hakim!' *al-Hayat*, 6 September 2003.

Chapter 2

Theory and System in Understanding Middle East International Politics: Rereading Paul Noble's 'The Arab System: Pressures, Constraints, and Opportunities'

F. Gregory Gause, III

As a graduate student in the early 1980s with an interest in both international relations as an academic discipline and the Middle East as a regional subject, I found myself in a bind. There were numerous, excellent narrative accounts of international politics in the region. There were more than enough theories out there in the academic literature with which to contend. But the efforts to put the two together—regional realities and international relations theory—were few and far between. I began to envy my comparative politics colleagues, who could read all sorts of theoretically informed accounts of the domestic politics of Middle Eastern countries. It was therefore literally a revelation when I read Paul Noble's 'The Arab System: Pressures, Constraints, and Opportunities.'[1] Here was what I was looking for: a work that was properly attuned to the nuances of the region's politics, but at the same time sought to use theoretical concepts in international relations to provide a larger framework for understanding those nuances. I had found a model for how to write about the international relations of the Middle East.

The influence of this article was not limited to one humble graduate student from south of the (Canadian) border. The recent literature that has attempted to understand the international politics of the Middle East from a systemic perspective is characterized by frequent citations to 'The Arab System: Pressures, Constraints, and Opportunities.'[2] This article requires a careful rereading for the insights it continues to generate about the application of international relations concepts to Middle East regional politics. I will highlight a number of those insights, raise an issue on which I have come to disagree with Noble's analysis, and then suggest some questions that remain to be addressed in efforts to develop a systemic understanding of 'regional international' politics.

Noble's Systemic Understanding of Middle East International Politics

When Noble published the original version of the article in 1984, academic debates about international systems were dominated by Kenneth Waltz's *Theory of International Politics*, the 'Ur-text' of neo-realism. Waltz identified three elements of any system: its ordering principles, the character of its units, and the distribution of capabilities among those units. In international systems, Waltz theorized, the ordering principle is anarchy, because states do not recognize any sovereign authority that has either the right or the capability to overrule their decisions. The only alternative ordering principle is hierarchy, but, short of a world empire, one will not find a hierarchically-organized international system. The units of an international system for Waltz are states, but he sees no differentiation of function among states. All states are alike, in that they all seek the same end: survival in the anarchic international system. In Waltz's theory, it is the third element, the distribution of capabilities, which does the heavy causal lifting. International systems change when the distribution of power among the states within them changes between multipolarity and bipolarity. Multipolar international systems, in his view, are more prone to conflict than bipolar systems.[3]

The great strength of Waltz's work was its parsimony, but that strength limits its applicability. While Waltz himself was very careful to specify the cases to which his theory applied—global international systems consisting of the great powers—the intellectual power of his model skewed discussions of all international systems, including regional systems, toward his monocausal focus on distribution of power as the driving force behind international outcomes. Noble's article had the great virtue of maintaining Waltz's basic outline of system definition (though using different terminology), while problematising what Waltz considered fixed: the organizing principle of the system and the nature of the units making it up.

Noble began his assessment of the Arab system with a focus on what he termed 'unit properties.' While Waltz saw no 'functional differentiation' among units in the international system, and thus dropped domestic political variables out of his definition of international systems, Noble identified the extensive changes in Arab society and the original weakness of post-colonial Arab states as common *domestic* characteristics among the units of his system that created regular patterns of *international* outcomes.[4] Domestic weakness and instability opened Arab states up to intervention—more political than military—by their neighbours, and helped explain what observers of the Arab world in the 1950s and 1960s saw as the chronic instability of regional politics. This observation was a truism of the empirical accounts of Arab politics of the period; Noble made it part of a more general and parsimonious understanding of the drivers of regional international politics. More importantly, Noble contends that changes in state-society relations in the Arab world dramatically affected international political outcomes. As states became stronger in the 1970s and 1980s, the Arab world was less characterized by the meddling in the domestic affairs of neighbours that was so ubiquitous in earlier decades.[5] Here a domestic political characteristic, the relative strength of the state over its society, varied in the same direction at the same time among almost all the Arab states, and produced an important change in Arab statecraft. Again, many analysts observed this change. Noble was the first, to my knowledge, to theorize its effects on regional international politics.

The second level of Noble's systemic framework is 'relational properties (the Arab setting).' He argues that the commonalities among Arabs across state borders, 'the homogeneity among the peoples and elites,' leads to qualitative differences in regional Arab politics when compared to other systems of developing states, in terms of the permeability of domestic political systems and the common political agenda to which all state leaders must react, be it Arab unity in the 1950s and 1960s, relations with Western powers, or the Arab-Israeli conflict.[6] This common Arab identity unifies the Arab states, both materially, in terms of the interchange of people and ideas, and metaphorically, in the sense that they cannot escape from the common agenda of issues that stems from being Arab. However, it also introduces elements of conflict, because an Arab leader can take other leaders to task for not fulfilling their 'Arab duties,' and can appeal to the citizens of other Arab states to oppose their leaders on the basis of the higher loyalty to Arabism. In effect, for Noble, Arabism sets the system apart.[7]

While he does not explicitly make this argument, I read his analysis here as an implicit criticism of Waltz's notion that the ordering principle of international systems, anarchy, is not a problematic concept. Waltz's anarchy is the flip side of Westphalian notions of sovereignty, where each unit is completely autonomous (at least in theory) within its own boundaries, and there is an absolute distinction between the domestic realm (a realm of hierarchic order) and the international realm (a realm of anarchy). Other scholars have questioned this absolute distinction between anarchy and hierarchy in international systems, arguing that there can be different qualities of formal anarchy, from more 'mature' anarchies where there is widespread agreement on principles of order to less 'mature' anarchies where conflict among the units is more endemic. In effect, the organizing principle of international systems is not a given, as Waltz contends, but a contested concept in itself.[8]

Noble's discussion of the unique 'relational properties' of the Arab states highlights the fact that Arabism, particularly in the 1950s and 1960s, presented for Arabs an alternative organizing principle to Westphalian sovereignty. Rather than accept the territorially distinct, separate, and legally equal states bequeathed to them by colonialism, many Arabs saw an alternative way of organizing their political geography, into a single, hierarchically-organized Arab unit. The Arab League represented an uneasy compromise between these two principles, basing itself explicitly on the desire for Arab unity while recognizing the sovereign rights of the Arab state members. This conflict over organizing principles helps us to understand the common origin of the Arab-Israeli conflict and inter-Arab conflicts, as both reflected not simply a rejection of the colonial territorial disposition in the region but the challenge presented to that status quo by an alternative organizing principle, Arabism. The 'instability' seen as so characteristic of regional politics can thus be understood theoretically as deriving from a clash between opposed organizing principles of the regional system, though the specifics of regional conflicts were undoubtedly affected by both regime security issues and by classical balance of power issues. By opening up what Waltz had declared closed, Noble helps us understand at a theoretical level the patterns of conflict that have characterized regional international relations.

If the organizing principle of an international system is not a given, but rather a contested concept, then understandings of that principle can change over time. Noble notes the effects of the 'decline' of Arabism since the 1970s.[9] In fact, one can see this period, as Noble depicts it, as a time when the ordering principle of the system became much less contested, as both elites and mass publics settled, however grudgingly, on Westphalian notions of sovereignty as the basis of regional politics. Noble interprets this post-1970 period as one in which the 'level of conflict and revisionism within the Arab system declined significantly;' moreover, he observes that Arabist notions justifying challenges to the territorial status quo had not completely disappeared – as evidenced by Iraq's 1990 invasion of Kuwait and by the continuing importance of the Palestinian issue in Arab politics.[10] One can question Noble's coding of regional politics from 1970 through 1990 as being less conflictual than earlier periods, but only in the context of a more general question about system definition which I will raise below.

Once again, Noble is not unique in his emphasis on the ideology of Arabism as the distinguishing feature of inter-Arab politics, nor in the contention that the waxing and waning of Arabism helps explain regional international political outcomes. He is, however, the first to try to theorize the role of ideology in the context of a systemic approach to the international relations of the Middle East.

Like Waltz, Noble makes the distribution of capabilities the third component of his definition of the Arab system. While largely agreeing with Waltz about the material bases of any definition of power, he opens that concept up to include the 'political capabilities' of states.[11] Particularly in analyzing relations among Arab states, where conflicts were more often pursued with political rather than overtly military means, understanding the power of states as still being materially based (economic levels, educational and cultural levels), but extending beyond simple measures of military power, is an important modification of realist and neo-realist understandings of power. Noble sees the distribution of capabilities in the Arab world as shifting from a 'virtual one-power situation' dominated by Egypt in the 1950s and 1960s to true multipolarity after 1970, with the new resources that oil wealth brought to Arab states like Saudi Arabia and Iraq.[12] Unlike Waltz, who sees multipolarity as a more conflict-prone distribution of power, Noble sees this shift to multipolarity as contributing to the lower levels of inter-Arab conflict after 1970.[13]

Noble, thus, sees three mutually reinforcing changes in the inter-Arab system occurring around the same time, in the late 1960s and early 1970s, leading to changes in important international political behaviours and outcomes. The 'hardening' of the Arab state, the declining relevance of Arabist ideologies, and the increasingly multipolar nature of the system together account for the decline in the power and prevalence of revisionist statecraft (including unionist projects), the decline of strategies based on the manipulation of the domestic politics of other Arab states, lower levels of inter-Arab conflict, and changing approaches to the Arab-Israeli conflict. Noble's article is the most sophisticated and theoretically informed effort to account for what has widely been recognized as a change in the way the international politics of the region has operated over the decades. By broadening the Waltzian definition of an international system, he provided a systemic explanation of a systemic change, rather than the *ad hoc* and reductionist explanations usually provided. That is the great strength of the article, and the source of its enduring influence.

A Controversy: System Definition

I contend that the major problem with Noble's systemic approach to understanding the international politics of the Middle East is his definition of membership in the system. Is it useful to consider all the members of the Arab League as belonging to a regional international system to which no other states belong? That depends upon the criteria by which system membership is determined. Noble does not dwell on this question, assuming that cultural affinities and self-definition (through membership in the Arab League) are sufficient characteristics upon which to determine membership.[14] But such a definition ignores one of the major international behaviours that systemic approaches try to explain: conflict. As geographical proximity is a leading correlate of international conflict, self-selection and cultural criteria that ignore geographical proximity will necessarily generate definitions of systems that cannot help analysts understand important patterns of inter-state conflict. Raymond Aron pointed out more than thirty years ago that it makes no sense to define an international system in such a way that states engaged in war with each other are not members.[15]

In this case, the absence of Israel, Iran, and the great powers from Noble's definition of the system makes it very difficult to offer a systemic explanation for international conflict in the Middle East. Noble recognizes this problem, identifying Israel and Iran as the 'periphery' of the system and noting that 'at the very stage that conditions within the Arab system became less threatening [after 1970], the larger regional environment was becoming more threatening.'[16] But the relegation of these two important regional players, against whom the Arab states have fought most of their wars, to the 'periphery' of the system causes important analytical problems for Noble. He defines the period between 1970 and 1990 as much less conflictual for Arab states than the period from the end of the Second World War through Jamal 'Abdel Nasser's regional dominance. This was so *among* the Arab states, by most definitions, but not *for* the Arab states. Two major Arab-Israeli wars (1973 and 1982), the onset of the first Palestinian *intifada*, and the longest, bloodiest conflict in modern Middle Eastern history (the Iran-Iraq War) involved numerous and important Arab actors in serious conflict. Certainly in terms of battle deaths, the period between 1970 and 1990 (before the Gulf War) was much *more* conflictual than the previous period. Even those Arab states not involved directly in the fighting were involved in these wars through their alliance choices.

Noble also defines the 1970 to 1990 period as being characterized by a reduction in the intensity of ideological conflict among the Arab states. Again, this is true *among* the Arab states, but not *for* the Arab states. While pan-Arabism as understood in the Nasser period was no longer the force that it had been, the rise of Islamist ideologies, particularly with the Iranian Revolution, subjected a number of Arab states to serious, trans-state ideological pressures that resonated in their domestic politics and greatly affected their foreign policies.[17] The Iraqi decision to go to war against Iran can only be understood in terms of the political pressures generated within Iraq by the Iranian Revolution. Likewise, Saudi, Egyptian, Jordanian, and Gulf state backing for Iraq in that war was, at least in part, a reaction to their fear of the contagious effects of Islamist radicalism. The rise of Islamist groups among Lebanese Shi'a and among Palestinians is another example; the former case, greatly attributable to direct Iranian involvement, had important effects on the Arab-Israeli dynamic as well.

Noble is correct to contend that the organizing principle of Middle East international relations is a contested concept, but he should have included pan-Islamist ideas along with pan-Arab ones among the contestants. In that way, while correctly identifying the consequences for inter-Arab politics of the declining salience of Arabism after 1970, he need not imply that this decline left the field clear for Westphalian notions of state sovereignty to dominate the region. Saddam Hussein's effort to combine Arabist and Islamist rhetoric and symbolism to rally support during the Gulf War is a testament to the continued prominence of both trans-state ideological challenges to Westphalian sovereignty in the region. The contested nature of the organizing principle of Middle Eastern international politics is a constant over the last 50 years, though the content of the challenging ideology has changed over time. That constant can help us understand the persistence of inter-state regional conflict since the end of the Second World War, not simply inter-Arab conflict but Arab-Israeli and Arab-Persian conflict as well.

Noble's exclusion of Israel and Iran from his definition of the regional system also has important analytical consequences in terms of the third element of system definition, the distribution of power. Noble argues that the Arab system changed from one-power dominance (Egypt) to multipolarity around 1970.[18] He attributes this change to multipolarity as an important element in the decline of inter-Arab conflict in the post-1970 period. Here he enters into one of the more contentious issues in the theoretical discussions of polarity in the international relations literature. The idea that multipolarity restrains inter-state conflict was common among classical realist scholars like Hans Morgenthau. However, Kenneth Waltz strongly argued in *Theory of International Politics* that just the opposite is true, that bipolar systems are less war-prone than multipolar ones, and that elements of multipolarity contribute directly to the increased likelihood of international conflict (the empirical evidence in this general debate is not conclusive).[19] It is not clear that the diffusion of power in the Arab system would lead naturally to a reduction in inter-Arab conflict. More damaging to Noble's argument, however, is the general theoretical agreement that unipolar systems are not conflict-prone, as no other state, by definition, has the resources to challenge the dominant state. By Noble's coding, Arab systemic unipolarity correlates with a high level of conflict. This is a theoretical anomaly that called for greater explication.

The inclusion of Israel and Iran in the regional system allows the analyst to avoid these sticky theoretical wickets, and provides a much more parsimonious explanation for the relatively high levels of international conflict in the region in the post-Second World War period. If Israel and Iran are included, then the regional system is consistently multipolar over time. The weight of various actors might change from period to period, but the structure of multipolarity is a constant. Following Waltz, then, one could argue that systemic multipolarity helps to explain the fact that the Middle East has been a conflict-prone region.

The alternative I suggest—a 'Middle Eastern' regional system rather than a purely 'Arab' one—better captures the realities of the area's international relations. Many of the Arab states, and certainly the states of the Arab Mashriq (east), devote large amounts of their foreign policy attentions and resources to their relations, both conflictual and cooperative, with their non-Arab neighbours. Analytically, a 'Middle Eastern' regional system conception provides a more parsimonious link between systemic characteristics and regional outcomes. The consistently high level of regional conflict can be explained by two important system-level continuities: the persistent challenges in the region to Westphalian sovereignty as an organizing principle, and regional multipolarity. A systemic change over time— the 'hardening' of state units as they have increased their control over their societies—can explain the decreasing ability of transnational ideological appeals to change the regional political status-quo. While there are important normative elements in conceptions of an Arab system that play an important role in understanding regional realities—many Arabs *want* there to be a strong and cooperative Arab state system—the empirical realities of regional conflict patterns require us to analytically define the system as a regional Middle Eastern one.

Questions: The Global System and Regional Economic Integration

The most difficult theoretical question, to my mind, in formulating a systemic understanding of any region's international politics is how the global system interacts with the regional system. Dependency theorists have a simple answer to this question: the regional system is economically dependent upon the global capitalist core, and thus is politically subject to the demands of the core capitalist states. This is the perspective, modified somewhat, taken by Bahgat Korany and Ali Dessouki in the volume in which Noble's article appears.[20] I do not find the dependency perspective adequate for understanding the relationship between the Middle Eastern system, or even the Arab members of that system, to the global system. More accurately, the relationship is one of *asymmetric interdependence*. Middle Eastern states have things that the great powers want: primarily oil and access to strategic locations. They can bargain with the leading capitalist states over those assets, gaining promises of protection, economic aid, and political support.

That bargaining is certainly not conducted on a level playing field. The power asymmetries between Arab states, and Middle Eastern states more generally, and the great powers are too wide for the relationship to be based on equality. However, the dependency perspective fails to capture important historical realities in the way regional states have interacted with the global system, on a number of levels. First, regional states have been able to defy great powers on enough occasions, in important ways, to call into question the premises of the dependency analysis. The outstanding example is the 1973-74 Arab oil embargo of the United States, implemented largely by America's Arab allies (Saudi Arabia in the forefront; Iraq did not participate). That embargo, unintentionally, led to a huge transfer of wealth from the core to those peripheral states, and greatly increased their power in the international system. Certainly global bipolarity assisted Arab states in the past in acts of defiance against the West, like Nasser's refusal to join the Baghdad Pact and subsequent turn to the Soviet Union for military and economic aid. However, even with the end of bipolarity we see a number of Middle Eastern regional states refusing to accept American dictates on important policy questions, be it Syria's refusal to accept the Israeli-American proposal for peace in 2000, Iraq's unwillingness to abide by UN Security Council resolutions, or Iran's general adversarial disposition toward the United States. The US-Israeli relationship, 'special' on numerous levels, also can hardly be seen as one of Israeli dependence on the United States, as that term is used by the theorists.

Second, continuing United States involvement in the Arab-Israeli peace process is testament to the fact that Arab states have some leverage over it; that is, they are not in a relationship of complete dependence vis-à-vis the United States. Once Egypt opted out of the confrontation with Israel and joined the American camp in the Cold War, one can imagine little strategic or material incentive for Washington to care what happened to Syria and Jordan, much less the Palestinians. Certainly one can fault Washington for, having decided to be involved, not doing enough to bring about a settlement that could assure stability with some amount of justice to all the parties. However, analytically, the puzzle of why the United States remains involved *at all* in the peace process can only be solved by recognizing that other Arab states, particularly Arab oil states, see their interests served by that American involvement. This remains true even with the end of global bipolarity.

Third, the very fact that the Middle East remains the region of the world least affected by the 'Washington consensus' of the 1990s—movement toward an open market economy and political democracy—is evidence of the bargaining power it retains in dealing with the global capitalist system and the United States in particular. One might argue that the autocrats who govern almost every Middle Eastern state are wrong to refuse to get on either the economic reform or the democracy trains. However, the fact that they *can* refuse, and remain in power, is a testament to their power to resist global pressures that their colleagues in other parts of the world either cannot or do not want to resist.

While rejecting the dependency framework for understanding the relationship between the global system and the Middle East regional system, I have no alternative to propose. The idea of *asymmetric interdependence* captures the reality that regional states retain some bargaining power against the global capitalist system, but provides no guidance in terms of systematic regularities in global-local interaction. Sometimes the regional state or states will succumb to the power of outside actors and behave the way dependency theorists would expect; other times they will not. The analyst can certainly explain the specific circumstances of individual acts of defiance, but there are no general principles suggested to explain what categories or types of defiance are more likely than others, or in what circumstances defiance is more likely to occur. In effect, *asymmetric interdependence* describes an empirical reality, but is too underdetermined to be a systemic concept. This could be a fruitful area for future research in the systemic tradition on Middle Eastern international relations.

Noble does not take on in an explicit way the relationship between the regional system and the global system. In the context of the volume to which he was contributing, that was someone else's job. Nor can he be faulted, given the time when the volume was published, for not dealing with the issue of the relationship, from a security rather than an economic perspective, between the structure of the global system and the effects of the global system on the regional system.[21] By 1991 the Middle East regional system had only existed, as a system of independent states, for four decades, during which the global system was bipolar. It was generally assumed that global bipolarity gave regional actors some freedom for manoeuvre. This assumption was both theoretically obvious and empirically ratified, so no one gave it much consideration. However, with the end of bipolarity, the question of how changes in the global distribution of power might affect the regional system came to the fore. The only sustained research on this question has been conducted by Benjamin Miller in his examination of the different effects of global systemic multipolarity and bipolarity on great power behaviour in regional crises and conflict situations.[22] The effects of unipolarity have generally been assumed—control by the hegemon of regional actors—but the past decade of systemic unipolarity and its impact on the Middle East has not borne out that easy assumption.[23] The interaction between global systemic change and regional politics remains an understudied element of Middle East regional politics.

A second important question raised by systemic approaches to Middle Eastern international politics is the impact of regional economic integration or interdependence on regional political outcomes. The 'dynamic density' of transactions among units in a system, according to John Ruggie and other international relations scholars, is properly understood as a characteristic not of the units themselves, but of the system to which they belong.[24] The 'dynamic density' of those interactions among states of the Arab Mashriq certainly increased dramatically during the 1970s and early 1980s, in terms of labour and capital flows.[25] Noble notes the interesting and counter-intuitive point that, when levels of economic integration were highest, the political pressures for unity and a common front on pan-Arab issues were much reduced from previous periods. He attributes this to the declining importance of Arabist ideologies.[26]

However, one could argue that the increased economic interdependence among the eastern Arab states actually was a contributing factor to the decline of unionist political agitation. Efficient economic exchange requires a common understanding of property rights. In the modern international system, sovereign statehood provides the basis for that understanding, facilitating economic interaction. When the costs of revisionism, in terms of disrupting existing economic networks, was low, as in the 1950s and 1960s, it was easier for leaders like Nasser to pursue those policies. As the importance of economic interaction among the Arab states increased, the costs for Arab leaders of challenging the regional status quo increased. Not only would aid flows from richer Arab states cease, but inter-Arab private investment could be seriously affected, as could the status of migrant workers from the country raising the revisionist claims.

This point is merely suggestive, however. The relative decline in the density of Arab economic links, from the oil price collapse in the middle 1980s and the labour pattern disruptions occasioned by the Gulf War, has not been matched by an increase in demands for Arab unity. The question of the impact of changes in the level of regional economic integration on regional political outcomes remains understudied, both regarding the question of regional conflict and/or cooperation, and regarding the appeal of transnational ideological platforms. Research on the systemic consequences of changing levels of economic interaction need not be limited to the Arab states. Iran and the Arab oil producers have experienced different levels of interdependence, in terms of their oil production decisions, in different world oil market conditions. Turkey's trade with the region has increased over the past two decades. The potential effects of Israeli economic integration into the region have been much debated, though with the collapse of the peace process this is a less immediate issue than they appeared to be in the middle 1990s.

Conclusion

Paul Noble's path-breaking article 'The Arab System: Pressures, Constraints, and Opportunities' remains a provocative guide to assessing regional international politics from a systemic perspective, and an important contribution to the theoretical literature on the international relations of the Middle East. It does what all good systemic-level analyses do: it makes big arguments about important continuities in the outcomes of Middle Eastern international relations, and provides parsimonious explanations for significant, region-wide changes in the way international politics works. Like all good articles, it raises more questions than it can answer and stimulates those who disagree with its conclusions to sharpen their counter-arguments. It is a model for how to study the international relations of the Middle East.

Notes

[1] Paul C. Noble, 'The Arab System: Pressures, Constraints and Opportunities,' in Bahgat Korany and Ali E. Hillal Dessouki, eds., *The Foreign Policies of Arab States*, 2nd ed. (Boulder: Westview Press, 1991). The original version of the article was in the first edition of that volume, published in 1984. All references here to the article are from the second edition.

[2] Just a few of the works that prominently cite Noble's article are: Michael Barnett, *Dialogues in Arab Politics* (New York: Columbia University Press, 1998); Raymond Hinnebusch, 'Introduction: The Analytical Framework,' in Raymond Hinnebusch and Anoushiravan Ehteshami, eds., *The Foreign Policies of Middle East States* (Boulder: Lynne Rienner, 2002); Avraham Sela, *The Decline of the Arab-Israeli Conflict: Middle East Politics and the Quest for Regional Order* (Albany: SUNY Press, 1998); Etel Solingen, *Regional Orders at Century's Dawn* (Princeton: Princeton University Press, 1998). My own work that owes the largest intellectual debt to the article is 'Sovereignty, Statecraft and Stability in the Middle East,' *Journal of International Affairs* vol. 45, no. 2 (Winter 1992).

[3] Kenneth N. Waltz, *Theory of International Politics* (Reading, MA: Addison-Wesley, 1979); see Chapter 5 for his conception of systems, and Chapter 8 for the relative stability of bipolar systems.

[4] Robert Jervis points out, supporting Noble's position, that if a domestic factor can have systemic effects, it becomes a legitimate element of a systemic analysis. *System Effects* (Princeton: Princeton University Press, 1997), p. 99.

[5] Noble, pp. 50-55.

[6] Noble, pp. 55, 58-59.

[7] He shares this position with Gamil Matar and 'Ali al-Din Hillal Dessouki, *al-Nizam al-Iqlimi al-'Arabi* [The Arab Regional System] (Beirut: Dar al-Mustaqbal al-'Arabi, 1983), p. 62, and is the precursor of Barnett's similar assertion, p. 44.

[8] The idea of a range of anarchies along a continuum from 'mature' to 'immature' is suggested by Barry Buzan, *People, States and Fear*, 2nd ed. (Boulder: Lynne Rienner, 1991), Ch. 4. More generally, Hedley Bull argues the elements of order can be found in differing degrees within formally anarchic international systems in *The Anarchical Society* (New York: Columbia University Press, 1977).

[9] Noble, pp. 75-80.

[10] Noble, quote from p. 75, discussion of post-1990 period pp. 90-92.

[11] Noble, p. 61.

[12] The decline in Egyptian relative power, which Noble sees as central to explaining changes in the Arab system in the 1970s, is a theme emphasized in other theoretically-grounded works on the region's international relations. See in particular Shibley Telhami, *Power and Leadership in International Bargaining: The Path to the Camp David Accords* (New York: Columbia University Press, 1990).

[13] Noble, p. 72.

[14] He is not alone in slighting this crucial analytical question in his construction of a systemic explanation for Middle Eastern regional international politics. The same criticism can be levelled at Barnett, *Dialogues in Arab Politics*; and Matar and Hilal, *al-Nizam al-Iqlimi al-'Arabi*. I develop this more general critique at greater length in F. Gregory Gause, III, 'Systemic Approaches to Middle East International Relations,' *International Studies Review* vol. 1, no. 1 (Spring 1999).

[15] Raymond Aron, *Peace and War: A Theory of International Relations* (New York: Praeger, 1967), p. 94. In his definition of regional security complexes as revoling around

'the pattern of amity and enmity among states,' Barry Buzan also includes conflict as a central element of system definition. See *People, States and Fear*, pp. 187-202.

[16] Noble, p. 80.

[17] Maridi Nahas argued that Arab nationalism and Islamic revolution not only presented similar challenges to the international order of the Middle East, but that they also had the same class basis in terms of their mass appeal. While that assertion is open to question, the analytic pairing of Nasser and Khomeini is a provocative one. 'State-Systems and Revolutionary Challenge: Nasser, Khomeini, and the Middle East,' *International Journal of Middle East Studies* vol. 17, no. 4 (November 1985).

[18] 'During this period [the 1950s and 1960s], the Arab system was also characterized by a distinctive pattern of power. Whereas in most Third World systems power and influence were relatively diffused, in the Arab system they were highly concentrated, giving rise to a virtual one-power situation.' Noble, p. 62.

[19] A summary of this debate can be found in Greg Cashman, *What Causes War? An Introduction to Theories of International Conflict* (Lanham: Lexington Books, 2000), Ch. 8.

[20] Bahgat Korany and Ali E. Hillal Dessouki, 'The Global System and Arab Foreign Policies: The Primacy of Constraints,' in Korany and Dessouki, eds., *The Foreign Policies of Arab States* (Boulder: Westview Press, 1991).

[21] The most ambitious effort to address this question is L. Carl Brown, *International Politics and the Middle East* (Princeton: Princeton University Press, 1984). For my critique of Brown's conclusions, see Gause, 'Systemic Approaches to Middle East International Relations.'

[22] Benjamin Miller, *When Opponents Cooperate: Great Power Conflict and Collaboration in World Politics* (Ann Arbor: University of Michigan Press, 1995); Benjamin Miller and Korina Kagan, 'The Great Powers and Regional Conflicts: Eastern Europe and the Balkans from the Post-Napoleonic Era to the Post-Cold War Era,' *International Studies Quarterly* vol. 41, no. 1 (March 1997); Miller, 'Great Powers and Regional Peacekeeping: Patterns in the Middle East and Beyond,' *Journal of Strategic Studies* vol. 20, no. 1 (1997).

[23] The only extended effort to assess the effects of global unipolarity on the Middle East regional system is Birthe Hansen, *Unipolarity and the Middle East* (New York: St. Martin's Press, 2001). Hansen's conclusion is that, while the systemic shift from global bipolarity to global unipolarity had important impacts on Middle Eastern politics, those impacts were not unidirectional. Both war (Gulf War) and peace (Arab-Israeli changes) resulted; civil wars were ended (Lebanon) and initiated (Yemen, Kurds in Iraq); states merged (Yemen) and broke apart (Iraq, Palestinian Authority in Israeli-occupied territory). See in particular Chapter 15 for the summary of the author's findings. While demonstrating that global systemic change is an important factor in explaining change in regional politics, this work does not move the debate forward on the key question of *how* changes on the two planes relate. To be useful, systemic explanations that posit a change in an independent variable (global system structure) should then anticipate variations in dependent variables (regional international outcomes) that move in a single direction. If global structural change leads to both more peace *and* more war in the same regional system, then from a systemic perspective the effects of global systemic change on regional systems are underdetermined. Things will change if the global system changes, but we cannot predict how or in what direction. We only know that they will change. This is hardly a satisfying systemic theory.

[24] John Ruggie, 'Continuity and Transformation in the World Polity: Toward a Neorealist Synthesis,' *World Politics* vol. 35, no. 2 (January 1983). See also Barry Buzan, Charles Jones, and Richard Little, *The Logic of Anarchy* (New York: Columbia University Press, 1993), pp. 69-80.

[25] A process documented by a number of regional scholars, including Malcolm Kerr and El Sayed Yassin, eds., *Rich and Poor States in the Middle East* (Boulder: Westview Press, 1982); Saad Eddine Ibrahim, *The New Arab Social Order* (Boulder: Westview Press, 1982); and Nadir Farjani, *Ruhhal fi Ard al-'Arab* [Migrations in the Land of the Arabs], (Beirut: Markaz Dirasat al-Wihda al-'Arabiyya, 1987).

[26] Noble, p. 58.

Chapter 3

Systemic Factors Do Matter, But… Reflections on the Uses and Limitations of Systemic Analysis

Paul Noble

Systemic approaches have enjoyed periodic prominence in the study of international relations over the past fifty years. These approaches have also been subjected to a variety of critiques which have questioned both their logic and usefulness. At the same time, new attempts have been made to undertake systemic analyses of regional international relations, particularly in the developing world. This chapter seeks to explore the scope as well as uses and limitations of such approaches both in general and in the study of Middle East international relations and foreign policy.

There is one preliminary conceptual issue which should be addressed, namely the meaning of the term *international system*.[1] This term can be used in two distinct senses, the concrete and the analytic. In the *concrete sense*, the term denotes a set of states and international actors who interact on a regular basis and consequently are interconnected to some extent (i.e., the condition and activities of each unit affect, and are affected by, those of other units). As a result, their interaction is characterized by some degree of mutual attentiveness and responsiveness (i.e., interdependent decision-making). In this sense the 'system' is the *concrete set of actors who are interconnected*. The term is used in this way when we refer to the global system, the dominant (i.e., major power) system, or the Middle Eastern system.

The term 'international system' may also be used in an *analytic sense*. Here it denotes the relationships and processes that have developed among a set of interconnected actors. More particularly, it refers to discernable patterns in these relations and processes. These include factors such as the pattern of power, the pattern and level of conflict or alignment, and the pattern and level of economic and social links. The 'system' here consists of the *pattern of relations among a number of interconnected actors* rather than simply the set of concrete actors themselves. It is in this analytic sense that the term 'system' will be used when we talk of systemic factors.

Scope, Uses, and Limitations of Systemic Analysis

Initial Framework of Analysis

Although other scholars, notably Morton Kaplan, had previously undertaken system-level and even structural analyses,[2] Kenneth Waltz is undoubtedly the best-known proponent of a systemic approach to the study of international relations. He makes a convincing case for the value of systemic inquiry, establishes a sound intellectual foundation for its pursuit, provides a basic, if parsimonious, framework of analysis, and develops one important dimension (the politico-military).[3] Yet paradoxically, for one so committed, Waltz failed to explore the approach's full potential, adopting instead a relatively narrow and unidimensional perspective.

Waltz's approach was overly narrow in several respects. To begin with, he adopted a restrictive interpretation of the basic feature of a *systemic variable*, namely that it involves the 'arrangement of the parts' (i.e., relationships between the units) as distinct from the characteristics of the individual units themselves.[4] As a result, Waltz limited the concept of 'systemic' variable to that of 'structure' and adopted a largely static politico-military view of the latter, namely the condition of anarchy in the international arena (a quasi-constant) and the overall distribution of capabilities therein, which varies over time.[5] All other variables were considered either unit-level (a vast residual category) or interactional. The latter, although relational in character, were not considered systemic variables.

This narrow realist conception of what constitutes a systemic variable gave rise to a sparse *unidimensional* (politico-military) analytical framework. In addition to its unidimensionality, Waltz's approach was also largely *unilevel* in character with its almost exclusive focus on the dominant (major power) system and neglect of other system levels.

A further limiting feature of Waltz's approach was its failure to explore fully the potential uses of systemic analysis. David Singer had argued earlier that a systemic approach could be particularly useful for analytic description but that its explanatory potential was sharply limited.[6] Waltz played down the descriptive value of a systemic approach and argued instead that it had significant explanatory potential with regard to system-level outcomes, notably international stability/instability.[7] However, he minimized the potential for systemic conditions to explain unit-level policy and behaviour.[8]

Expanded Framework of Analysis

Despite the strong case which Waltz made for systemic analysis, he failed to explore its full potential. In fact, system-level theorizing is a much broader and richer endeavour than Waltz envisaged. Such an expanded and enriched systemic analysis rests on a less restrictive interpretation of the basic criterion for system-level variables, namely that they involve 'relational' rather than unit-level conditions. While Waltz believed that this included only structural characteristics, other analysts interpret it as covering a much broader range of relational conditions.[9]

These additional sets of system-level variables include, first, a number of *pre-interactional conditions* that serve primarily as explanatory variables. Some of these are *additional realist-style structural variables*, notably the equality or inequality of power relations, the level and type of military capabilities and their distribution,[10] and finally, the dynamics of power relations (structural dynamics, i.e., power approaches/transitions and long cycles).[11] Others are *realist-style distributional variables,* notably the extent of substantive differences regarding the state and territorial framework and other distributional issues as well as the resulting degree of compatibility or incompatibility of interests between system members.[12] These too have an important 'relational' aspect.

In addition to these realist systemic factors, there are important *liberal and Marxist* systemic variables. One such set of *textural systemic factors* is the *range and intensity of inter-societal links*, particularly economic links, and the international political-economic system generally. This arises from the fact that states are not simply politico-military units operating in an international system characterized by anarchy but also economic units in increasingly interconnected (transnational) global and regional economies. Barry Buzan, John Ruggie, and Joseph Nye have all noted the systemic character of the 'dynamic density of interaction' and inter-societal linkages generally.[13] Moreover, both liberal and Marxist scholars (Immanuel Wallerstein, world system, and dependency theorists) have attempted to use system-level political economy explanations of international economic relations and states' economic policies.[14]

There are also what might be termed *constructivist* systemic variables. These *ideational* textural variables include both widely held sets of norms, values, and beliefs; and the homogeneity or heterogeneity of identities, ideologies/values, and political-economic systems. This type of systemic variable has been emphasized by Alex Wendt and others who have extended the meaning of the term 'structure' to cover the ideational and normative ethos of a period.[15] These factors meet the 'relational' criterion for systemic characteristics either by cutting across many units (especially major units), or by involving a comparison of units. The similarities and differences in the political institutions of states are a relational (i.e., systemic) factor, while the specific form of homogeneity or heterogeneity (e.g., democratic or authoritarian systems) is a unit-level factor.

Apart from these pre-interactional systemic variables, a *broad range of inter-state interactions and relationships* also qualify as system-level variables. Waltz had treated these as 'interactional' rather than 'systemic' in part because inter-state relations constituted the outcomes he sought to explain. Nevertheless, they meet the criterion for systemic variables since they are relational rather than unit-level in character. These interactional variables include the patterns and quality of relations (conflict, war, accommodation, alignment, and cooperation), the state of the regulatory framework (norms, rules, regimes, and institutions), and the level of stability or instability (vulnerability to structural and other change) in a system. These serve primarily as outcome variables: results which analysts seek to explain.

However, they can also serve as explanatory variables either for state behaviour, or for inter-state relations (e.g., the level of conflict in a system could help explain the pattern of alignment or vice-versa).

In addition to these full-fledged system-level variables, there are unit-level variables that have a potential systemic aspect. Various *pre-interactional unit-level* variables (e.g., the degree of fit between State and nation, the strength or weakness of 'states,' the level of domestic political stability or instability, types of political and economic institutions, the strength of ideological orientations, and the nature of domestic coalitions) can be partly systemic in character. This occurs when similar conditions prevail across a number of units, especially important units, and these conditions have systemic effects.[16]

Unit-level behavioural variables (foreign policy/state behaviour) can have similar features. These normally serve either as unit-level outcome variables or as unit-level explanatory variables for inter-state relations. However, when a similar pattern of policy or behaviour prevails among several states, especially key ones, there is a systemic aspect to otherwise unit-level behaviour.

This broader conception of what is 'systemic' gives rise to an expanded *multidimensional* framework of analysis which is richer than Waltz's in terms of both explanatory and outcome variables. Moreover, this enriched systemic analysis is not only multidimensional but also *multilevel* since it encompasses both the dominant major power system as well as relevant regional and sub-regional systems.[17] Systemic conditions at all these levels shape state policies and the relations between them.

Uses and Limitations of Systemic Analysis

Another important feature of this expanded form of systemic inquiry is the broader range of *uses* to which it can be put, including not only analytical description but also the explanation of both systemic outcomes and foreign policy/state behaviour.

Analytical Description

One benefit of all forms of systemic analysis is that it gives us a broader perspective on international relations. It does so by forcing us to look at the larger strategic picture (i.e., the shape of the forest not just the individual trees) as well as by sensitizing us to the interconnectedness of developments.[18] Secondly, the expanded analytical framework enables us to engage in a much fuller analytic identification of the basic patterns of inter-state and inter-societal relations, thereby providing us with a deeper level of knowledge of international relations. Waltz was less useful in this regard given the skeletal nature of his framework.

Figure 3.1 International Systems: A Framework of Analysis/Explanation

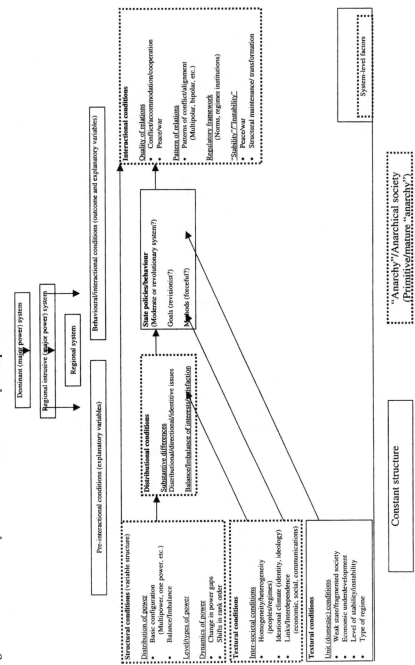

Explanation

Systemic Outcomes The most difficult and challenging use of systemic analysis is explanation. Waltz maintained that his basic systemic explanatory variables (anarchy plus the distribution of power) could primarily explain systemic outcomes (notably war or peace, and the durability of particular structures), rather than unit-level policies and behaviour. While his overall argument is questionable, Waltz does have a point. System-level variables, which are themselves relational, are better at explaining patterns of inter-state relations which persist over a period of time (e.g., conflict, alignment, cooperation, and regime formation) than they are at explaining specific state decisions. With a broader range of systemic explanatory and outcome variables, there is a greater potential for system-level explanations of the outcomes of interstate relations. In particular, a multi-factor systemic argument is more likely to provide a satisfactory explanation of system outcomes than is a single-factor argument like Waltz's. As Aaron Friedberg has pointed out, in the post-Cold War period several regional systems may have the same basic power structure (multipower), but they will in all probability experience different systemic outcomes (levels of revisionism, conflict, violence, accommodation, and cooperation) due to differences in other structural, distributional, and textural features, as well as the level of development of the regulatory framework.[19]

Foreign Policy/State Behaviour System-level variables are also capable of explaining foreign policy/state behaviour in varying degrees. Despite his disclaimer, Waltz attempted himself to use system structure to explain state behaviour. In particular, he sought to explore the logic of a two-power structure, deducing the broad strategies and behaviour of the two superpowers and the resulting systemic outcomes (war or peace, structural maintenance or transformation).[20] Morton Kaplan attempted something similar in his discussion of the 'essential rules' of various types of system but provided a more differentiated analysis of state behaviour based on various positional characteristics and systemic conditions.[21]

One important caveat is in order regarding the explanation of foreign policy, namely that one cannot logically argue directly from systemic characteristics to state policies and behaviour. There is an important intervening variable that must be added: the *positional characteristics* (a mixed systemic and unit-level factor) of the state whose policy is being analyzed.[22] One such positional factor is a state's power position within the system. Other positional characteristics include a state's membership, or not, in alliance structures, and its degree of vulnerability in a network of economic links (dependent or interdependent). These positional characteristics are the crucial link in understanding the impact of systemic factors on the strategies and behaviour of particular types of states. It should also be noted that foreign policy is not one single phenomenon but rather a range of phenomena, including the interests and preferences underlying policy, the broad lines of policy, the basic modes of behaviour, and specific decisions and actions.

Modes of Explanation

It is important to realize when using systemic factors as explanatory variables that several distinct types of causality can be involved.[23] *Permissive causality* is one form. Here systemic factors serve either as *constraints* or *opportunities,* obstructing or facilitating the pursuit of certain types of objectives, modes of behaviour, or relationships and outcomes. These shape what states can or cannot do. *Stimulus causality* is operative when certain conditions or actions serve as a *catalyst* for a state's reassessment of existing policies and relationships. *Efficient causality* is present when conditions and actors generate strong *pressures* toward particular courses of action or types of relationships ('because of' causality). Finally, *motivating causality* refers to the purposes and motives for which states act ('in order to' causality). If permissive causality shapes what states can and cannot do, motivating causality shapes what states *want to do.*

Flowing from these considerations, several questions arise which will be addressed in this chapter. What are the most important systemic (and other) explanatory factors for the purposes of understanding foreign policy behaviour and inter-state relations in the Middle East? Whose policy or behaviour and what aspects of it can systemic factors best explain? What types of causality are featured in this process? Our task here will be to ascertain the respective roles played by systemic, positional, and domestic factors as sources of the stimuli, pressures, constraints, opportunities, and motives of foreign policy behaviour/international relations.

System Levels

A full-fledged systemic explanatory framework will not only be *multidimensional* but also *multilevel* in character. Our first task therefore is to sketch the basic contours of the main systems that shape Middle Eastern international relations and foreign policy, notably the global major power system (the core or dominant system), and the Middle Eastern regional system.

Major Power (Dominant) System

The global system consists of two main spheres of activity. The first is the *politico-military* sphere, which is made up primarily of state units operating in a state system characterized by a framework of anarchy. Realism in its various forms is the pre-eminent theoretical perspective here, although liberal-institutionalism and—to some extent—constructivism also have their proponents. The *economic sphere,* or international politico-economic system, consists of varying types of economic units, from states to intergovernmental organizations and multinational enterprises, functioning in an increasingly interconnected international/transnational world economy. Liberalism, institutionalism, Marxism, and realism constitute the competing theoretical approaches here. Finally, there is a less-clearly delineated *societal-ideational sphere* where constructivism and sociological approaches constitute the main forms of analysis.[24]

Within this multisectoral global system, it is the *major power sector* that constitutes the *core or dominant system*.[25] It is often assumed that this dominant system takes the same form across the globe. In fact, there can be significant variations in the levels and patterns of major power involvement, both politico-military and economic, in different regions of the world. Consequently, the basic features of the major power system in any given region may differ from those in the global major power system as well as those in other regions (see Tables 3.1 and 3.2). For example, the global major power system currently has a pronounced (strong) one-power structure (US) in the politico-military sphere and an unbalanced two-power to multipower structure (US–EU–Japan) in the economic sphere. In the East Asian region, however, there is an unbalanced two-power pattern (US–China, with US advantage) in the politico-military sector and an unbalanced multipower pattern (US–China–Japan–EU, with US advantage) in the economic sector. In both sectors there are high levels of major power involvement. The Middle Eastern major power intrusive system, for its part, has roughly similar features to the global major power system, namely a one-power pattern in the politico-military sector and an unbalanced two-power to multipower pattern (US–EU [Germany–France–UK]–Japan, with US advantage) in the economic sphere.

It is the characteristics of the *major power intrusive system in a given region*, in this case the Middle East, that constitute the relevant global-level systemic variables for purposes of explaining international relations/foreign policy in that region.

Middle East Regional and Sub-Regional Systems

The regional system constitutes the second main level of our multilevel explanatory framework. For decades, scholars have disagreed not only over the geographic contours of the Middle Eastern region but also over the most appropriate focus for systemic analyses of the international relations of the area. Many analysts have focused on the *region as a whole* although their definitions of the region often diverge (Brecher, Brown, Binder, Cantori and Spiegel, Gause).[26] Others have chosen to concentrate their attention on particular *sub-regional systems*. In most cases this has meant the Arab sub-system (Kerr, Noble, Mattar and Dessouki).[27] In some cases it has involved the Arab-Israeli sub-system (Brecher to some extent), or Gulf sub-system (Ramazani, Buzan and Rizvi), or the two together (Buzan).[28] For the purposes of this analysis, the Middle Eastern regional system will be defined basically along the lines set out by Gause (in line with Cantori and Spiegel), namely Egypt, the Arab states of west Asia, and the three non-Arab perimeter powers: Israel, Iran, and Turkey. The great powers will not be included in the regional system proper but rather will be treated as forming a major power intrusive system. Since there are no resident great powers in the Middle East (unlike East Asia), the two system levels are analytically distinct, though practically intertwined.

Table 3.1 Regional Intrusive System Structures: Politico-Military Sphere

	Middle East[a]	Africa/North Africa	East/ Southeast Asia[b]	South Asia	South/ Central America/ Caribbean
Major power military presence / force projection capacity (2000)					
Level	High	Low (Africa) to medium (N.Africa)	High	Medium low	High (C.America/ Caribbean) to low (S.America)
Pattern	One power (US)	Multipower (France, US, UK)	Unbalanced two-power (US, China)	Unbalanced tripower (US, China, Russia)	One power (US)
Major power arms transfers (1995 to 1997)					
Level (US$ bil.)	57.0	3.3	24.9	2.7	3.9
Transfers to developing world (%)	62.2%	3.6%	27.1%	2.9%	4.2%
Distribution *(% of transfers to region)*					
US	49.8	17.9	57.1	18.4	45.5
UK	25.3	3.6	6.4	1.3	10.6
France	9.7	11.7	17.2	14.3	5.5
Russia	3.7	21.3	5.8	28.7	4.0
China	1.5	11.8	2.5	17.3	1.5
Other powers	10.0	33.7	11.0	20.0	32.9
Pattern	One power (US)	Multipower (Russia, US, France, China)	One power (US)	Multipower (Russia, US, France, China)	One power (US)
Overall pattern	One power (US)	Multipower	Very unbalanced two-power (US, China)	Tripower (US, China, Russia)	One power (US)

a. Includes Iran, Turkey, Israel, Arab states of Southwest Asia, and Egypt.
b. Excludes Japan, South Asia, Pacific Area.

Sources: Major power regional military presence and force projection capacity drawn from data on individual major power force deployments and bases, and on foreign force presence data in individual developing countries in International Institute of Strategic Studies, *The Military Balance 2000-2001* (London: Oxford University Press, 2000). Data on arms transfers adapted from US Department of State, Bureau of Verification and Compliance, *World Military Expenditures and Arms Transfers, 1998* (Washington: Department of State, 2000), Table III.

Table 3.2 Regional Intrusive System Structures: Economic Sphere

	Middle East[a]	Africa/North Africa	Asia/Pacific Developing Countries[b]	South/Central America/ Caribbean
Major power trade with developing regions (exports + imports, 2000)				
Level (US$ bil.)	360.5	167.4	1630.6	525.2
Distribution (% of major power trade with region)				
US	19.4	20.7	27.4	72.0
EU (and members)	54.9	66.4	25.3	18.6
Japan	17.1	5.3	21.9	5.5
China	6.5	7.0	25.0	3.5
Russia	2.1	0.6	0.4	0.4
Pattern	Weak one power (EU)	Strong one power (EU)	Multipower	Strong one power (US)
Major power aid to developing regions (1999/2000 Combined)				
Level (US$ bil.)	7.688	23.262	23.279	8.263
Distribution (% of major power aid to region)				
US	52.1	17.8	10.9	31.3
EU (and members)	30.4	68.2	29.0	48.1
Japan	11.9	11.7	58.8	19.5
Other donor countries (China, Russia, etc.)	5.6	2.3	1.3	1.0
Pattern	Unbalanced two-power (US, EU)	Strong one power (EU)	One power (Japan)	Unbalanced two-power (US, EU)
Overall pattern	Two-power (US, EU)	One power (EU)	Unbalanced multipower (Japan, EU, US, China)	One power (US)

a. Includes Iran, Turkey, Israel, Arab states of Southwest Asia, and Egypt.
b. Excludes Japan but includes Asia and Pacific.

Sources: Adapted from International Monetary Fund (IMF), *Direction of Trade Statistics Yearbook 2001* (Washington: IMF, 2001), regional tables (Part B) (Trade) and from Organization for Economic Cooperation and Development (OECD), *Geographic Distribution of Financial Flows to Developing Countries 1996-2000* (Paris: OECD, 2002), Donor Country and Regional Tables (Aid).

Within these geographic limits, the *framework of interaction* has undergone considerable change over the years. For much of the post-war period, the Middle East was a *segmented* regional arena consisting of a number of distinct but overlapping sub-regional clusters of states. Until the late 1960s there were two main clusters (sub-regional systems): the Arab-Israeli and the inter-Arab. By the

1970s, a new sub-regional system had developed in the Gulf area. A number of factors contributed to this, notably the achievement of independence by several small Gulf Arab states following Britain's withdrawal from the area, periodic tensions between Iraq and these smaller states (especially Kuwait), the heightened importance of the area's oil, Iran's growing ambitions in the Gulf, the subsequent Islamic Revolution in Iran and the outbreak of the long and bloody Iraq-Iran war (1980-1988). All these developments served to intensify interaction and turn the Gulf into the primary focus of attention for the states of the area. Elsewhere in the region, Turkey, after decades of relative inattention to the Middle East, became increasingly involved with its regional neighbours in the 1980s and 1990s over a range of issues (oil supplies and pipelines, trade, water issues, the Kurdish problem, the Islamic revolution in Iran, the Iraq problem, and Syrian territorial claims).[29] This gave rise to a new northern sector (encompassing Turkey, Syria, Iraq and Iran).

For much of the post-war period then, the main 'systems' were sub-regional: interaction within each sector was relatively intense while cross-sector and region-wide interactions were much weaker. Since the late 1970s, there has been a slow but steady *expansion and diversification of interaction between sub-regional sectors*. The most important contributing factor has been the expanding range and scope of involvement of the non-Arab perimeter powers within the region. In recent decades, both Israel and Iran have extended their reach and activities beyond their immediate neighbourhoods to other parts of the region. This was facilitated by developments in military technology and an emerging 'peace process' in the case of Israel, and by a combination of the growing appeal of Islamic ideas and movements and the resurgence of Shi'a consciousness across the region in the case of Iran. Turkey, for its part, found itself involved not only in increased friction with its regional neighbours but also in closer politico-military ties with Israel. In addition to the expanded potential for hostile interaction, the post-Gulf war period witnessed the development of a variety of other contacts between Arab states and perimeter powers in both the Arab-Israeli and Gulf sectors. This expanding regional reach and activity of the perimeter powers has brought them into more intensive contact with Arab states near and far, as well as with each other.

The growing *regionalization of interaction* has created a *genuine region-wide security complex* characterized by increasing military, politico-diplomatic, and transnational political linkages.[30] In the *military* sphere, key states have acquired, or are likely to acquire, a region-wide military power projection capacity (Israel, Iran). Others (Syria, Saudi Arabia) have developed some shorter-range delivery capacity. With Middle Eastern states increasingly exposed to military pressures from outside as well as inside their respective sectors, a region wide military-security complex is emerging.

Increased linkages have also been in evidence in the *politico-diplomatic* sphere. The launching of the 'peace process' following the Gulf war led to a substantial expansion of Israeli politico-diplomatic contacts with Arab front-line states as well as those of the Gulf and North Africa. The vast majority have subsequently been suspended but some contacts do remain even if downgraded for now. Since the Gulf war, Iran has made considerable progress in restoring relations with Saudi Arabia, the Gulf Cooperation Council (GCC) states, Egypt, and Turkey, in addition to maintaining ties with Syria, Lebanon and Sudan.[31] While many of these links are sporadic or limited, a region-wide politico-diplomatic chessboard is clearly in the process of formation.

Transnational political links constitute another dimension of expanded regional interaction. Previously such links were largely limited to the Arab system where they were extremely intense. By the 1990s the growing appeal of Islamic ideals and the strength of Islamic movements along with the sharpening of identitive cleavages within societies (Sunni vs. Shi'a; Kurds vs. Turks, Arabs, and Iranians) served to draw Iran, Turkey, and the Arab world into a broader, more diversified network of transnational ties. On the other hand, *economic ties*, at least in their traditional form (trade), remain relatively limited within the region.[32] However, in addition to inter-Arab financial and labour flows, there are some economic links between perimeter powers and the Arab world involving the oil industry, shared water systems, and more broadly-based links between Israel and Palestine, Jordan, and Turkey.

This emerging region-wide security complex has not eliminated the sub-regional sectors. In fact, they not only persist but arguably remain the locus of the most intense interaction in the area. However, they are all increasingly enmeshed in a wider network of regional relations. The Arab system continues to function but is experiencing an increasing erosion of its boundaries and heightened permeability to a broad range of pressures and activities from the perimeter powers. Still, the Middle Eastern regional system is not a single undifferentiated arena but rather a complex of partly distinct but overlapping and interrelated sectors. In many ways, it remains a 'system of systems.'

System-level Explanations

The key test for any systemic approach is its explanatory power. Let us examine the most promising regional and global systemic explanatory factors as well as their impact on regional foreign policies and relationships.

Regional and Sub-Regional Systemic Factors

The Middle East and Asia are the regions that have been characterized by the highest levels of revisionism, conflict, and militarization in the developing world.[33] They have also experienced the most frequent and damaging wars and, in the case of the Middle East, the most extensive permeability of states and the most intensive transnational political processes of any developing region. What regional factors best account for such behaviour and outcomes?

Key Regional Systemic Explanatory Factors

At the regional level, the main systemic variables are two sets of *realist* factors (structural and distributional) and two sets of *textural* factors (identitive factors and social communications links). The first key systemic explanatory factor is *structure*, the most basic realist variable. This is really a set of factors rather than a single factor. Apart from the condition of anarchy, it encompasses the overall distribution of power, the equality or inequality of power, the level and types of power, and the dynamics of power (power approaches and transitions). In the overall region, there is a highly *unbalanced multipower pattern*, with Israel and to a lesser extent Turkey enjoying the strongest capabilities, particularly in the military sphere.[34] This imbalance is exacerbated by the Israeli-Turkish politico-military partnership. There are also high levels of conventional military power, nuclear weapons (an Israeli monopoly), and widespread bacteriological and chemical weaponry, plus an emerging region-wide delivery capacity on the part of some states. Under these conditions, military strength is not only useful for deterrence and defence but continues to be usable for other coercive purposes, as evidenced by the recurrent resort to force and coercive diplomacy in recent decades, particularly between the perimeter powers and Arab states. While limited uses of force are likely to continue, the regional build-up of weapons of mass destruction (WMDs) and missile delivery systems, with the substantially higher levels of damage they generate, is likely to operate increasingly as a constraint on the resort to large scale or extreme forms of force by regional States.

The impact of structural factors is greatest, however, at the sub-regional level. In the *Arab-Israeli sector*, the pronounced imbalance is heightened by Israel's nuclear monopoly and region-wide delivery capacity. Moreover, the military power gap between it and Arab frontline states appears to be widening rather than narrowing. This gives Israel an opportunity to maintain revisionist claims and engage in the recurrent use of force and coercive diplomacy to maintain control over occupied territories, intervene in some adjacent territories, and destroy emerging nuclear forces. However, the regional build-up of missile delivery systems and WMDs by some Arab states and Iran should eventually operate as a constraint on Israel's resort to large-scale conventional or nuclear force. The nuclear monopoly and pronounced imbalance of military power also serve as a deterrent and constraint on the use of large-scale military force by Arab states. However it is by no means an absolute deterrent against an attempt to regain lost Arab territories (as distinct from an attack on Israel proper), as was evidenced by Egypt and Syria's initiation of a war for that purpose in 1973. It is also not an absolute deterrent against resistance activities in the occupied territories or low intensity attacks on Israel (e.g., by the Palestinians or Hizbullah).

In the *northern sector*, the imbalance in Turkey's favour combined with the Israeli entente provides it with opportunities for assertiveness and coercive diplomacy, including military pressures on Syria and intervention in northern Iraq. At the same time, this deters military pressure by neighbouring states. In the *Gulf sector*, the situation was more complex prior to the recent US-Iraq war (2003) with more of a balance between Iraq and Iran coupled with some imbalances between each of these and Saudi Arabia/the GCC states. Now that Iraq's military capabilities have been virtually destroyed, the imbalances predominate. There are generally more constraints in this sub-region, emanating especially from the major power arena. However, the power hierarchy is more fluid here than in other sectors and with this fluidity there is greater danger of revisionism and assertiveness.

Finally, in the *Arab sector*, the pattern of power now and for the foreseeable future is a relatively balanced multipower configuration. However, it is a balance of weakness rather than a balance of power, despite the high levels of military power in several states and elements of financial strength in others. This condition is likely to persist due to the lack of consistency in the capability profiles of the leading Arab states (i.e., those with the strongest military capabilities tend to have much weaker economic capabilities and vice-versa), the declining soft power resources of these states, and the domestic problems that weaken them all. At one level this diffusion of power and balance of weakness serve to dampen revisionism and conflict. No single state has the capacity to engage in extensive revisionism or achieve a hegemonic position. Nevertheless, there have been problems in the past with power approaches and transitions in the Arab system, more recently regarding Iraq, and these could recur. The diffusion of power also contributes to the fragmentation of the system, since without the mobilizing pressures and inducements of a pre-eminent power, there has been a strong tendency for Arab sub-system members to go their own way.

In short, there are different structural conditions within the Middle Eastern arena. These operate primarily as *permissive causes* (constraints and opportunities) in shaping modes of behaviour (methods) as well as regional policies and relations. Where significant power dynamics occur, however, this can serve as a *motivating* rather than simply a permissive cause for revisionism and conflict.

The second key systemic explanatory variable is another realist-style factor which may be termed the *distributional factor*. This refers to the *extent of substantive differences* regarding the state and territorial framework, the allocation of resources and populations, as well as status, influence, and power relations in the area.[35] The protracted unsettled character of these issues and the resulting imbalance of interests and satisfaction is a major problem not only in the Middle East but also throughout much of the developing world with the possible exception of Latin America. These conditions in turn generate substantial revisionism, conflict, and (periodically) war.

These problems are especially acute in the Middle East where not only is the territorial framework challenged (in the Gulf area, Arabian peninsula and Levant) but also the state framework itself (and consequently the national existence of some states).[36] This challenge has occurred bilaterally in the cases of some Arab states vs. Israel, Israel vs. Palestine, Iraq vs. Kuwait, Syria vs. Lebanon, between Jordan and Palestine, and between the two Yemens. The problem has subsided in some cases but remains active in others.

The problem assumes a broader multilateral form in the Arab arena where the sense of common Arab identity and resulting pan-Arab national consciousness have given rise to recurrent plans for 'mergers and acquisitions' which challenge the independent national existence of one or more Arab states. This type of challenge is more or less unique to the Arab world. In short, the Middle East is characterized not only by significant imbalances of power but also by *serious imbalances of interest and satisfaction* which serve as an important *motivating cause* of state behaviour and ultimately inter-state relations. While all states experiencing significant dissatisfaction are potentially disruptive regardless of their power levels (e.g., the Palestinians), it is those who have substantial power relative to others, and especially quickly rising power (a positional factor), who will tend to be the greatest source of revisionism, conflict, and violence.

A third key set of systemic explanatory variables is *textural* and primarily *identitive-constructivist* in character. Here identitive differences (ethnic-linguistic, cultural, and religious) between the Arab world, Israel, Iran, and Turkey create fault lines which contribute to conflict. However, these are not much more serious than in other regions and indeed may even be less serious than in Asia where at least four of Samuel Huntington's cultural/'civilizational' fault lines lie.[37] What is distinctive about the Middle East is the high degree of identitive homogeneity which characterizes much of the region, primarily the Arab states (linguistically and culturally) but also Iran to some extent (through Islam). This is much more extensive than in other regions: only Latin America comes close. This homogeneity of peoples has led to a clear sense of kinship and even common identity, particularly in the Arab sector. This in turn has generated a preoccupation of Arab governments and peoples with certain common issues and a sense of solidarity when any segment of the Arab world finds itself in conflict with non-Arab actors. Paradoxically, the prevailing sense of kinship and common identity has also led to intense and critical scrutiny of each other's policies and behaviour, sharp criticisms of policy deviations or lack of solidarity and, at times, challenges to the legitimacy of existing state units combined with pressures for political union. In so doing, it has served to amplify the bases for revisionism and conflict already inherent in the unsettled state and territorial framework of the region.[38]

Widespread identitive homogeneity has also contributed to another important systemic characteristic of the region, namely *extensive transnational societal and political links*, particularly between Arab countries (a liberal sociological variable).[39] These links take several forms including the extensive movement of persons (see Table 3.6), the intense circulation and resonance of information, opinion and ideological currents, the emergence of cross-frontier ties between religious and political movements, and the development among attentive and mass publics of some identification with, and responsiveness to, leaders and movements in other regional states.

In particular, developments in communications technology (satellite communications) combined with the prevailing identitive homogeneity have strengthened regional communications links. This is evident in the rapid proliferation of transnational Arabic satellite TV channels serving region-wide audiences (see Table 3.3).[40] The regional impact is especially strong in the case of channels featuring news, public affairs, and talk shows dealing with politics, religion, and social issues (e.g., *al-Jazira*). The substantially increased flow of information and opinion helps to generate greater mutual awareness among Arab elites and peoples. It also serves to mobilize public opinion on issues of common concern (e.g., the Israeli-Palestine and Iraq conflicts, and the Western campaign against Islamic 'terrorism').[41] As a result, the Arab world resembles a vast sound chamber in which information and currents of thought circulate widely and enjoy considerable resonance across state frontiers. This dilutes narrower national and sub-regional perspectives and sensitizes populations to a broader Arab perspective. Overall then, the Arab world (and to a lesser extent, the Middle East) are characterized by extensive transnational social and political links as well as a *pervasive permeability* of societies and states. This in turn has given rise to a *transnational political process* encompassing not only governments but also groups and individuals, engaged in a broad range of activities, including transnational appeals, cross-frontier alliances, and the trans-border penetration and manipulation of domestic politics.[42] Such efforts can be used to delegitimize and destabilize regimes, to reshape the basic policy directions of states, and even to undermine their political autonomy. This transnational political activity, whether undertaken by governments or by religious and political movements, has constituted the main form of cross-frontier behaviour in much of the region.

Overall then, the relative homogeneity of peoples, especially in the Arab world, and the permeability of societies and states to which it gives rise, not only shape the predominant *mode of behaviour* in the region (transnational political activity) but also expand the scope of *revisionism* to include the targeting of not only state interests but even *regime interests* (i.e., regime survival) as well.

Table 3.3 Arab World/Middle East: Satellite TV Communication Links (2001)

	TV Homes (millions)	Satellite TV receivers (millions)	Population with access to satellite TV	
			Millions[a]	% of total pop
Turkey	13.670	3.140	15.700	25
Israel	1.600	0.110	0.550	10
Egypt	12.410	0.890	4.450	7
Saudi Arabia	3.910	2.200	11.000	55
Gulf Arab States	N/A	N/A	5.790	65
Lebanon	0.830	0.590	2.950	85
Jordan	0.710	0.330	1.650	25
Syria	2.870	1.060	5.300	30
Algeria	4.470	4.120	20.600	65
Morocco	4.050	1.120	5.600	20
Tunisia	1.900	0.330	1.650	17

a. The estimate of access to satellite broadcasts is based on the number of satellite TV receivers multiplied by a factor estimating the number of people who watch TV on each dish (about 5).

Sources: EUTELSAT 2002, 'The Cable and Satellite TV Market 2001,' <www.eutelsat.com>; data for the Gulf Arab States are based on estimates by Hussein Amin in Alterman, *New Media, New Politics?* (Washington: Washington Institute for Middle East Policy, 1998), p.15; estimates of total population (2000) used as a reference point are drawn from Economist Intelligence Unit (EIU), *Country Reports 2001*, <www.eiu.com>.

Questionable Regional Systemic Explanatory Factors

Thus far we have emphasized four sets of system-level explanatory factors: the structural (realist), distributional (realist), and two closely related sets of textural factors, the identitive (constructivist) and social/communications links (sociological liberalism). It is noteworthy that none of these, with one possible exception, involve the usual alternative system-level variables employed in the study of international relations, at least among developed countries, namely *liberal* and *institutionalist* variables of various types (economic links and interdependence, communities of democratic regimes, or international regimes and institutions).[43] None of these factors, which serve as significant constraints on revisionism, conflict, and violence in the developed world, are really in evidence in the Middle East at the present time, although there are some limited regional (horizontal) economic links and even stronger vertical links to the global economic system (see Tables 3.4 and 3.5).

Liberals and institutionalists nevertheless insist that, if not the Middle East, then other developing regions (Latin America, Southeast Asia, and East Asia) are experiencing some transformation (i.e., economic development), leading to some degree of *economic if not political liberalization/democratization, growing regional economic links*, and *emerging regional institutions*.[44] This, they argue, will serve to mitigate the potential for revisionism, conflict, and violence or even to generate incentives for accommodation and cooperation. Thus realist-style problems may persist in some areas but their importance is steadily diminishing and giving way to other types of concern, notably economic. As these processes deepen and spread, more of the developing world, it is argued, will experience similar transformations. For now, these processes are very weak in the Middle East, although links to the global economic system are developing. As a result, liberal and institutionalist systemic variables have extremely limited explanatory power in the area, either for regional outcomes or state behaviour.

Alternative Explanations: Unit-level Explanatory Factors

The real alternative in the Middle East and developing world to existing systemic approaches is therefore not liberal and institutionalist (systemic) approaches but rather unit-level approaches, arising from conditions of political and economic underdevelopment. The most prominent of these is the *weak state-fragmented society model* which emphasizes that developing societies are characterized by deep vertical (ethnic/religious, communal), horizontal (class), and ideological cleavages as well as by institutions and regimes lacking legitimacy and capacity.[45] The result is widespread internal conflict and instability, with severe challenges not only to regimes and their basic ideological direction but also to state institutions themselves and to national cohesion and territorial integrity (due to the poor fit between State and nation).[46]

In the Arab world and Middle East, the national unity and territorial integrity of several States have been severely challenged by violent conflict (Lebanon, Iraq, Sudan, and Yemen). However, in many States some state consolidation has been occurring in recent decades. This has been due in part to the oil boom of the 1970s which strengthened both the coercive and co-optive capacities of national governments, the preoccupation of societies and states with their own problems, the focusing of the attention of populations and elites on their individual States as the framework for the resolution of these problems, and the growth of national communications media and institutions of higher education—all factors which have tended to strengthen national identities. While challenges from within to national unity and territorial integrity remain, the problem in the Arab world is more one of weak regimes than of weak states. The most widespread and frequent challenges have been to regimes and/or the basic ideological direction of states and societies (i.e., Islamist fundamentalism vs. secularist or moderate Islamist orientations). Whatever their precise form, these domestic divisions and challenges give rise to widespread internal instability, conflict, violence, and accentuate the permeability of States and societies, thereby generating serious internal and transnational political security concerns for governments. These internal and transnational threats, it is argued, constitute the most pervasive as well as most immediate and acute security problem confronting the Middle East and the developing world today.

More significantly, the weak state-fragmented society perspective has emerged as an important *alternative paradigm* for *foreign policy/international relations* in the developing world. In the first place, domestic cleavages and turbulence weaken the State internationally by preventing it from mobilizing the full range of resources it needs to carry out its external responsibilities, and by hampering it from concentrating its attention and energies on the international arena in a sustained and effective manner (permissive causality). Second, internal divisions and conflicts affect foreign policy behaviour in a number of ways, ranging from introversion in the case of weaker regional states through policy rigidity toward traditional opponents or even diversionary aggressiveness for stronger regional states (motivating causality).[47] Internal instability and conflict have also been used to explain a wide range of regional international relations starting with conflict, for example outlet and diversionary theories (motivating causality),[48] spill-over and splashback theories (efficient causality?), and magnet theories (internal conflicts drawing external intervention: permissive causality).[49] In addition, domestic political competition and conflict has been used to explain international alignments,[50] and even cooperation (with shared internal political security concerns as the motivation) or the lack thereof (cooperation obstructed by the lack of domestic cohesion).[51] In general, internal instability and conflict is viewed as having a decidedly negative effect on foreign policy and regional international relations.

Economic underdevelopment/dependence approaches constitute a second set of alternative approaches (mixed unit-level and positional) to foreign policy/international relations in the contemporary periphery. Like economic liberalism, such approaches maintain that developing countries are not simply State units operating in an international system characterized by anarchy, but also economic units functioning in an increasingly interconnected transnational world economy. Unlike the liberal school, which emphasizes interdependence with its mutual benefits and constraints, this approach stresses the pronounced hierarchy of the world economy and consequent relationships of inequality, dependence, and vulnerability.[52] Internal political threats may be the most immediate (and acute) security concern facing developing states. However, economic difficulties are both equally pervasive and more fundamental, since they are a major source of virtually all security concerns in the developing world today (human security, regime security, State security).[53] Moreover, economic difficulties contribute to turbulence in much of the periphery by fuelling domestic political unrest and generating discontent with the status quo. The overall effects, however, are likely to be more mixed in terms of international relations since poor economic conditions also generate weakness, which limits the ability to translate discontent into forceful action. Substantial economic needs may also lead to accommodative, even compliant, foreign policy behaviour to attract economic assistance or devote attention and resources to internal development.

Economic growth is also likely to have mixed (rather than simply negative) effects.[54] The *pessimistic perspective* is that such growth could significantly increase the economic and ultimately the military capabilities of a State. This would increase its ambitions as well as the power available to achieve them (motivating and permissive causality). Economic growth also creates losers as well as winners and this could generate substantial dissatisfaction among important domestic interests (motivating causality). All of this can contribute to rigidity or even assertiveness in foreign policy. *The optimistic perspective* foresees more positive results in terms of foreign policy/international relations. First, it is argued that economic growth will produce more satisfaction within a society both in terms of standard of living and economic position relative to other societies (motivating causality). Second, economic development and modernization will lead to the predominance of economic cost-benefit calculations and economic welfare values over nationalist and heroic values among populations and elites (motivating causality*).*[55] Third, economic growth means that populations have more to lose if the country engages in adventurous moves (motivating causality). Such developments serve to limit aggressive behaviour. Finally, economic growth will probably produce more economic interdependence and hence more constraints on assertiveness and adventurous behaviour (permissive causality).

Global Systemic Factors

Global systemic factors, both politico-military and economic, also play a key role in shaping foreign policy behaviour/international relations in the Middle East.

Politico-Military Sphere

Extra-Regional Policies and Relations. One area where the dominant system has a definite impact is regional policies and relations vis-à-vis the major powers (vertical relations). Here the combination of the *power structure, pattern of alignment,* and *quality of relations* in the dominant system shape not only the flow of major power resources and pressures to a region, but also the range of options open to regional states in dealing with these powers and the ensuing patterns of relations.[56]

In the Cold War period, the Middle Eastern intrusive system was characterized by a *two-power, two-bloc pattern with intensely competitive and conflictual relations* between the two leading powers. This increased the *flow of resources* to the area as the two powers competed for influence by offering military and economic assistance as well as diplomatic support to regional states.[57] In theory, these conditions provided regional states with a *broad range of options* in their dealings with the intrusive powers (i.e., non-dependence, unidependence on one power or the other, or bi-dependence). In reality, the amount of latitude turned out to be less than expected. To begin with, *non-dependence* was not really an option in light of the regional situation, which generated high-level politico-military needs on the part of virtually all regional states. *Bi-dependence* ceased to be an option after a while due to the same high level of national needs as well as the policies of the superpowers and the nature of the military sector itself.[58] In effect, the more extensive a country's needs, the more concentrated its pattern of dependence, since regional states were prepared to accept close relationships with an intrusive power to ensure its full support. The superpowers for their part were unwilling to provide the high levels of support sought by many Middle Eastern states unless they were assured of a quasi-exclusive relationship. Moreover, military relationships are more sensitive and inherently less divisible than economic relationships. Intrusive powers were reluctant to furnish advanced military technology to states if military advisors of an opposing power were present, for fear of loss of technological secrets. Finally, the policies of the superpowers with regard to major regional conflicts were not neutral or even-handed. Hence, regional states involved in such conflicts were very unlikely to obtain the necessary levels of support from both superpowers. For all these reasons, balanced relationships seemed out of the question and regional states were basically forced to choose between reliance on one superpower or the other *(unidependence)*. Unidependence in turn tended to lead to *quasi-alignment* as a result of pressures exerted by the superpowers combined with the acute needs of regional states. There was, of course, still the potential for switching from one power to the other (e.g., Egypt) but this could presumably be done only once.

In the post-Cold War period, the shape of the dominant system changed substantially. What emerged was a *one-power, quasi-unipolar* pattern centred on a US-led Western core coalition with periodic collaboration from Russia and China. The nature of relations also shifted from intense competition and conflict to a spectrum ranging from muted competition to acquiescence or even active collaboration. The pre-eminent power (US) has remained heavily involved in the region but the core coalition has tended to erode over time as evidenced by the recent divisions over how to deal with Saddam Hussein's Iraq as well as Iran. Despite the decline in competition, the *flow of military resources* has continued, given the important US interests in the region. The decline in competition also reduced the overall *flow of major power pressures* somewhat but the absence of any effective counterweight to the US has opened the door to increased pressure against states which oppose it. In this situation, the range of options available to regional states seeking extra-regional support has been limited.[59] Given their high level of politico-military needs, these could only be met by one power (the US). Other major powers could supply some arms but only the US could provide the full range of required services (military protection, arms supplies, and diplomatic support in achieving an honourable settlement to protracted regional conflicts). The only options were to turn to the pre-eminent power or proceed with little outside assistance. Some had little choice but to accept the latter (e.g., Iraq). Most, however, gravitated to relations of *unidependence* not just upon one side, but upon one power alone (the US). This was accompanied by pressures for military cooperation and the alignment of regional policies with its own. The former were usually acquiesced to, at least in part (i.e., use of military facilities, prepositioning of military equipment, participation in military exercises). The alignment of policies has met with greater resistance due to divergences in threat perceptions and in the regional policies themselves. As American policies came to be perceived as less responsive to Arab interests, even relatively close Arab associates of the US have felt obliged to demonstrate their autonomy and maintain some distance in the face of domestic pressures and concern for their respective regional positions, for example Egyptian and Saudi Arabian policies toward the US prior to the 2003 Gulf War.

Regional Policies and Relations Conditions in the dominant system also have an impact on policies and relations in the regional system itself (horizontal relations). Benjamin Miller's work is arguably the most thorough and insightful in this regard.[60] He begins by acknowledging that a combination of *regional systemic conditions* (extensive substantive differences over the state/territorial framework) and *unit-level conditions* (the lack of fit between State and nation) are the factors primarily responsible for the *outbreak* and, to a lesser extent, *level of conflict* in a region, as well as for the *outbreak of hot war* and potentially also the achievement of a *warm peace*.

Miller emphasizes, however, that *global systemic factors* play a key role in shaping regional conflict intensity and persistence, war avoidance and termination, as well as accommodation or cold peace. During the Cold War period, the combination of a *two-power, intensely competitive* major power relationship along with a *high level of major power involvement* intensified and prolonged Middle East conflicts due to the superpowers' continuing efforts to bolster the position of their respective clients through arms supplies and supportive diplomatic efforts. This led parties to regional conflict to *put off attempts at accommodation or conflict resolution*, even when in a very weakened condition, due to the belief that their superpower patron would rebuild their strength to enable them to negotiate or fight again from a more equal position (permissive causality). Great powers at times also contributed to a *further intensification* of regional conflict or even the *outbreak of regional wars* by permitting or encouraging assertiveness and adventurous moves (permissive causality-opportunity) on the part of their clients, e.g., the US with regard to Israel in 1982 (Lebanon) and 2002 (Palestine) and even to some extent in 1967. More often though, they had strong incentives to *discourage adventurous moves or wars* between their respective allies for fear that they themselves might be drawn in (permissive causality-constraint). This concern tended to be operative more in the case of the superpower backing the weaker party. The great powers also played a key role in *war termination* (efficient causality) based largely on these same fears. Hence, under conditions of intense great power competition (whether two-power or multipower) and high-level involvement in a region, global systemic factors will have mixed but primarily harmful effects on regional inter-state relations.

Conversely, in situations of *hegemony* or *great power cooperation*, along with *substantial involvement* in a region, the impact of global systemic factors on regional relations tends to be more favourable. Under conditions of hegemony, as in the post-Cold War Middle East, the pre-eminent power, at the very least, is in a position to prevent cold wars from turning into hot wars by using its superior resources and connections to restrain the parties, although this was only attempted at a much later stage of the most recent phase of the Israeli-Palestinian conflict. Its pre-eminent position and connections will also be a decisive factor (efficient causality) in turning cold or even hot war conditions in regional conflicts into accommodation and peace agreements (cold peace) if it is so inclined. Global systemic conditions of great power cooperation can also generate similar positive results. On the other hand, *great power disinterest/ disengagement*, whatever the power structure of the dominant system, will have damaging effects on regional relations by removing some important restraints on conflict as well as potential incentives for accommodation.

Economic Sphere

In the Middle East, the dominant economic system continues to be characterized by an *unbalanced two-power to multipower pattern* (US–EU, with a lesser level of Japanese involvement). This has been combined with a *quasi-unipolar pattern of alignment* centred on a core coalition of developed Western powers led by the US. The latter was partly *diluted by trilateral tendencies*: the existence of three major power-centred regional economic groupings (EU, NAFTA, and, the East/Southeast Asian network).[61] The economic sphere is arguably also characterized by *more competition and rivalry* than the politico-military sphere.

The better-balanced and more competitive situation provides Middle Eastern states with a *range of options* in pursuing their economic interests.[62] While these options are clearly greater than in the politico-military sphere, they are more limited than might otherwise appear. To begin with, the competing powers' capacity to provide desired economic resources (markets, goods, technology, aid, investment, and debt relief) is by no means equal. The US is still the leading supplier and mobilizer of economic resources for the region, while its main competitor (the EU) is not even a fully unified economic actor. Moreover, Japan's economy has slipped badly and it is not as active an economic player in the area as before. Second, the competing European and Asian powers are not as heavily involved in the area as their overall economic resources might warrant. They believe that the US enjoys a decided economic advantage arising from its protective responsibilities in regard to Gulf oil producers and its central role in handling the Arab-Israeli conflict. Its ensuing special relationships with key Middle Eastern states tend to restrict the ability of potential economic rivals to compete in establishing markets or enhancing their trade and influence through economic assistance. Moreover, better opportunities to achieve such aims are perceived to exist in regions closer to home (Eastern Europe and Africa in the case of the European powers, and Asia in the case of Japan). Hence there is less intrusive power economic competition in the area than might appear. Finally, in spite of some trilateral and tripolar tendencies, the leading economic powers have tended to act in concert economically on several issues of importance to Middle Eastern states, such as debt rescheduling, aid conditionality, and some energy issues. They have gone different ways on other issues, such as the US attempt to isolate Iran economically. Nevertheless, while there are fewer options in terms of economic relationships than might appear in theory, Middle Eastern states are still able to diversify relations with the major economic powers. *Multidependence* therefore is much more prevalent in this sphere than unidependence (permissive causality).

Beyond these structural and 'quality of relations' arguments, some have argued that globalization has become the new paradigm for international relations.[63] Whether or not this is true, any study of global systemic factors and their impact on the policies and relationships of Middle Eastern states must take *economic globalization* into account. This phenomenon has still to be explored systematically in the context of the Middle East. In any case, the technology and processes that promote greater interconnectedness in the world appear to have contrasting results when it comes to the Middle East. In the *economic sphere* they have served to connect the region much more strongly to the dominant system and larger world (see Tables 3.4 and 3.5). In the *communications and socio-cultural sphere*, however, they have intensified the links between regional societies (at least Arab societies), much more than between the Middle East and the larger world (see Tables 3.3 and 3.6).

Even in the economic sphere, where Middle Eastern states, with a few exceptions, are more closely linked to the dominant system than they are to each other, they are far less connected to the global system than virtually any other region, with the possible exception of Africa. This weaker linkage helped to limit some of the direct negative effects of the Asian, Mexican, and Russian financial crises of the 1990s. Nevertheless, the indirect effects of the Asian crises, and the subsequent economic downturn in the developed states, were strongly felt in terms of demand for oil and consequently oil prices and revenues for Middle Eastern states.

Table 3.4 Developing World (regions): Trade Links (2000)

(Destination of trading activity (exports + imports) of main regional groupings)

	Middle East[a]		Africa/North Africa		Asia[b]		South/Central America/ Caribbean	
	US$ bil.	%	US$ bil.	%	US$ bil.	%	US$ bil.	%
Trade with major powers/developed countries[c]	339.6	66.3	164.9	69.0	1233.8	50.3	586.2	74.9
Intra-regional trade	41.2	8.1	24.4	10.2	977.4[e]	39.5[e]	134.0	17.1
	(31.2)[d]	(6.8)[d]						
Trade with other regions	131.2	25.6	49.7	20.8	241.1	9.8	62.3	8.0
	512.3	100	239.0	100	2,451.6	100	782.5	100

a. Arab States of Southwest Asia, Egypt, Iran, Turkey, and Israel.
b. East, Southeast and South Asia except for Japan and China (major powers).
c. All major powers (including Russia & China) plus Western developed countries.
d. Data in parentheses represent absolute level and percentage of trade among Eastern Arab states (including Egypt).
e. Intra-Asian regional trade including China but not Japan.

Sources: Adapted from International Monetary Fund, *Direction of Trade Statistics Yearbook 2001* (Washington: International Monetary Fund, 2001), regional tables (Part A).

Table 3.5 Developing World (regions): Investment Links (2000-01)

(Destination of world investment flows, by main regional groupings)

	LEVEL	
	US$ bil.	%
Middle East[a]	13.9[d]	3.1
(Eastern Arab World)[b]	(4.4)[e,f]	(1.0)
Africa/North Africa	24.0	5.4
Asian Developing Countries[c]	225.4	50.8
South/Central America/Caribbean	180.7	40.7
	444.0	100.0

a. Arab States of Southwest Asia, Egypt, Iran, Turkey, and Israel.

b. Arab States of Southwest Asia and Egypt.

c. East, Southeast and South Asia except for Japan.

d. Investment flows to Israel represent over half ($7.4 billion) of investment directed to the Middle East and 1.7 per cent of total investment flows to the developing world during this period.

e. Gross investment flows to Eastern Arab world; net investment flows (after outflows from Saudi Arabia and Yemen) equal $1.9 B.

f. FDI (Foreign Direct Investment) flows to eastern Arab states amount to $0.77 B (gross) and $0.13 B (net) for 2000/2001. Since some part of these originates outside the region, it is obvious that intra-regional (Eastern Arab world) official FDI flows account for only a small portion of overall FDI flows to the Middle East/Eastern Arab world.

Sources: United Nations Conference on Trade and Development, *World Investment Report 2002* (New York and Geneva: United Nations, 2002), Annex, Table B.1.

Table 3.6 Developing World (regions): Travel Links (1997)

(Outbound Travel: Region of Destination)

	Eastern Arab World		Sub-Saharan Africa		East/ Southeast Asia/ Pacific		South Asia		South/ Central America/ Caribbean	
	Total[a]	%	Total	%	Total	%	Total	%	Total	%
Europe/North America	1.685	19.8	2.536	19.8	22.902	25.0	1.645	31.2	85.059	73.7
Intra-regional	5.571	65.5	7.549	58.9	59.59	65.2	1.198	22.8	22.107	19.1
	(6.322)[b]	(74.3)[b]								
Other destinations	0.493	5.9	2.732	21.3	8.935	9.8	2.412	46.0	8.231	7.2
	8.5	100	12.8	100	91.4	100	5.3	100	115.4	100

a. Number of travellers in millions.
b. Number and percentage of travellers from the Eastern Arab World to the Eastern Arab World and Arab North Africa combined.

Sources: World Tourism Organization, *Yearbook of Tourism Statistics 1999* (Madrid: World Tourism Organization, 1999), Regional Tables, Outbound Travel by Region of Destination.

Table 3.7 Developing World (regions): Cyber-communication Links (2000-01)

(PCs/Internet users in the developing world by main regional groupings)

	PCs per 1000 people		Internet Users	
	Number	%[d]	Number (millions)	%[d]
Middle East[a]			8.126	7.3
Arab world[b]	19	22.3	(4.329)	(3.9)
Sub-Saharan Africa	8.0	9.4	4.962	4.4
East/Southeast Asia/Pacific[c]	17	20.0	56.035	50.2
			(106.286)[e]	
South Asia	3.0	3.6	8.534	7.6
South/Central America/Caribbean	38.0	44.7	32.904	29.5
	85.0	100.0	116.624[f]	99.0[f]

a. Arab States of Southwest Asia, Egypt, Turkey, Iran, and Israel.
b. Arab States of Southwest Asia, Egypt, and Arab North Africa.
c. Excludes Japan, China, Australia, and New Zealand.
d. Regional percentages of PCs per 1000 people and internet users in the developing world.
e. East/Southeast Asia including China.
f. 1.067 million internet users in Arab North Africa are not counted in the overall figures. This represents the missing 1.0 per cent of internet users in the developing world.

Sources: United Nations Development Programme and Arab Fund for Economic and Social Development, *Arab Human Development Report 2002* (New York: UNDP, 2002), Statistical Annex, Table 21, p. 156 (PCs per 1000 people): NUA.ie, *Internet Trends and Statistics*, <www.nua.ie/surveys/how_many_online/index.html>, Regional Tables (internet users).

As previously noted, the *weak intra-regional (horizontal) economic linkages* in the Middle East, especially across the main axes of conflict, mean that one potential source of constraints on conflict and war in the region is inoperative. Still, the actual as well as hoped-for *vertical economic links* between some conflicting regional states and the dominant economic powers may serve as a substitute constraint. Even these are not yet strong enough, however, to prevent adventurous moves or war. Nevertheless the parties are aware that such moves could prove harmful to them in terms not only of their political but also economic relations with these powers.

Conclusion

This chapter has attempted to explore the uses and usefulness, as well as the limitations, of systemic analysis in the study of international relations/foreign policy both in general and in the Middle East. Systemic analysis clearly has a number of important uses. One of these is to provide a broad strategic picture of the world or region, thereby helping us to discover (or perhaps construct?) the basic patterns of inter-state and inter-societal relations therein *(analytical description)*. This in turn generates a deeper knowledge of regional international relations. The real test, however, lies in the area of *explanation*. Here we have seen that systemic factors are able to provide an understanding and explanation not only of *inter-state relations and systemic outcomes* but also of *foreign policy behaviour*. This was subject, however, to a number of limitations and qualifications.

To begin with, systemic variables are better at explaining *patterns of relations* than foreign policy behaviour. They are also better at explaining broad patterns of inter-state relations which persist over a period of time than they are at explaining relations between specific states. Bilateral system characteristics would have greater applicability here.

With respect to *foreign policy behaviour*, systemic variables can explain important aspects of such behaviour *(pace* Waltz), but certain limitations apply. The most important is the need for an *intervening variable* in the form of relevant *positional characteristics* (a mixed systemic and unit-level factor) of the state in question. These provide the crucial link in understanding the impact of systemic factors on state strategies and behaviour. Systemic factors also explain and predict *a range* within which state policies and action will be selected, reducing the degree of indeterminacy therein rather than pinpointing precise decisions or actions. Moreover, like everything in the social sciences, they operate only in a *probabilistic* manner, not deterministically.

Within these parameters, systemic factors are able to explain *certain aspects of foreign policy behaviour* better than others:

1)   Systemic factors are better able to explain and predict the policies and behaviour of *types of states*, or even states in general, than those of *specific states*.

2)   Systemic factors can tell us something about the *interests,* and perhaps even the *preferences*, of states but what they tell us will be very general in character. *Positional characteristics* of the units will tell us much more about state interests and preferences, as will *domestic factors*.

3)   Systemic factors are better able to explain and predict *broad lines of policy* and *recurrent modes of behaviour* than *specific decisions or actions*.

4)   Systemic factors are better able to explain and predict the *outcomes* of decisions and actions than the specific decisions and actions themselves. This is because specific decisions will depend more

heavily on domestic factors and/or the interests, values, beliefs, and perceptions of decision-makers, while outcomes (especially the success or failure of a decision) will depend heavily on the reactions of others, the distribution of power, and broad conditions in the regional or global arenas. Needless to say, these reactions and conditions will feed back and have important effects on subsequent decisions and actions.

Several conclusions can also be drawn about the *types of explanation* that systemic factors provide both for foreign policy behaviour and inter-state relations/systemic outcomes. To begin with, systemic factors operate most often as *permissive causes* (a weaker form of causality). That is to say, they serve either as *constraints* or *opportunities*, obstructing or facilitating certain types of objectives, modes of behaviour, or relationships and outcomes. In effect, they shape what states can or cannot do. Several key systemic variables operate largely in one or another of these ways. Thus regional and global structural variables (the overall distribution of power, the equality or inequality of power, and the type of military capabilities), some textural variables (economic links and interdependence), the condition of the regulatory framework, and conditions in the major power intrusive system, serve either to dampen or enhance the probability of revisionism, violence, accommodation, peace, or cooperation. Domestic conditions can also serve as permissive causes of state behaviour/international relations, but systemic and positional factors figure more prominently in this role.

Stimulus causality (another weak form of causality) is operative when systemic or other external conditions serve as a catalyst for a state's reconsideration of existing policies and relationships. Such catalysts stem more often from systemic or external sources than domestic sources. *Efficient causality* (a much stronger form of stimulus causality) is present when actors or conditions generate *strong pressures toward particular courses of action* or types of relations. One example at the systemic level would be pressures emanating from the major power intrusive system, which shape the behaviour of lesser powers. These pressures, however, may stem as much from domestic or positional factors as from systemic or external factors.

Motivating causality is another strong form of causality. As we have seen, several systemic factors can generate motivations for action. Distributional factors (in the form of important substantive differences over the state and territorial framework or other distributional issues) tend to generate an imbalance of interests and satisfaction as well as conflicting national claims, which provide the motivation for revisionism and ultimately conflict or violence. Structural dynamics (i.e., power approaches and transitions) and systemic textural factors, such as ideological and identitive differences, can also provide motives for revisionism and conflict. Other systemic textural factors, in particular economic interdependence or shared values, can generate the interests and motives for accommodative behaviour, peace, and even cooperation. However, many, if not most, of the interests and preferences of states, and consequently the motives behind state behaviour and inter-state relations, arise either from positional factors (mixed) or domestic factors (including the interests of decision-makers and elites).

Since any meaningful explanation of regional foreign policy behaviour and international relations will involve not only *motivating* causes but also *stimulus/efficient* and *permissive* causes, all explanations are bound to be multifactoral. Systemic factors are therefore very good starting points but only partial end points in the search for explanation and understanding. Positional and domestic factors are necessary ingredients of any explanation.

Notes

The author wishes to thank FCAR/FCRSQ (Québec) and the Inter-University Consortium for Arab and Middle Eastern Studies (ICAMES) for their research support.

[1] Robert Jervis, *System Effects* (Princeton: Princeton University Press, 1997), p. 6 ff.; Hedley Bull, *The Anarchical Society* (London: MacMillan, 1997), pp. 9-16; Kay Boals 'The Concept-Subordinate International System: A Critique,' in Richard Falk and Saul Mendlovitz, *Regional Politics and World Order* (San Francisco: W.H. Freeman & Co, 1973), pp. 399-411.

[2] Morton Kaplan, *System and Process in International Politics* (New York: Wiley, 1957) and 'Variants on Six Models of the International System,' in James Rosenau, ed., *International Politics and Foreign Policy*, 2nd ed. (New York: The Free Press, 1969); Richard Rosecrance, *Action and Reaction in International Politics* (Boston: Little Brown, 1963), Ch. 1; Rosecrance, *International Relations: Peace and War* (New York: McGraw-Hill, 1973), Chs. 4 and 7; Raymond Aron, *Peace and War* (Garden City, N.Y.: Doubleday, 1966), Chs. 4 and 5. For assessments of these views, see Stanley Hoffmann 'International Relations: The Long Road to Theory,' *World Politics* vol. XI, no. 3 (1959); Robert Weltman, *System Theory in International Relations* (Lexington, MA: D.C. Heath, 1973), Chs. 2 and 4; Kenneth Waltz, *Theory of International Politics* (Reading, MA: Addison-Wesley, 1979), Ch. 3.

[3] Waltz, *Theory of International Politics*, Ch. 3 (pp. 38-40), Ch. 4; and Waltz, 'Reflections on Theory of International Politics: A Response to My Critics,' in Robert Keohane, ed., *Neo-Realism and Its Critics* (New York: Columbia University Press, 1986).

[4] Waltz, *Theory of International Politics,* p. 80 and Ch. 5 generally.

[5] Barry Buzan, Charles Jones, and Richard Little, *The Logic of Anarchy* (New York: Columbia University Press, 1993), pp. 24-28.

[6] David Singer, 'The Level of Analysis Problem in International Relations,' in Klaus Knorr and Sidney Verba, eds., *The International System: Theoretical Essays* (Princeton: Princeton University Press, 1961).

[7] International stability/instability proved to be a problematic dependent variable since it had two potentially distinct meanings: the level of violence/war in a system and the degree of durability/change in the system's basic structural characteristics, see Jervis, *System Effects*, pp. 94-98. This became evident at the end of the Cold War when Waltz, in assessing his basic argument about the greater 'stability' of bipolar systems, had to acknowledge that he had failed to distinguish between the two meanings, see Waltz 'The Emerging Structure of International Politics,' *International Security*, vol. 18, no. 2 (1993). He should also have acknowledged that bipolar systems, although less susceptible to major power wars, were

nevertheless less durable than multipower systems (45 years for the post-Second World War bipolar system versus 450 plus years for the traditional European multipower system).

[8] 'An international political theory *serves primarily to explain international political outcomes*' (emphasis mine), Waltz, *Theory of International Politics,* p. 38, see also pp. 72 and 122-123.

[9] Buzan, Jones and Little, *The Logic of Anarchy,* pp. 48-50, 66-73; Jervis, *System Effects* pp. 92-93, 109-110; Joseph Nye 'Neorealism and Neoliberalism,' *World Politics* vol. 40, no. 2 (1988).

[10] John Mearsheimer, 'Back to the Future: Instability in Europe After the Cold War,' *International Security* vol. 15, no. 1 (1990); Waltz, *The Spread of Nuclear Weapons: More May Be Better,* Adelphi Papers, 171 (London: International Institute for Strategic Studies, 1981); James Goldgeier and Michael McFaul, 'Tale of Two Worlds: Core and Periphery in the Post Cold War Era,' *International Organization* vol. 46, no. 2 (1992).

[11] A.F.K. Organski, 'The Power Transition,' in *World Politics* (New York: Knopf, 1968), Ch. 14; Robert Gilpin, *War and Change in World Politics* (Cambridge: Cambridge University Press, 1981), Ch. 5; William R. Thompson, *On Global War* (Columbia, S.C.: University of South Carolina Press, 1988); Jack Levy, 'Long Cycles, Hegemonic Transitions, and the Long Peace,' in John T. Gaddis, *The Long Peace* (New York: Oxford University Press, 1987); Douglas Lemke, *Regions of War and Peace* (Cambridge: Cambridge University Press, 2002); George Modelski, 'The Long Cycle of World Leadership,' in William R. Thompson, ed., *Contending Approaches to World System Analysis* (Beverly Hills, CA: Sage, 1983).

[12] This is a variable that is often overlooked in the study of international systems but has been featured by some analysts. Henry Kissinger, for one, noted the importance of the 'legitimacy' factor (referring to the international status quo) in the post-Congress of Vienna European system. Henry Kissinger, *A World Restored* (Boston: Houghton Mifflin, 1973), Chs. IX and XVII. Paul Schroeder, a diplomatic historian, emphasized that the 'balance/imbalance of interests' was as important as the balance/imbalance of power in an international system. Organski and power transition theorists incorporated the satisfaction/dissatisfaction factor into their explanatory framework, see Organski, *World Politics,* pp. 363-376 and Ronald L. Tammen, Jacek Kugler, Douglas Lemke *et al., Power Transitions: Strategies for the 21st Century* (New York: Chatham House Publishers, 2000), pp. 9-13, 21-28. Kal Holsti stressed the importance of the 'issues' which generate conflict/war (as distinct from 'ecological,' structural, or unit attribute factors), see Kalevi J. Holsti, *Peace and War: Armed Conflicts and International Order 1648-1989* (Cambridge: Cambridge University Press, 1991). Arie Kacowicz characterized this factor as an important overlooked variable in his recent study of the war-proneness/peacefulness of regional state systems in the developing world, Arie Kacowicz, *Zones of Peace in the Third World* (Albany N.Y.: State University of New York Press, 1998).

[13] Buzan, Jones and Little, *The Logic of Anarchy,* Ch. 4; John Gerard Ruggie, 'Continuity and Transformation in the World Polity,' in Keohane, *Neorealism and Its Critics,* pp. 148-152; Nye, 'Neorealism and Neoliberalism,' *World Politics* vol. 40, no. 2 (1988).

[14] Immanuel Wallerstein, 'The Rise and Future Demise of the World Capitalist System: Concepts for Comparative Analysis,' in *The Capitalist World Economy* (Cambridge: Cambridge University Press, 1979); Wallerstein, *The Politics of the World Economy* (Cambridge: Cambridge University Press, 1984); and Wallerstein, *Geopolitics and Geoculture: Essays on The Changing World System* (Cambridge: Cambridge University Press, 1991); Christopher Chase Dunn, 'International System and Capitalist Economy,' *International Studies Quarterly* vol. 25, no. 1 (1981); Holsti, *The Dividing Discipline* (Boston, MA: Allen and Unwin, 1985), Ch. 4; V. Kubalkova and A. Cruickshank, *Marxism and International Relations* (New York: Clarendon Press, 1985), Introduction, Ch. 10;

Barrie Axford, *The Global System* (New York: St. Martins Press, 1995), Chs. 7 (pp. 46-62), 4; Joshua Goldstein, *Long Cycles* (New Haven: Yale University Press, 1988).

[15] Alex Wendt, *Social Theory of International Politics* (Cambridge: Cambridge University Press, 1999), especially Ch. 1.

[16] Paul Noble, 'The Arab System: Pressures, Constraints, and Opportunities,' in Bahgat Korany, Ali E. Hillal Dessouki *et al.*, *The Foreign Policies of Arab States*, 2nd ed. (Boulder, Colorado: Westview Press, 1991), pp. 50-55; F. Gregory Gause, III, 'Systemic Approaches to Middle East International Relations,' *International Studies Review* vol. 1, no. 1 (1999).

[17] Michael Brecher, 'International Relations and Asian Studies: The Subordinate State System of South Asia,' *World Politics* vol. 15, no. 2 (1963).

[18] Jervis, *System Effects*, Ch. 1.

[19] Aaron Friedberg, 'Ripe for Peace: Prospects for Peace in a Multipolar Asia,' *International Security* vol. 18, no. 3 (1993).

[20] Waltz, 'The Stability of a Bipolar World,' *Daedalus* vol. 93, no. 3 (1964).

[21] Kaplan, 'Variants on Six Models of The International System;' and Kaplan, *System and Process*, especially Preface, Chs. 1, 2, 3, 6, 8.

[22] Waltz himself implies this at certain points, *Theory of International Politics*, pp. 61, 80.

[23] Waltz introduced the distinction between permissive and efficient causality in his first major work, *Man, The State and War* (New York: Columbia University Press, 1959), particularly in the last chapter. Holsti underlined the importance of 'issues' (substantive differences) as motivating causes in his explanation of conflict and war, *Peace and War*, pp. 12-19.

[24] Axford in *The Global System* identifies three main spheres of activity (functional systems): a political (Ch. 5), an economic (Ch. 4), and a socio-cultural (Chs. 3, 6) system.

[25] Louis Cantori and Steven Spiegel, *The International Politics of Regions* (Englewood Cliffs, N.J.: Prentice Hall, 1970). They distinguish between the dominant system itself and its regional manifestations (major power intrusive systems).

[26] Brecher, 'The Middle East Subordinate System and Its Impact on Israel's Policy,' *International Studies Quarterly* vol. 13, no. 2 (1969); L. Carl Brown, *International Politics and the Middle East* (Princeton: Princeton University Press, 1984), pp. 7-11; Leonard Binder, 'The Middle East as a Subordinate International System,' *World Politics*, vol. X, no. 3 (1958); Cantori and Spiegel *The International Politics of Regions*; Gause, 'Systemic Approaches to Middle East International Relations.'

[27] Malcolm Kerr, *The Arab Cold War* (London: Oxford University Press, 1971); Noble 'The Arab System;' Gamil Matar and Ali Al-Din Hilal (Disuqi), *al-Nizam al-Iqlimi al-'Arabi* [The Arab Regional Order] (Beirut: Dar al-Mustaqbal al-'Arabi, 1983).

[28] Brecher, 'The Middle East Subordinate System;' Rouholla K. Ramazani, *Revolutionary Iran* (Baltimore: Johns Hopkins University Press, 1986); Barry Buzan, *People States and Fear,* 2nd ed. (Boulder: Lynne Rienner, 1991), Ch. 5 (pp. 199, 214); Barry Buzan and Gowher Rizvi, *South Asian Insecurity and The Great Powers* (London: MacMillan, 1986), Chs. 1, 6.

[29] Kemal Kirisci, 'Turkey and the Muslim Middle East' and William Hale, 'Economic Issues in Turkish Foreign Policy,' in Alan Makovsky and Sabri Sayari, *Turkey's New World* (Washington, DC: Washington Institute for Near East Policy, 2000).

[30] See Buzan, *People, States and Fear,* 2nd ed., Ch. 5 for the concept of regional security complex.

[31] Gary Sick, 'Iran's Foreign Policy: A Revolution in Transition' and Asef Bayat and Bahman Baktiari 'Revolutionary Iran and Egypt,' in Nikki R. Keddie and Rudi Mathee, eds., *Iran and The Surrounding World* (Seattle: University of Washington Press, 2002).

[32] For an analysis of economic ties within the Arab world, see Michael C. Hudson, ed., *Middle East Dilemma* (New York: Columbia University Press, 1999), chapters by Noble (pp. 80-83), Roger Owen, Yusif Sayigh, Antoine Zahlan, Nemat Shafik, and Atif Kubursi.

[33] For data on comparative militarization, see Keith Krause 'Arms Imports, Arms Production, and the Quest of Security in the Third World,' in Brian Job, ed., *The Insecurity Dilemma* (Boulder: Lynne Rienner Publishers, 1992); For data on conflict and wars, see Holsti, *The State, War, and the State of War* (Cambridge: Cambridge University Press, 1996), Table 2,1 (p. 22), and Appendix: Major Armed Conflicts by Region and Type, 1945-1995.

[34] For a more extensive discussion of the distribution, levels, and types of power in the Middle Eastern and Arab systems, see Noble, 'From Arab System to Middle Eastern System: Regional Pressures and Constraints,' in Bahgat Korany and Ali E. Hillal Dessouki *et al.*, *The Foreign Policies of Arab States*, 3rd ed. (forthcoming). This chapter also contains updated comparative tables on levels of military and economic capabilities in various regions of the developing world.

[35] For a discussion of the importance of this factor in shaping conflict, war and peace, particularly in regions of the developing world, see Kacowicz, *Zones of Peace in the Third World*, particularly Chs. 2, 5.

[36] Binder, 'The Middle East as a Subordinate International System;' Noble, 'The Arab System,' pp. 70-83.

[37] Samuel P. Huntington, *The Clash of Civilizations and The Remaking of World Order* (New York: Simon & Schuster, 1996).

[38] Noble, 'The Arab System,' pp. 55, 57-59.

[39] Noble, 'The Arab System,' pp. 56-57, 59-60.

[40] For the development of Arabic language satellite television and the role of particular channels, see S. Abdallah Schleifer, 'Media Explosion in the Arab World: The Pan-Arab Satellite Broadcasters,' *Transnational Broadcast Studies Journal* no. 1 (Fall 1998), <www.tbsjournal.com>; Jon B. Alterman, *New Media, New Politics?* (Washington: Washington Institute for Middle East Policy, 1998), Ch. 3; Edmund Ghareeb, 'New Media and the Information Resolution in the Arab World,' *Middle East Journal* vol. 54, no. 3 (Summer 2000); Schleifer, 'The New MBC: The Marriage of Elegant Professionalism and Emirati Glitter,' *Transnational Broadcast Studies Journal* no. 9 (Fall-Winter 2002), <www.tbsjournal.com>.

[41] For an analysis of the impact of pan-Arab satellite TV on Arab societies, political systems, attitudes and policies, see Alterman, *New Media, News Politics?*, Ch. 5, pp. 54-66; Alterman, 'Transnational Media and Regionalism,' *Transnational Broadcast Studies Journal* no. 1 (Fall 1998), <www.tbsjournal.com>; Alterman, 'The Effects of Satellite Television on Arab Domestic Politics,' *Transnational Broadcast Studies Journal* no. 9 (Fall-Winter 2002), <www.tbsjournal.com>; Mamoun Fandy, 'Information Technology, Trust, and Social Change in the Arab World,' *Middle East Journal* vol. 54, no. 3 (Summer 2000).

[42] Noble, 'The Arab System,' 56-60, 75, 80; F. Gregory Gause, III, 'Sovereignty, Statecraft and Stability in the Middle East,' *Journal of International Affairs* vol. 45, no. 2 (Winter 1992).

[43] Goldgeier and Mc Faul, 'Tale of Two Worlds.'

[44] Kacowicz, *Zones of Peace in the Third World*, Chs. 1, 5; Emmanuel Adler and Michael Barnett, *Security Communities* (Cambridge: Cambridge University Press, 1998), chapters by Amitav Acharya (Southeast Asia) and Andrew Hurrell (South America).

[45] Mohammed Ayoob, *The Third World Security Predicament* (Boulder: Lynne Rienner, 1995), Chs. 2, 8, 9; Buzan, *People States and Fear*, Ch. 2. For an application of this weak state-fragmented society model to the Middle East, see Benjamin Miller, 'The International System and Regional Balance in the Middle East,' in T.V. Paul, James J. Wirtz, and Michel

Fortmann, eds., *Balance of Power Revisited: Theory and Practice in The 21ˢᵗ Century* (forthcoming).

[46] Here, as elsewhere in this chapter, I have used the capitalized form of 'State' to designate those political entities which are characterized by a defined territory and population as well as sovereign governing institutions. This is distinguished from the non-capitalized 'state,' which consists of the governing institutions themselves.

[47] Noble, 'The Arab System,' p. 50-51.

[48] Levy, 'The Causes of War: A Review of Theories and Evidence,' in Philip E. Tetlock, Jo L. Husbands, Robert Jervis *et al.*, *Behavior, Society, and Nuclear War*, vol. 1 (New York: Oxford University Press, 1989), pp. 271-274; Levy, 'The Diversionary Theory of War,' in Manus I. Midlarsky, ed., *Handbook of War Studies* (Boston: Unwin, Hyman, 1989).

[49] Michael Brown, ed., *The International Dimensions of Internal Conflict* (Cambridge, MA: MIT Press, 1996), Introduction, Ch. 17.

[50] Stephen David, 'Explaining Third World Alignment,' *World Politics* vol. 43, no. 2 (1991).

[51] Yezid Saygh, *Confronting the 1990s: Security in the Developing Countries*, Adelphi Papers, 251 (London: International Institute of Strategic Studies, 1990), pp. 68-72; Ayoob, *The Third World Security Predicament*, pp. 61-64.

[52] Gilpin, *The Political Economy of International Relations* (Princeton: Princeton University Press, 1987), pp. 67, 72, 82-85, 92-97; Kubalkova and Cruickshank, *International Inequality* (New York: St. Martin's Press, 1981), Ch.3; Robert Packenham, *The Dependency Movement* (Cambridge, Mass: Harvard University Press, 1992), particularly Ch. 5.

[53] Barry Buzan, Ole Waever, Jaap de Wilde, *Security: A New Framework for Analysis* (Boulder: Lynne Rienner, 1998), Ch. 5; Balder Raj Nayar 'Political Mainsprings of Economic Planning in the New Nations,' *Comparative Politics* vol. 6, no. 3 (April 1975); Laurie Brand, 'Bridging the Gap between Political Economy and Security Studies' (Ch. 1), in *Jordan's Inter-Arab Relations: The Political Economy of Alliance Making* (New York: Columbia University Press, 1994).

[54] Richard Betts, 'Wealth, Power, and Instability,' *International Security* vol. 18, no. 3 (Winter 1993-94).

[55] Carl Kaysen, 'Is War Obsolete?' *International Security* vol. 14, no. 4 (Spring 1990).

[56] There are at least two distinct dimensions to relationships between lesser and major powers. The first or *material* dimension refers to the *level and pattern of material dependence* (military, economic) of the weaker on the stronger power (non-dependence [self-reliance] vs. dependence, unidependence vs. multidependence). The second or *policy* dimension involves the degree of *military or political alignment/affiliation* of the weaker with the stronger power (including alliances, major power bases/facilities, politico-military coalitions, diplomatic common fronts, coordinated policy positions/diplomatic activities, non-alignment vs. alignment).

[57] Neil MacFarlane 'The Impact of Superpower Collaboration on The Third World,' in Thomas Weiss and Meryl Kessler, eds., *Third World Security in The Post Cold War Era* (Boulder: Lynne Rienner, 1991).

[58] For an analysis of the impact of conditions in the Middle Eastern intrusive system on the foreign policy options of regional states, see Shibley Telhami, 'The Superpowers and the Preference of States' (Ch. 3), in *Power and Leadership in International Bargaining* (New York: Columbia University Press, 1990).

[59] For a discussion of the politico-military characteristics of the post-Cold War Middle Eastern intrusive system and their impact on the foreign policy options of regional states, see Noble, 'The Prospects for Arab Cooperation in a Changing Regional and Global System,' in Hudson, ed., *Middle East Dilemma*, pp. 66-72.

[60] Miller, 'The International System and Regional Balance in the Middle East,' in Paul, Wirtz and Fortmann, *Balance of Power Revisited*; Miller, 'When Regions Become Peaceful: Explaining Transitions from War to Peace,' *REGIS Working Papers* (Montreal: McGill University, 2001); Miller, 'The Global Sources of Regional Transitions from War to Peace,' *Journal of Peace Research* vol. 38, no. 2 (March 2001); Miller, 'Between War and Peace: Systemic Effects on the Transition of the Middle East and the Balkans from the Cold War to the Post-Cold War Era,' *Security Studies* vol. 11, no. 4 (Autumn 2001).

[61] For an extensive analysis of the trilateral/tripolar features of the post-Cold War dominant economic system and their impact on the position, policies, and economic results of regional groupings of developing states, see Barbara Stallings, ed., *Global Change, Regional Response: The New International Context of Development* (Cambridge: Cambridge University Press, 1995).

[62] For a discussion of the *economic* characteristics of the post-Cold War Middle Eastern intrusive system and their impact on the position and options of regional states, see Noble, 'The Prospects for Arab Cooperation,' pp. 68-72.

[63] Thomas Friedman, *The Lexus and the Olive Tree* (New York: Anchor Books, 2000).

Chapter 4

Between Conflict and Cooperation: Accommodation in the Post-Cold War Middle East

James Devine

This chapter focuses on accommodation in the post-Cold War Middle East. It examines strategies pursued by 'regional challengers': states engaged in protracted conflicts or enduring rivalries with local allies of the United States. The first half of this chapter offers a framework of analysis that links strategic choices made by these states at the regional level with factors from multiple analytical levels (global, regional, and domestic). The framework also considers the interaction of different types of security concerns (realist political/military, economic, and domestic political) and different types of causal relationships (stimulus, permissive, and motivating causality). The second half focuses on one type of causal relationship—motivating causality—in the context of Iran's policy of accommodation towards Saudi Arabia.

Accommodation involves an effort to avoid conflict and reduce tensions, and it is of interest for a number of reasons. Accommodation has rarely been studied as a strategic policy distinct from cooperation, yet the two are not the same. Accommodation has its own distinct causes and dynamics. After the Cold War, it became an increasingly common policy choice in the Middle East: in addition to Iran, Syria has pursued on again/off again accommodation with Israel, and while the Palestinians have not achieved a formal state, the PLO's policy towards Israel also fits the pattern. The timing of this trend underscores the impact of globalization and the global balance of power on regional conflicts such as those in the Middle East. However, the persistence of conflict in the region suggests that this is a complex and ongoing interaction. It is thus important to understand not only why accommodation was initiated, but also why there are particular dynamics and outcomes of accommodation.

Accommodation: Between Conflict and Cooperation

As a description of foreign policy, the term accommodation is often used interchangeably with cooperation, yet they differ in significant ways. Simply stated, accommodation involves an effort to avoid conflict and resolve differences. Unlike cooperation, it does not involve shared interests (beyond peace) or the pursuit of mutual gains. While a cooperative relationship involves some elements of partnership, states in an accommodative relationship pursue their own interests, for the most part, separately.

On the other end of the spectrum, accommodation needs to be distinguished from conflict. Although the two terms are not as frequently confused, the border between them can be ambiguous. There is a significant body of literature devoted to the issue of conflict de-escalation. William Zartman, for instance, argues that conflicts have three distinct stages: escalation, stalemate, and de-escalation; and that in the latter stage, one or both parties qualitatively reduce the level of conflict either in terms of their goals or their methods.[1] In cases where de-escalation is intended to end a conflict and avoid future hostilities, it constitutes an accommodative policy. In many cases, however, it is intended only to reduce the level of conflict to a more bearable level. Rather than accommodation, this type of de-escalation can be better understood in terms of conflict management.

Relative to conflict, an accommodative strategy represents a significant yet limited change in policy direction. According to Charles Herman, foreign policy change can be divided into four analytically distinct categories. *Adjustment changes* involve alterations in the level of effort or in the scope of a given policy, while the means and ends remain the same. Changes that address the means or ends of foreign policy can be referred to as *program changes* or *problem/goal changes*, respectively. Finally, *international orientation changes* involve a fundamental reorientation in the direction of a state's foreign policy.[2]

Accommodative strategies can be considered in terms of this typology. Accommodation may involve limiting the intensity of a given foreign policy, or possibly limiting its scope. In order to accommodate a rival, a regional challenger may stop some forms of behaviour in that particular relationship but continue it in others. The most important adjustments will likely occur in the form of program changes. Accommodation requires diplomacy and negotiation rather than coercion and force, even if the regional challenger maintains its commitment to contentious issues. As accommodation deepens, it may involve some adjustment to the actual goals of foreign policy (problem/goal changes): some issues may be sacrificed or compromised to avoid conflict in the larger relationship.

A change in international orientation may also have an impact on regional rivalries. A fundamental reinterpretation of interests may lead to the emergence of a cooperative relationship: as policy orientation changes, there may be a convergence on previously divisive issues, or new shared interests may emerge. This may not happen immediately, however, or it may not happen at all: accommodation, in the end, may be the preferred coping strategy. It may take some time for enough trust to develop to underwrite cooperation. If there is a fundamental reorientation of policy, the incompatibilities in interests may even prove persistent. It is worth noting, though, that while a change in international orientation may not be 'sufficient' to produce cooperation in and of itself, such a change may prove to be 'necessary' for the emergence of cooperative strategies.

Framework of Analysis

The shift from conflict to accommodation is too complex to be accounted for by a simple mono-causal explanation, and thus a number of potential causal factors and several levels of analysis need to be taken into account. Moreover, the dependent variable, accommodation, is itself a multifaceted phenomenon: it is not only necessary to explain the initiation of accommodation, but also the dynamics and the outcomes. To do all of this, a multidimensional framework will be necessary (summarized in Figure 4.1 at the end of this chapter).

Dependent Variables

The starting point of this framework is the *initiation* of accommodation. For the purposes of this chapter, initiation does not mean that the challenger is the first state to make a gesture. Although this may prove analytically significant in other respects, initiation in this context refers to the point where the challenger signals that it is willing to consider changing its policy.[3]

The second category of dependent variable is *dynamics*. Within this classification there are two specific variables: the direction of accommodation and its depth. Regional challengers to clients of the United States are locked into conflict triads rather than dyads, and there are thus two potential directions along which it can pursue accommodation: horizontally towards its regional rival, and vertically towards Washington. In practice, both routes are likely to be important, yet there may be differences in emphasis or timing.

The second aspect of this variable is *depth*. Accommodation can either be procedural or substantive. Procedural accommodation does not address the issues at the heart of the conflict, but rather attempts to regulate behaviour so that crises and war can be avoided. In terms of policy change, this would run the range from adjustment changes to program change. Procedural accommodation would therefore involve limiting the scope or intensity of a policy, or using diplomacy rather than coercion. It might also involve the creation of institutions that facilitate communication. Substantive accommodation involves problem/goal changes, and requires that states deal with the issues of contention themselves.

The final dependent variable to be included in this framework is the *outcome*. The accommodative process may be unstable and break down in relatively short order, or it may prove stable and enduring. Under the right circumstances, accommodation may even give way to a fully developed cooperative relationship.

In order to analyze the causal relationships that shape accommodation, the framework will include factors in the operating environment as well as the policy-making environment. The operating environment includes events, actions and conditions that define the circumstances in which a state operates, within both the domestic and international arenas. The policy-making environment includes factors that influence perceptions, planning, and the implementation of policy. Frequently, analytical frameworks organize the operating and policy-making environments as independent and intervening variables respectively, but this approach does not capture many of the processes that shape accommodation as it casts factors in the policy-making environment as passive. Instead, the framework proposed in this chapter examines the explanatory factors in terms of different modes of explanation; that is, in terms of different types of causal relationships.

Modes of Explanation

To explain the process of accommodation, it is necessary to ask what—if anything—acted as a trigger (stimulus causality), what choices were available when policy was being formulated (permissive causality), and what the regional challenger wanted from the policy (motivating causality). Stimulus causality involves events, changes, or pressures in the environment (domestic, regional, or global), which act as an impetus for states to re-evaluate old policies or consider new ones. This is often considered a sufficient explanation of 'cause,' yet states are not exclusively reactive: they can also be purposive, setting goals and trying to manipulate the environment to their advantage. Motivating causality therefore involves explaining behaviour in terms of what states are trying to accomplish. Finally, permissive causality shapes behaviour by determining which policies are or are not possible, and which are relatively more or less costly. Two types of permissive causality should be considered: opportunity and constraint.

Operating Environment

There are three types of explanatory factors in this category. The first is external political/military: essentially realist considerations relating to the balance of power, national security, influence and status. They originate from a variety of analytical levels: the global system, the regional system, or bilaterally. In the post-Cold War context, the emergence of a one-power system is an obvious consideration. At the regional level, the presence or absence of other conflicts may have an important impact, particularly if they involve the regional challenger or its rival. Bilaterally, the balance of power is also likely to be an important factor.

The second type of factor is domestic politics, which includes political instability, either in terms of competition for control of the state, or in terms of threats to national integrity, such as separatist movements. The third type is economics. The economy and conflict are connected in a number of ways: the state may lack the resources to continue the conflict, or the cost of continuing the conflict may undermine the overall health of the economy, and resolving the conflict may help the state escape sanctions or improve its position with international investors. For states confronting US clients, this is likely to be a serious consideration.

Policy-making Environment

There are three types of factors that need to be considered in this category. First, there are different types of goals that can be pursued through accommodation. They can be divided into four types. The first three correspond to factors in the operating environment discussed above: states may be pursuing political/military (relative power/security), economic (security/wealth) or domestic goals (regime security/state-building). In addition, they may also focus on goals defined by ideology/identity. Goals can also be discussed in terms of avoiding losses or realizing gains: realism predicts that states will be primarily concerned with relative gains, while neo-liberalism emphasizes the importance of absolute gains, and prospect theory suggests that states will try to avoid losses.[4] Depending on each respective theory, states may react differently to the stimuli and permissive features of their environment.

The second factor is expectations, which involves the way decision-makers believe the environment will change over time, or in response to their actions. The first factor in this category that needs to be considered is the perception of time: how a state responds to a particular stimulus may depend, at least in part, on how long the regime thinks it has to react. Expectations also involve anticipated change: the same static state of affairs (in terms of the factors discussed earlier: external security, domestic politics, and economics) may produce different reactions depending on whether decision-makers see the situation improving or deteriorating in the future. Finally, the anticipated response expected by policy makers should be taken into account. Specifically in the context of conflict resolution, Richard Lebow suggests that anticipated reciprocity may be a key consideration, as states will not be willing to engage in accommodation unless they expect their rivals to reply in kind.[5]

The third factor is the policy-making process. States where decision-making is dominated by a single person may differ systematically from those where decisions are influenced by bureaucratic or factional politics. Not only might this influence decision-making, but command and control may also be affected in cases where there are significant divisions in the regime or state institutions. Implementing foreign policy decisions may therefore be just as difficult as arriving at them.

For the most part, the operating environment comprises factors involved in stimulus and permissive causality. Accommodation may be in response to stimuli in the political/military, domestic or economic spheres. Once initiated, opportunities and constraints in those spheres shape how accommodation is pursued (i.e., the dynamics of accommodation). The policy-making environment also plays a part in these two causal roles: goals influence which factors in the operating environment are most salient, both in terms of their stimulus and permissive roles, and expectations are a factor in how states deal with the permissive environment. Policy-making includes some consideration of how the permissive environment changes over time.

Motivating causality, on the other hand, involves primarily the policy-making environment. Goals are particularly important in this regard. However, motivating causality may also involve bargaining between various factions and/or bureaucratic actors. The decision-making process is therefore another significant variable. This may also be influenced by what decision-makers feel is realistically possible, thus expectations and permissive factors are also implicated.

Iranian Accommodation vis-à-vis Saudi Arabia: Motivating Causality

In the post-Cold War period, Iran fits neatly the profile of a regional challenger. Since the revolution, Tehran has been at odds with both the United States and one of its most important regional partners, Saudi Arabia. Although Iran has not directly engaged Saudi Arabia in a military dispute, the rivalry between the two states has been long and intense. Iran's relationship with Washington has been even more strained. The revolution that brought the clergy to power was as much directed against US influence as it was against the Shah. As a result, anti-Americanism has become one of the revolution's defining features.

Iran has made two separate attempts at accommodation with Saudi Arabia: President Hashemi Rafsanjani's 'Good Neighbour' policy (1989-1992), and President Mohammad Khatami's policy of *détente* (1997 and onwards). Although the first attempt failed amid disagreements over regional security and OPEC policies, the second has been much more successful. Attempts at vertical accommodation, however, have been less successful. Although they have been able to achieve short term, tactical accommodations in times of crisis—such as the 1991 Gulf War—US-Iranian relations continue to be characterized by mistrust and hostility.

Several previous studies suggest that the goals involved in accommodation will be complex and involve a mix of domestic-level motivations (economics and/or domestic politics) and external security interests. Both Lebow and Janice Stein have also argued that accommodation will necessarily be linked to programs of domestic political or economic reform. Conflict resolution may allow the state to redirect its resources toward the economy and better position itself for trade and investment. This may be an end in itself, or it may be part of a larger plan to reform the economy and shore up the domestic position of the regime. If the reform program is more ambitious, accommodation may also be instrumental in establishing a new political order. Ending the conflict will undermine those elites who used it to justify their position, and reforming the economy empowers new elites to replace them.[6]

Lebow's and Stein's studies—which focused primarily on Soviet accommodation of the US at the end of the Cold War, and Egypt's accommodation of Israel after the 1973 war—also suggest that accommodation is motivated by a desire to avoid losses rather than attain gains. In the Soviet Union, the goal was to revive a failing economy, and in so doing maintain the state's position as a world power. In Egypt, Anwar Sadat faced growing political unrest as a result of a deepening economic crisis: as a consequence of the Camp David peace treaty, Egypt received vital foreign aid and was able to reduce its defence budget, also securing the return of land lost in the 1967 war. This pattern is consistent with prospect theory, but is in contrast with traditional models of decision-making, which argue that behaviour is driven by the pursuit of relative (realism) or absolute (neo-liberalism) gains.[7]

These studies suggest several questions about Iranian motivations. Is Iranian accommodation intended to achieve a mixed set of goals, and if so, what is the nature of the mix? To what extent is domestic reform a necessary part of the process? Has Iran been motivated by loss-avoidance, either in terms of domestic (economic and/or political) or external issues? Finally, it is also useful to ask if the goals of accommodation are consistent with the regime's other motives.

The goals of Iranian accommodation do in fact appear to be complex. Although ideological goals and domestic politics are part of the mix, the two key motives which stand out in its policies towards Saudi Arabia appear to be improving the country's political/military position in the Persian Gulf and improving its influence in OPEC. The evidence for this conclusion comes largely from correlating the degree of friction in these issue areas with the stability of accommodation.

Iran's first attempt at accommodation, President Rafsanjani's 'Good Neighbour' policy, went astray in 1991-92 when Iran was unable to reach agreement with Riyadh on either regional security arrangements or on quotas and pricing in OPEC. Signs that Iran and Saudi Arabia had different security agendas became evident almost immediately following the defeat of the Iraqi military in Kuwait. Iran's 'positive neutrality' during the conflict was expected to significantly improve its position with the Persian Gulf states, and there were discussions concerning Iran-GCC (Gulf Cooperation Council) coordination.[8] Instead, the six states looked outside the Persian Gulf to Egypt and Syria for protection. The Damascus Declaration, signed in 1991, would have seen a standing force established in the Gulf comprised of troops from the six GCC states plus Egypt and Syria. This agreement, also known as the 'six-plus-two agreement,' was never implemented, but it gave the impression that the Saudis and the other GCC states still intended to keep Iran isolated in the region.[9] The GCC protested that the agreement was not an anti-Iranian alliance, but when it collapsed they turned to the United States to guarantee their security. For Tehran, which continued to argue that Persian Gulf security was the business only of the littoral states, this was even worse.[10] The formal and informal arrangements made between Washington and the

GCC states, as well as the sale of relatively advanced arms, gave the US a permanent foothold in Iran's most vital strategic region.[11]

At approximately the same time, Iran and Saudi Arabia began to clash in OPEC. In March 1991, Iran deferred to Saudi Arabia's position on price cuts,[12] but in 1992, Iran wanted production slashed to push the price of oil to $21 per barrel.[13] In January of that year, Saudi Arabia announced that it would cut production, but at the February OPEC meetings, the two states were still far apart:[14] Iran was unwilling to sign-off on the final agreement, and Iran's oil minister singled out the Saudis as the cause for the meeting's 'failure.'[15] The dispute was put on hold though, because the Saudis eventually changed their position in response to Western policies on emission controls and alternative energy sources.[16] The result was more in line with what the Iranians were looking for, even if it was only delaying the inevitable: the two sides continued to differ fundamentally on quota and output issues and Iran exceeded its production quota for most of the next year.[17]

As these two issues began to drive a wedge between Iran and Saudi Arabia, Tehran's behaviour became decreasingly accommodative. Iran immediately criticized the Damascus Declaration and the subsequent bilateral agreements as illegitimate and destabilizing. They renewed their criticism of Riyadh's close relationship with the United States, and mounted a series of military manoeuvres in the Persian Gulf. The final break was a dispute over the small island of Abu Musa in the strategic Strait of Hormuz. The dispute was expanded to include two small adjacent islands, the Greater and Lesser Tunbs, and reached its peak in December 1992 when President Rafsanjani threatened the GCC that they would have to 'cross a sea of blood' to reach the islands.[18]

When accommodation was revived in 1997, oil was once again a key issue. In 2000, an agreement was reached between Iran and Saudi Arabia to control output and thus keep the average price of oil at $24 per barrel with upper and lower limits of $28 and $22 respectively.[19] This agreement boosted the price of oil and kept Iran's economy afloat, which was on the brink of crisis before the price of oil rose.[20] Realist political/military issues were also addressed: although there is still no settlement in the Abu Musa dispute, Saudi Arabia has downplayed the UAE's claims while its relationship with Iran improved.[21] This is significant because Iran has taken its territorial claims in the Persian Gulf very seriously, and the dispute offended Iran's sense of nationalism. Perhaps more importantly, it also signalled that Saudi Arabia was not going to use the issue to keep Iran isolated in the region. Tehran and Riyadh have still not been able to arrive at a regional security formula, but the situation in the Persian Gulf was not as acute as it seemed in the early 1990s. The presence of the United States was troubling for the Iranians, but the two sides avoided confrontation. Moreover, the US military effectively neutralized Iraq and gave Iran time to rebuild its military.

Security and economics have tended to compliment each other in Iran's relationship with Saudi Arabia. Power and influence in the Persian Gulf are considered essential to safeguard the free flow of Iranian oil. Conversely, oil revenues are necessary as Iran attempts to rebuild its military after the Iran-Iraq war and maintain its position as a regional power. This is especially the case for Tehran given that oil is the main source of Iran's export earnings and the single most important source of government revenue.[22]

In addition to being the backbone of Iran's economy, petrodollars have also had a pay-off in terms of regime security. This concern, however, has not been as consistently salient as economics and security. When Rafsanjani began to pursue his 'Good Neighbour' policy, the domestic scene was relatively quiet. There was significant competition between the various political factions, but Iran's economic situation did not appear to be undermining the stability of the regime. In 1997, when the second round of accommodation began, the situation was different. The economy had stagnated through the middle 1990s, oil revenue was low, and—as evidenced by the election of Mohammad Khatami—there was growing opposition to the political order. The political impact of petrodollars was more likely to be important at this point in time.

Ideology has also played a limited or secondary role in setting the goals of accommodation. Most importantly, accommodation has opened the way for Iranian pilgrims to attend the *Hajj* from which they had been barred since 1987. However, Iran was willing to put the ideological benefits of accommodation on hold when its oil and security interests were frustrated. Moreover, in 1991, when Tehran was forced to choose between ideology and realist security concerns, it made a pragmatic decision and pursued a policy of 'positive neutrality.' Through the rest of the 1990s, Iran continued to put security ahead of ideology. Even though the United States pursued a policy of 'dual-containment' against Iran and Iraq, Tehran adopted a pragmatic outlook on the American presence in the region. In fact, one former Iranian diplomat described the post-Desert Storm period as a *de facto* alliance between Iran and the United States.[23]

Domestic reform has also played a role in Iranian accommodation. However, reform does not seem to have been a necessary condition for accommodation as Lebow suggests.[24] When Rafsanjani took over as President in 1989, rebuilding the state's economy was one of the main pillars of his political platform.[25] In fact, the President's supporters were referred to as the 'servants of the reconstruction.' Rafsanjani's agenda also included some limited political reforms, but it was a program of adjustment, not an attempt to restructure the system.

Achieving an accommodation with Saudi Arabia would further this agenda in several ways. First, it would have helped improve Iran's image abroad, making it more attractive to international investors. While this was not likely to have much influence over the United States, it may have helped Tehran's relationship with Europe, which has preferred engagement to isolation. Improving Iran's image might also entice wealthy or skilled expatriate Iranians to return home and help rebuild the country. Most importantly, relations with Saudi Arabia were important in terms of oil revenue, which would fuel the country's reconstruction.

The program pursued by President Khatami has been more ambitious. The reform movement that emerged in 1997 sought not only to restructure the economy, but also targeted the Islamic Republic's political system. Although reform was supposed to take place within the parameters of the constitution, deepening the democratic institutions of the state was bound to fundamentally change the nature of the regime. In terms of foreign policy, President Khatami's version of economic reform has had the same implications for Iranian-Saudi relations as Rafsanjani's. His political reforms, however, also seem to have crossed over into his foreign policy. R.K. Ramazani has argued that Khatami's foreign policy is informed by a conception of democratic peace.[26] Accommodation in the Persian Gulf would undermine the position of isolationists and ideological hard-liners, and tip the balance of power at home toward the moderates.

Nevertheless, it is difficult to argue that accommodation was a necessary condition for reform. The conservative elements of Iran's clergy, who stand to lose the most from reform, have supported an accommodative policy toward Saudi Arabia.[27] While the reformers could see accommodation as a pathway to change, conservatives could see accommodation as a way to avoid change. When oil revenues began to rise at the end of the decade, petrodollars reinvigorated the economy, obviating the need to undertake reforms that would hurt their supporters or threaten the political status quo. The discrepancy between reform and accommodation is clearer when the timing of the second phase is scrutinized closely: although the success of the second period of accommodation coincided with President Khatami's time in office, it was initiated by the Saudis just before the end of Rafsanjani's last term.[28] Accommodation did not await a reformist president: it waited for an opening in Riyadh.

The third question raised by previous studies involves the importance of avoiding losses as opposed to achieving gains. Although most of the evidence is inferential, it would seem that Iranian behaviour is consistent with prospect theory. Rather than relative or absolute gains, Iran has been trying to maintain the status quo while recouping what it had lost in the 1980s.[29] As the first period of accommodation began, Iran needed to rebuild after eight years of war, and this was a prominent theme in Iranian politics at the time. The need for reconstruction was particularly apparent in Iran's oil industry, which had decayed badly during the 1980s. Iran had also lost ground in terms of its regional position, going from the 'gendarme' of the Persian Gulf to a virtual outcast. The situation with Iraq was the most dire: not only was Iran's military inferiority a loss relative to the situation in the 1970s, it had the potential to lead to further losses in the future.

Many of these concerns continued to be relevant during the second period of accommodation. In 1997, Iran's oil industry was still in a state of disrepair, and while its regional position was better than it had been during the 1980s, it was still isolated relative to the 1970s. Iraq was pinned down by the US at the time, but there was no guarantee that this situation would be permanent. Most importantly in the late 1990s, growing dissatisfaction with the political system represented a serious threat to the future of the regime.

The final question about motivations concerns the coherence of the Islamic Republic's various goals. Although accommodation appeared to be directed at improving Iran's oil income and regional position, other aspects of its policies seemed to contradict these goals. Despite the desire to increase oil revenue, Iran has set strict limits on the type of deals that Western oil companies are allowed to sign. Laws protecting Iran's sovereignty over its resources also limited efforts to rebuild Iran's old oil infrastructure. Since the middle 1990s, the government has dodged these laws through 'buy-back' plans, but even these are a significant impediment to Iran's oil industry. Relative to longer-term arrangements, buy-back deals attract reduced revenue and older, less efficient technology.[30] Had Iran been willing to compromise on these deals, its ability to generate income would have been significantly higher, even if its production quota and world oil prices had stayed the same.

The same type of inconsistencies can be seen in Iran's diplomatic relations. While Iran courted Saudi Arabia in the early 1990s, it could not distance itself from Islamist militants in the region. In 1992, the Algerian government expelled Iran's diplomatic representatives for alleged connections with Algeria's outlawed Front Islamique du Salut, and Egypt continued to accuse Iran of supporting Islamic groups in the Sudan.[31] To Riyadh, this seemed eerily similar to Iran's earlier attempts to export its revolution in the Persian Gulf. Perhaps most importantly, Iran has not been able to deal with its troubled relationship with Washington. Iran and the United States reached short-term tactical accommodations during the 1991 Gulf War, the campaign against the Taliban, and even the 2003 invasion of Iraq, but they have not been able to translate any of this into a lasting relationship. To be fair, Washington's attitudes and behaviour have contributed to this situation, but Iran has not been able or willing to refrain from antagonistic behaviour. Iran's arms acquisitions—perhaps including a nuclear weapons program—have certainly been a bone of contention between Tehran and Washington, but these purchases are not surprising considering Iran's geo-political neighbourhood. Yet Iran's continued involvement in the Arab-Israeli conflict is a different matter. Despite subordinating ideological goals at other times, Iran continues to allow its involvement with Hizbullah, Hamas and Islamic Jihad in Palestine to undermine vertical accommodation. Better relations with Washington would not only simplify the situation with Riyadh, it would ease Iran's strategic predicament in the region and improve its access to international markets and investment.

These contradictions can be understood only when concerns about regime security are taken into account. Regime security has probably been the dominant motivation in Iranian policy, both foreign and domestic. Despite the obvious pay-offs, a rapprochement with America would undermine its legitimation formula, which is based in large part on ideology. The clerical leadership of Iran have presented themselves as the guardians of the revolution and Ayatollah Khomeini's legacy. This has enabled them to justify their power and maintain the loyalty of their followers. Permitting Iran to re-establish its relationship with the United States would leave them essentially irrelevant, as it would mean surrendering the political agenda to the pragmatists and reformers, and would undermine their relationship with their support base. Other foreign policy issues with the same type of ideological significance have a similar role in domestic legitimacy. One example is Iran's support for Hizbullah: although it does not define Iran's revolution in the same way as anti-Americanism has, it is a barometer of the regime's fidelity to its values. The impact of abandoning them would have a similar effect as compromising on US relations, although it would be less pronounced.

Iranian accommodation reflects a complex balance of interests and domestic political forces. In the short term, there is a consensus among both the conservatives and reformers on the value of accommodation, even if in the long term they have divergent agendas. As accommodation continues and perhaps deepens, it is not clear that the consensus will continue to hold. The reformers are likely committed to reform in the long term. The conservatives, on the other hand, will have to be able to balance the competing demands of regime security. It is worth noting that this consensus does not always apply to the means by which the policy is pursued: there were frequent criticisms of Rafsanjani's management of foreign policy, suggesting that he was not tough enough.[32] Rafsanjani and Ayatollah Ali Khamenei—the *Velayat-e Faqih*—also clashed over the way Iran's representative in OPEC conducted negotiations. Rafsanjani argued that Oil Minister Gholam Aqazadeh, who was close to the conservatives, was too heavy handed.[33]

Conclusion

The first part of this chapter made a distinction between accommodation and cooperation, and offered a framework that breaks accommodation into its component parts, suggesting that a variety of explanatory factors need to be considered. This is useful for descriptive purposes: disaggregating the dependent variable makes it possible to map out the specific features of accommodation and allows for better comparisons across cases. In terms of analysis, the framework makes it possible to isolate and identify the causal relationships that shape the initiation and dynamics of accommodation, as well as the eventual outcomes.

The second part of the chapter examined one of three types of causal relationship identified in the framework: motivating causality. The motivations involved in this case of accommodation were similar in some respects to those identified by Lebow and Stein in other contexts. Iran's motivations, like the USSR's and Egypt's, have been complex, involving goals at both the external and the domestic levels. Iran pursued security agreements and a larger share of the pie in OPEC, and although regime security was also involved, its role was more complex. The economic pay-off buttressed the regime in the late 1990s, but its largest impact was probably as a constraint. Conflicting goals generated by the demands of regime security have complicated the accommodation process. Iran's motives also seemed to be orientated toward recouping past losses and preventing future losses. Yet Iranian accommodation differed from the previous cases in that it was only weakly related to economic and political reform. Although accommodation coincided with reform-minded administrations, changing the political/economic system was not a necessary condition for its initiation or its stability.

These conclusions are important for a number of reasons. In terms of theory-building, they support the contention that foreign policy choices are influenced by domestic-level issues as well as realist security concerns. However, they call into question the importance of reform. They also call into question the impact of globalization: although the reformers have justified accommodation in terms of increasing Iran's international competitiveness, the economic pay-off for the conservatives has simply been petrodollars. Integrating Iran into the world economy would in fact be threatening to the conservatives. Iranian accommodation also differs from expectations in terms of the American role. Powerful third parties are usually expected to facilitate conflict resolution, yet the US has been very wary of an Iranian-Saudi rapprochement. To the extent that it has been involved, Washington has been an impediment.

These conclusions also have implications for the future of Iranian-Saudi relations, in particular regional security arrangements and OPEC. First of all, for accommodation to continue, Iran needs reciprocity in both of these issue areas. The two goals are both important in their own right, and in some ways interrelated. Consequently, reciprocity in just one area will not be sufficient. In 1997, Iran did not receive the security agreement it wanted in 1991-92, but Saudi Arabia put the Abu Musa issue aside and there were security contacts between Tehran and several GCC states.[34] Between these developments, and—ironically—the US pressure on Iraq, Iran's minimum requirements would seem to have been satisfied.

Despite the success of the latest period of accommodation, it is also possible to identify limits and tensions in the relationship. One problem area is the contradictions between regime security and Iran's other policy goals. Accommodation may be threatened if the Iranian domestic environment becomes radicalized. Although the relationship between Saudi Arabia and the United States has been strained in the post-9/11 environment, they are still strategic allies. Growing anti-Americanism among the more extreme conservative groups in Iran may make it more difficult for the Saudi leadership to maintain the relationship. Like Iran's connections to Islamist groups, it may also make Riyadh wary of Iran's long-term intentions. Accommodation may also be threatened from the other side: if the US escalates its pressure on Iran, Saudi Arabia may simply find it impossible to find a comfortable balance between the two.

Even if the regime is able to maintain the balance between these concerns, the nature of the two state's interests will likely put limits on their relationship. The Iranian-Saudi agreement on oil pricing splits the difference between their preferences. It removed a source of friction, but it does not appear that there is enough common ground for this to be the basis of a cooperative relationship. Moreover, it cannot be taken for granted that the agreement would survive major changes in international oil markets. Their relationship in the security sphere is similar. Although both seem willing to tolerate each other, they are natural rivals in the Persian Gulf. Moreover, the two sides are divided by long standing ethnic and religious tensions. Also, while both regimes use Islamic symbolism to legitimize their rule, their regime types are incompatible.

Saudi Arabia has traditionally tried to maintain a balance in its relations with its two powerful neighbours (Iraq and Iran) and the United States. By the middle 1990s the Saudis felt that they had moved too close to the United States.[35] Their willingness to engage Iran in 1997 can be seen as a way of recalibrating this balance. If this is the case, then it is unlikely that they will want to get too close to Iran even if domestic reforms continue, and even if there is a change in the 'international orientation' of the Islamic Republic's foreign policy.

There is still considerable work to be done on the issues examined above, both in terms of the case study and theory-building. The preceding discussion focused on only one of the three types of causal relationship identified in the framework. Without exploring stimulus and permissive causality, the picture is incomplete. In the Iranian case, the complex demands of regime security clearly demonstrate the need to examine how the different causal relationships interact. More casework will also be necessary before any generalizations can be made. As noted above, domestic reform, globalization, and powerful third parties did not play their expected roles in Iranian-Saudi accommodation, and without looking at other cases it is not clear if this is part of a larger pattern, or simply Iranian 'exceptionalism.'

Modes of explanation	Explanatory Variables		Dependent Variables

• Stimulus causality
• Permissive causality
• Motivating causality
	Operating environment
	• Political/military
	• Domestic
	• Economics
		Policy-making environment
		• Goals
		• Expectations
		• Policy-making process
			• Initiation
			• Dynamics
			  o Direction
			  o Depth
			• Outcomes
			  o Instability
			  o Stability
			  o Cooperation

Figure 4.1 Framework of Analysis

Notes

I would like to thank Paul Noble who played a vital role in the writing of this chapter. Not only did he provide invaluable feedback while this chapter was being written, the definition of accommodation and the distinction between substantive and procedural accommodation should be attributed to him. Also, the distinction between different types of causality is based on those made in his chapter of this volume.

[1] See I. William Zartman, *Ripe for Rivalry: Conflict and Intervention in Africa* (New York, Oxford: Oxford University Press, 1989).

[2] Charles Herman, 'Changing Course: When Governments Choose to Redirect Foreign Policy,' *International Studies Quarterly* vol. 34, no. 1 (March 1990), pp. 5-6.

[3] In the course of a protracted conflict or enduring rivalry, diplomatic initiatives will come and go. For instance, Syria was presented with numerous peace initiatives, peace conferences and the like. What is significant in this context is that Syria chose to attend the Madrid talks, when it had let other opportunities pass.

[4] Janice Gross Stein, 'International Co-operation and Loss Avoidance: Framing the Problem,' *International Journal* XLVII (Spring 1992), pp. 208-209.

[5] Richard Ned Lebow, 'The Search for Accommodation: Gorbechev in Comparative Perspective,' in Richard Ned Lebow and Thomas Risse-Kapan, eds., *International Relations Theory and the End of the Cold War* (New York: Columbia University Press, 1995), p. 174.

[6] Lebow, 'The Search for Accommodation,' p. 173; Stein, 'International Co-operation and Loss Avoidance.'

[7] Stein, 'International Co-operation and Loss Avoidance,' p. 203.

[8] F. Gregory Gause, III, *Oil Monarchies: Domestic and Security Challenges in the Arab Gulf* (New York: Council on Foreign Relations Press, 1994), p. 134.

[9] Gause, *Oil Monarchies*, p. 134.

[10] Gause, *Oil Monarchies*, p. 134.

[11] Gause, *Oil Monarchies,* p. 143.

[12] *Wall Street Journal*, pp. 3-18, C10, *The Gulf/2000 Project Members' Page*, 3 December 1991, School of International and Public Affairs, Columbia University, 13 August 2002 <https://www1.columbia.edu/sec/cu/sipa/GULF2000/chronology/data/91-03.html>.

[13] Michael Shields, 'Saudis in Driver's Seat as OPEC Plans Oil Output,' in Reuters Vienna, *The Gulf/2000 Project Members' Page*, 19 May 1992, School of International and Public Affairs, Columbia University, 13 August 2002 <https://www1.columbia.edu/sec/cu/sipa/GULF2000/chronology/data/92-05.html>.

[14] *New York Times*, pp. 1-22, D1, 4, *The Gulf/2000 Project Members' Page*, 21 January 1992, School of International and Public Affairs, Columbia, 13 August 2002 <https://www1.columbia.edu/sec/cu/sipa/GULF2000/chronoloy/data/92-01.html>.

[15] See 'Aqazadeh on "Saudi Failure to Agree,"' *Voice of the Islamic Republic of Iran First Program Network*, 15 February 1992, found in Foreign Broadcast Information Service, Near East and South Asia (FBIS-NES-92-032), p. 10.

[16] Reuters, *The Gulf/2000 Project Members' Page*, 23 May 1992, School of International and Public Affairs, Columbia University, 18 July 2003 <https://www1.columbia.edu/sec/cu/sipa/GULF2000/chronology/data/92-05.html>.

[17] Reuters Vienna, *The Gulf/2000 Project Members' Page*, 22 May 1992, School of International and Public Affairs, Columbia University, 18 July 2003 <https://www1.columbia.edu/sec/cu/sipa/GULF2000/chronology/data/92-05.html>; Reuters, *The Gulf/2000 Project Members' Page*, 22 May 1992, School of International and Public Affairs, Columbia University, 18 July 2003 <https://www1.columbia.edu/sec/cu/sipa/GULF2000/chronology/data/93-05.html>; and Reuters, *The Gulf/2000 Project Members' Page*, 5 May 1993, School of International and Public Affairs, Columbia University, 18 July 2003 <https://www1.columbia.edu/sec/cu/sipa/GULF2000/chronology/data/93-05.html>.

[18] Reuters, *The Gulf/2000 Project Members' Page*, 25 December 1992, School of International and Public Affairs, Columbia University, accessed 18 July 2003 <https://www1.columbia.edu/sec/cu/sipa/GULF2000/chronology/data/92-12.html>.

[19] Kayhan Barzegar, 'Khatami's Presidency and Iranian-Saudi Relations,' *Discourse* vol. 2, no. 2 (2000), p. 169.

[20] See 'Pinning Hopes On Economic Reforms,' *Middle East Economic Digest, The Gulf/2000 Project Members' Page*, 2 June 2002, School of International and Public Affairs,

Columbia University, 25 August 2002 <https://www1.columbia.edu/sec/cu/sipa/GULF2000/newsframes/gulf2000-2.html>.

[21] Sherine Bahaa, 'GCC fractures over Tehran ties,' *Al-Ahram Weekly* no. 434 (17 - 23 June 1999), 18 July 2003 <http://weekly.ahram.org.eg/1999/434/re5.htm>.

[22] Oil and gas represented approximately 77% of exports in 1998/99 and approximately 37% of General Government Revenue. See International Monetary Fund 'Islamic Republic of Iran: Statistical Appendix' IMF Staff Country Report No. 99/37 (Washington D.C.: International Monetary Fund Publication Services, May 1999), p. 27 and p. 52.

[23] Abbas Maleki, personal interview by the author (Tehran: 20 December 2001).

[24] See Lebow, 'The Search for Accommodation,' p. 181.

[25] Rafsanjani's agenda also included some limited political reforms, but it was a program of adjustment, not an attempt to restructure the system.

[26] R.K. Ramazani, 'The Shifting Premise of Iran's Foreign Policy: Towards a Democratic Peace?' *Middle East Journal*, vol. 52, no. 2 (Spring 1998), p. 182.

[27] Ali Emani, personal interview by the author (Tehran: 20 November 2001).

[28] Mahmood Vaezi, personal interview by the author (Tehran: 10 December 2001).

[29] Although the current status quo is the most likely reference point, losses relative to the status quo at an earlier point may be the relevant reference point. Stein, 'International Co-operation and Loss Avoidance,' p. 215.

[30] See Peg Mackay 'ANALYSIS-Infighting Stymies Iran oil and Gas Investment,' Reuters, *The Gulf/2000 Project Members' Page*, 6 August 2002, School of International and Public Affairs, Columbia University, 13 August 2002 <https://www1.columbia.edu/sec/cu/sipa/GULF2000>; and Valerie Mason, 'Foreign Investment Law to Finally Take Effect Next Month,' World Markets Analysis, *The Gulf/2000 Project Members' Page*, 20 August 2002, School of International and Public Affairs, Columbia University, 25 August 2002 <https://www1.columbia.edu/sec/cu/sipa/GULF2000>.

[31] See 'Algerian Decision to Severs Ties "Irrational,"' *Islamic Republic News Agency*, 28 March 1993, found in Foreign Broadcast Information Service, Near East and South Asia (FBIS-NES-93-058); and 'Mubarak Interview on Iran, Peace Process Reported' *Middle East News Agency*, 30 March 1993, found in Foreign Broadcast Information Service, Near East and South Asia (FBIS-NES-93-058), p. 54.

[32] See, for example, 'Press Criticism Cited,' *Agence France Presse*, 12 September 1992, found in Foreign Broadcast Information Service, Near East and South Asia (FBIS-NES-92-178); and 'Karrubi on Majlis Elections,' *Tehran Bayan*, January-February 1992, found in Foreign Broadcast Information Service, Near East and South Asia (FBIS-NES-92-039), p. 46.

[33] *Al-Sharq Al-Awsat, The Gulf/2000 Project Members' Page*, 15 December 1993, School of International and Public Affairs, Columbia University, 18 July 2003 <https://www1.columbia.edu/sec/cu/sipa/GULF2000/chronology/data/93-12.html>.

[34] Jim Muir, 'Khatami Concludes Historic Gulf Tour,' *BBC News*, 20 May 1999, *BBC Online Network*, 18 July 2003 <http://news.bbc.co.uk/1/hi/world/middle_east/349033.stm>.

[35] Mahmood Vaezi, personal interview by the author (Tehran, 10 December 2001).

Chapter 5

Regime Autonomy and Regional Foreign Policy Choices in the Middle East: A Theoretical Exploration

Bassel F. Salloukh

The nexus of domestic and foreign politics has always been a central concern of the Montréal school of Middle East international relations, a school of which Paul Noble is a founding member. The need to integrate domestic politics and international relations has become recently a core concern for many students of comparative politics and international relations.[1] This interest in the impact of domestic factors on foreign policy and alliance choices is predominant in studies of system- and domestic-level (or *Innenpolitik*) theories of state behaviour.[2] Similarly, there is a substantial literature on Middle East international relations—catalogued in the next section—that examines the origins of foreign policy and alignment choices. Nevertheless, this latter literature has hitherto failed to address important questions in the study of Middle East comparative and international politics. These are: why do some regimes in the Arab Middle East enjoy more independence than others when taking foreign policy and alignment choices? How does the organization of state-society relations constrain or enable a regime's foreign policy independence? Finally, how are the foreign policy and alignment choices of some regimes deployed for domestic political uses?

To address these theoretical questions, this chapter bridges theories from comparative politics and international relations. It supplies a new method of examining the relationship between domestic and foreign politics in non-democratic political systems through an examination of the impact of *regime autonomy* (the independent variable) on *foreign policy independence* (dependent variable) in the Arab Middle East.[3] This analysis is undertaken in two steps. The first unpacks the independent variable by examining the organization of state-society relations in a particular state. After all, in the context of non-democratic political systems, regime autonomy is determined by the manner in which a regime organizes its relations with the active sectors of society to ensure its survival and inhibit the emergence of viable alternatives to its rule. Unpacking the different ways in which regimes organize state-society relations allows us to judge *a priori* whether or not they enjoy autonomy from the active sectors of society.

The second step looks at whether or not a regime enjoys independence in taking foreign policy and alignment choices. This entails examining the underlying logic of a regime's foreign policy and alignment choices, allowing us to causally relate the independent and dependent variables. Where the organization of state-society relations ensures the regime a considerable degree of control over the active sectors of society, the regime enjoys substantial autonomy. Consequently, it also enjoys foreign policy independence. In this case, and in line with neorealist predictions, we expect the regime's foreign policy and alignment choices to reflect responses to its external security environment, namely shifts in the regional balance of power. This is the case even when such choices are deeply unpopular with significant sectors of the population and elicit the ire of public opinion. Alternatively, when the organization of state-society relations does not guarantee the regime thorough control over society, the regime's autonomy is incomplete. Subsequently, the regime's foreign policy independence is compromised. In this latter case, we expect foreign policy and alignment choices to have domestic origins and uses.

More than a revision of neorealist theorizing, and in a departure from idiosyncratic, domestic structure, or constructivist approaches to the study of state behaviour, this study contends that a contextual and historical analysis of regime autonomy in non-democratic political systems explains whether or not regimes enjoy independence in taking foreign policy and alignment choices, and, concomitantly, whether or not these choices will have domestic origins and uses. Unpacking the effects of regime autonomy on foreign policy independence in the Arab Middle East also contributes to developing a first-cut theory of state behaviour in non-democratic political systems.

The map of this chapter assumes the following contours. The next section advances a critical cataloguing of contending theoretical explanations of state behaviour in the Middle East, and pertinent examples from idiosyncratic-perceptual, realist-neorealist, domestic politics, and constructivist theories are evaluated. This section establishes the inability of these theories to explain foreign policy independence in some contexts but not in others. It is followed by a brief theoretical explanation of the different domestic political uses of foreign policy in the developing world. The chapter then examines some recent system- and domestic-level theories of state behaviour. It interrogates the utility of the domestic variables deployed in this literature to the study of regime autonomy and foreign policy independence in the Middle East. The comparative politics side of the argument is explored next. It makes an argument for unpacking the determinants of regime autonomy (the independent variable) by examining how regimes organize their relations with the active sectors of society. It also develops a model for examining the effects of regime autonomy on foreign policy independence in the Arab Middle East. The chapter closes with an operationalization of the model on a paired comparison involving Jordan and Syria.

The Study of Middle East State Behaviour

Analysis of the foreign policy and alignment choices of Middle East states fails to address two overlapping theoretical questions: how do different configurations in the organization of state-society relations affect regime autonomy, and how, in turn, does regime autonomy affect foreign policy independence and the use of foreign policy for domestic purposes? The following review of this literature establishes the theoretical case for the research questions advanced in this chapter. It first examines idiosyncratic theories of Middle East state behaviour.

Idiosyncratic (or psychological) theories focus on the belief systems of the decision-making elite. On this view, personalities and beliefs, rather than bureaucratic positions and the bland calculations of rational actors, play a causal role in determining decision-makers' foreign policy choices.[4] Studies applying this type of individual-level theories to the analysis of Middle East state behaviour explain foreign policy and alignment choices by reference to the belief system or 'operational code' of the principal decision-taker or the decision-making elite, reducing foreign policy analysis to a consequence of idiosyncratic predilections.[5] Yet as Bahgat Korany has noted, this 'overemphasis on the psychological environment [leads] ... to the exclusion of the operational environment (that is, 'the real world' as distinct from the image or perception of this world),' resulting in 'a psychological reductionism verging on monovariable analysis.'[6] Consequently, the domestic political institutional structures sustaining elites as decision-makers in the first place have only minimal input, if any, on the research design used by idiosyncratic theories.

Adeed Dawisha's study of Syrian decision-making during the Lebanese civil war of 1975-76 is representative of idiosyncratic analysis of Middle East state behaviour.[7] He argues that the Lebanese civil war constituted a 'crisis situation' for Syria's foreign policy-making elite, and applies Michael Brecher's crisis decision-making model to explain the motives behind the Syrian political elites' decision to intervene in Lebanon in 1976. Yet Dawisha's study, like others employing individual-level theories, does not unpack the effects of regime autonomy on foreign policy independence. The price of such an omission is evident in the reasoning Dawisha offers to explain the ability of the Syrian regime to intervene in Lebanon on the side of the Christian Lebanese, despite popular discontent expressed by most Syrians, whose sympathies were with fellow Palestinian and Lebanese Muslims. Dawisha argues that 'the persistence of the Syrian leadership with its Lebanese policy and the confidence with which it executed the policy could only suggest that the popularity of the Asad-Ba'thist regime was able to gradually transcend religious and sectarian schisms and conflicts.'[8] Rather, this paradox is better explained by reference to how the corporatist institutional organization of state-society relations in Hafiz al-Asad's Syria allowed the regime considerable autonomy and, consequently, foreign policy independence.

System-level analysis of Middle East state behaviour is dominated by realist and neorealist theories. These theories explain foreign policy and alignment choices either by reference to the security dilemma deriving from systemic regional anarchy, or by systemic, balance-of-power or balance-of-threat variables.[9] Stephen M. Walt's *The Origins of Alliances* is representative of the latter genre. In this influential study, Walt explains the foreign policy choices of Arab states in terms of the pattern of inter-Arab alliances between 1955 and 1979. He does so by employing an improved structural neorealist method, arguing that in determining their alliance choices, states engage in both balance of power *and* balance of threat behaviour. Despite this theoretical leap, Walt's argument does not amount to a comprehensive explanation of the foreign policy and alignment choices of Arab states, with some of his interpretations failing to pass an accurate test of the historical record.[10] In addition to the malleability of his notion of threat, Walt neglects to consider the impact of transnational, ideological, and domestic factors on alliance choices.[11] Moreover, his analysis 'overlooks how changes in state-society relations ... shape the foreign policies of states,' and how foreign policy and alignment choices may have domestic origins and political uses, that is, how foreign policy may be used 'as a tool of statecraft' in the Arab world.[12] Consequently, the realist-neorealist paradigm also neglects the impact of regime autonomy on foreign policy independence, and the domestic use of foreign policy and alignment choices.

One further example deserves consideration before a survey of domestic-level theories is undertaken. In his 'omnibalancing' theory, Steven R. David attempts to incorporate domestic considerations to determine Third World alignment shifts and, more broadly, foreign policy choices.[13] According to David, we fail to understand alignment decisions of Third World leaders unless we consider the role of internal threats to the leadership. Moreover, omnibalancing assumes that the main determinant of alignment choices is the intensity of threat to the leadership of the state, not whether the threat is internal or external. Despite its welcome corrective, David's theory 'focuses more narrowly on the domestic political interests of the elite in power and minimizes the impact of economic variables,' specifically, 'dynamics rooted in the domestic political economy.'[14] Nor does it consider the effects of regime autonomy on foreign policy independence.

The privileged position long enjoyed by idiosyncratic and systemic theories of Middle East state behaviour has recently been challenged given the greater attention paid to domestic level theories by students of Middle East international relations. Sharing the same insistence on the causal power of domestic variables in shaping state behaviour, these explanations emphasize the impact of domestic socio-political constraints,[15] political economic exigencies,[16] state-society relations,[17] sectarian considerations,[18] regime security and instability,[19] political liberalization and the concomitant pressures from domestic coalitions,[20] democracy,[21] capital accumulation crises,[22] or state-building imperatives,[23] on the foreign policy and alignment choices of Middle East states. Other studies explore the impact of interrelated domestic and external security threats on regime survival and alliance choices.[24] While some of these studies relate the vague and static notion of 'domestic structure' to foreign policy choices, none investigates the effects of regime autonomy on foreign policy independence.[25] Moreover, they do not unpack the domestic uses of foreign policy and alignment choices.

Fred Lawson's *Why Syria Goes to War* is one pertinent example of domestic-level explanations of Middle East state behaviour. Lawson's objective is to understand how domestic political-economic dynamics affect the strategies regimes adopt during confrontations with external adversaries. He proposes a connection between 'accumulation crises, high levels of domestic political conflicts, and contradictory regime responses on the one hand and belligerent foreign policies on the other.'[26] Lawson argues that whenever Syrian regimes confronted internal challenges to their ruling coalition, at a time when contradictory responses were being deployed to resolve a burgeoning capital accumulation crisis, they responded with an aggressive foreign policy (as in 1948, 1967, 1970, 1976, and 1982). In these cases, Lawson argues, foreign aggressiveness was judged by the ruling regime to be 'less costly than further measures to prop up a crumbling political-economic order at home.'[27] When, on the other hand, the regime did not face a crisis of capital accumulation, it opted to defuse foreign confrontation, as with Turkey in 1994.

Lawson's neo-Marxist thesis is not without fault. His proposed connection between accumulation crises, high levels of domestic political conflict, contradictory regime responses on the one hand and belligerent Syrian foreign policies on the other is assumed to be mechanical. In so doing, Lawson commits the political equivalent of what Antonio Gramsci derides as 'economism,' that is, 'an overestimation of mechanical causes' in relating two phenomena to each other.[28] Nor is it at all clear from Lawson's narrative how domestic crises actually affect foreign policy choices. After all, to accept Lawson's argument one has to assume that successive Syrian regimes have been preoccupied by intricate economic calculations, an assumption denied by this very leadership.[29] Another fault with Lawson's argument pertains to the static image of state-society relations he presents. By applying the capital accumulation argument to both the pre-Ba'thi and Ba'thi phases of Syrian history, he excludes any possible impact of changing levels of regime autonomy on foreign policy independence. In sum, the emerging school of domestic-level analysis of Middle East state behaviour also fails to consider the effects of regime autonomy on foreign policy independence. Nor does it theorize the domestic political uses of foreign policy and alignment choices in the Middle East.

Constructivism is the most recent arrival on the menu of theories of state behaviour. This approach places causal value on intangible variables such as ideas, norms, and identities in the shaping of state behaviour. Social constructivists fault neorealists for taking state interests for granted and for locating the origins of national security policies and alignment choices in rational calculations derived primarily from material factors. Instead, they point to the way cultural and institutional structures of constructed meaning, embodied in 'norms' and 'identities,' affect national security interests and policies, alliance choices and, hence, state behaviour.[30]

Constructivist studies of Middle East state behaviour explore the impact of changing norms, public sphere deliberations, and identity on foreign policy choices.[31] Michael Barnett's *Dialogues of Arab Politics* makes a strong claim for the explanatory power of this approach. Barnett argues that Arab politics is best understood as a series of dialogues between Arab states concerning the desired regional order. These dialogues create the norms of Arabism, which in turn shape the foreign policies of Arab states. Consequently, changes in the foreign policy behaviour of Arab states and in regional security patterns are explained in terms of changes in the normative structure of Arabism, rather than in systemic military capabilities or in domestic state-society relations. On this view, Arab politics is best fathomed in terms of symbolic interactions, such as competition over symbolic capital and sanctions, attempts at impression management, and symbolic entrapment. On this constructivist view, symbolic, not strategic, considerations explain the Arab states' participation in the 1948 War, the 1958 union between Egypt and Syria, King Hussein's alignment with Egypt's Jamal 'Abdel Nasser on the eve of the 1967 War, and Nasser's involvement in the events that culminated in the 1967 fiasco.

Barnett's constructivist narrative of Arab politics is salutary in at least one respect: it offers a refreshing reinterpretation of Arab politics without lapsing into culturally-reductionist arguments.[32] Nevertheless, the anomalies dotting his work cannot be ignored. They are rooted in the tension running throughout Barnett's work between, on the one hand, the supposedly determining role of norms and, on the other hand, the exigencies of regime survival. According to Barnett, the dominant norm in any specific period should determine state behaviour. However the anomalies to this general rule are impressive: Lebanon and Jordan invoked Western protection in the 1950s when the norm against such action was at its zenith after the struggle over the Baghdad Pact; in 1961 Syrian politicians dared exit a union which they had convinced a sceptical Nasser into joining when the norm for unity was strong; and Sadat made peace with Israel when the norm against that was still strong in Arab politics. Moreover, if, as Barnett claims, symbolic capital enabled Jordan and Syria to stake their legitimacy on Arab nationalism, how then could King Hussein unleash his troops against the Palestinians in Jordan in a period when Arabism was defined by the Arab-Israeli conflict, or how could Asad intervene against the Palestinians in Lebanon in 1976 and make, or sponsor, war with them in 1983 and 1985? As Gregory Gause notes in a searching engagement with Barnett's book, 'It is not clear from Barnett's account when states will be constrained by the norms of Arabism, and when they will ignore them.'[33] Nor is it clear when strategic considerations will outweigh symbolic ones, or when the converse will hold.

True, symbolic entrapment best explains Nasser's participation in the 1967 War. But it is clearly the logic of regime survival, not symbolic politics, that explains King Hussein's participation in the 1967 War. Moreover, there was nothing symbolic in Asad's turn to Iraq in late 1978. The move was based on

Asad's attempt to counter the geopolitical fallout created by the Camp David Accords and Sadat's impending peace with Israel.

Most problematic, however, for the purposes of this chapter, is Barnett's analysis of state behaviour in terms of symbolic struggles among states to define the norms of Arabism. This assumes that Arab regimes are suspended from their institutional bases and the constraining or enabling impact of the organization of state-society relations. Surely this is not the case. After all, even Nasser, a magician in the art of symbolic politics, could not afford to ignore building corporatist institutional structures that organized relations between his regime and the active sectors of Egyptian society.[34] Indeed, a better appreciation of the constraining and enabling effects of different levels of regime autonomy on foreign policy independence helps explain some of the anomalies raised by Barnett's constructivist account of Arab politics. For if, as Barnett argues, the game of symbolic capital and sanctions renders Arab regimes accountable to public opinion, how then can regimes take foreign policy choices that are domestically unpopular—as did Sadat in his 1977 trip to Jerusalem, and Asad by intervening in Lebanon in 1976 and by aligning with Iran in 1980—without fear of domestic retribution? In fact, attention to the constraining or enabling effects of different levels of regime autonomy on foreign policy independence allows for an analysis of the 'linkage between domestic configurations and foreign policy outputs,' something that Barnett argues is 'difficult to provide' due to 'foreign policy and domestic policy substitutability.'[35] Finally, Barnett's use of the term 'symbolic capital,' though close to this chapter's investigation of the domestic political uses of foreign policy, is only deployed for regime-legitimating, but not state-building, purposes.

The foregoing survey suggests that neither idiosyncratic, realist-neorealist, domestic-level, or constructivist theories of Middle East state behaviour explain this chapter's kernel theoretical question: why do some regimes enjoy more foreign policy independence than others? Nor do they theorize about the domestic uses of foreign policy in the Middle East. The next section undertakes this latter task.

The Domestic Uses of Foreign Policy

Be it to balance against power or threats, realism and structural realism assume that foreign policy and alignment choices are taken to maximize state power against *external* threats. In part, this line of reasoning has dominated international relations theorizing because the 'explananda of mainstream [international relations] theory ... have been structures (international, organizational, cognitive) and processes, rather than purposes. The purposes of foreign policy, to the extent that they have been mentioned at all, have been assumed rather than investigated.'[36] A growing body of literature, however, has begun appreciating what Franklin Weinstein, some time ago, labelled the domestic 'political uses of foreign policy.'[37] For example, in his study of Lebanon, Nassif Hitti catalogued four foreign policy choices—'forced accommodation,' 'confrontation,' 'passive preventive accommodation,' and 'active preventive accommodation'—of which at least two may be deployed for domestic political uses.[38] On this view, foreign policy and alignment choices are tools in the hands of regimes deployed for domestic political purposes. These may be any, or a combination, of the following overlapping goals: to bolster a regime's state-building efforts, thus consolidating its rule and ensuring its survival;[39] to legitimate nascent ruling regimes;[40] to secure a consensus among political actors whose support for the ruling regime is pivotal for the successful implementation of regime policies;[41] to attract foreign aid to deflect demands for greater political accountability;[42] and/or to neutralize, through 'two-level games,' the ability of opposition groups to strengthen their local positions by invoking the support of external powers.[43] A central theme of this new research strategy, then, is that regimes shape their foreign policy choices to maximize their chances for survival.[44] It invites a shift away from realism's overemphasis on decision-makers' concern with the maximization of state power. Consequently, this research strategy dissolves realism's presumed epistemological binary distinction between a domestic, order-like 'inside' sphere and an external, anarchy-governed 'outside' sphere, viewing them instead as overlapping terrains.[45]

Neoclassical Realist and *Innenpolitik* Explanations of State Behaviour

The preceding survey established the inability of existing theories of Middle East state behaviour to explain why some regimes enjoy foreign policy independence while others do not. It also theorized about the domestic political uses of foreign policy choices. But does recent international relations theorizing relate to the questions raised in this chapter? Are the determinants of regime autonomy deployed in this literature exportable to the Middle East? Or are other, more context-sensitive, determinants needed? This section takes up these questions.

Despite their insistence on systemic pressures, some neorealists have begun tracing how systemic incentives are translated, through unit-level (intervening) domestic variables, into foreign policy choices. Gideon Rose labels this new school 'neoclassical realism' because, as realists, its adherents argue that 'the scope and ambition of a country's foreign policy is driven first and foremost by its place in the international system and is specified by its relative material power capabilities.' They are neoclassical since they contend that 'the impact of such power capabilities on foreign policy is indirect and complex, because systemic pressures must be translated through intervening variables at the unit level.'[46] Fareed Zakaria has operationalized one such intervening variable, 'state power,' to explain why, until the 1890s, decision-makers were unable to expand American interests abroad despite distinct opportunities to do so.[47] After surveying fifty-four such opportunities between 1865 and 1908, Zakaria concludes that 'the United States could not expand because its policymakers presided over a weak, divided, and decentralized government that provided them with little usable power.' In the

1870s and 1880s, however, 'as industrialization proceeded and the need arose for an extensive regulatory state, the scope and strength of the central government increased. Power shifted from the states to the federal government and from the legislative branch to the executive branch. By the 1890s, the expansionist pipe dreams of the 1860s and 1870s would become reality.'[48] The theoretical implications of Zakaria's conclusions are inescapable: 'the structure, scope, and capacity of the state are crucial factors in explaining the process by which nations become increasingly active on the world stage,' that is, in shaping their foreign policies.[49] However by conceiving state structure in terms of the relationship between the federal government and the different states, on the one hand, and the legislative and executive branches, on the other, Zakaria limits the utility of his suggested first-cut theory (dubbed 'state-centred realism') across regions with different political systems. Where the political system is not fully institutionalized *à la* Western liberal democratic model, the relationship between state structure and foreign policy is better investigated in terms of the organization of state-society relations.

In contrast to their system-level counterparts, domestic-level (or *Innenpolitik*) theorists have always insisted on the causal power of domestic variables in shaping state behaviour.[50] These theories have undergone a renaissance in recent years. They may be further divided into two subtypes. The first engages in rigorous comparative studies of the relationships between, on the one hand, foreign policy and alignment choices, and political (and economic) institutions, on the other.[51] The second is best identified with the 'democratic peace' school. Adherents of this school contend that the similar institutional composition and normative inclinations of democratic dyads—transparent decision-making processes, division of powers, public debates, the potential for electoral defeat—constrain political elites and hence permit the peaceful resolution of conflict among democracies.[52] On this view, the threat of being elected out of office by domestic constituents is sufficient cause for democratic decision-takers to avoid risking war, preferring the peaceful resolution of disputes except when victory is assured.[53] This line of reasoning is being subjected increasingly to critical scrutiny, however, for it erroneously assumes that similar institutions have the same constraining effects on national leaders in different national contexts.[54] The assumption—made by both traditional realists and neorealists—that democracies have similar foreign policy behaviour because of the overriding power of systemic pressures ignores the impact institutional, procedural, and normative differences among democracies have on their ability to conduct foreign policy autonomously from the constraints of domestic opinion.[55] This critique of the democratic peace thesis is best expressed in Norrin Ripsman's study of American, British, and French foreign security policies towards 'the curious case of German rearmament' after the Second World War.[56]

Ripsman examines the impact of the structural autonomy of the foreign policy executive (independent variable) in the United States, Great Britain, and France on two dependent variables: 'the degree to which national leaders could make controversial decisions in the face of domestic opposition (*policy independence*); and their ability to use domestic political opposition as a means of securing concessions in international negotiations *(domestic constraint projection)*.'[57] The level of structural autonomy possessed by a foreign policy executive is in turn determined by three variables. The first is the 'institutional structures,' such as constitutional provisions that set the boundaries of the domestic decision-making environment. These include the structural features of the political system (presidential, parliamentary, or mixed; the type of electoral system employed; and the frequency of elections); and the structural features of the foreign policy apparatus (who are the foreign policy decision-makers, who appoints them, and how often do they report to democratically-elected bodies). The second variable refers to 'decision-making procedures,' such as 'routinized patterns of behaviour and informal rules that govern actors' conduct, but do not necessarily stem from the structure of the institutions within which they operate.' These include the Westministerian tradition of party discipline (an enabling factor), and the recent American tradition whereby the executive consults the legislature before dispatching troops to war (a constraining factor). 'Procedural norms' make up the third variable. These are 'widely accepted standards that constitute a consensus on the way politics ought to be conducted in terms of the rights and obligations of political actors.' Legislative, judicial, and public norms that grant the executive substantial freedom in conducting foreign policy affect decision-making procedures and subsequently the autonomy possessed by the foreign policy executive. Furthermore, strong norms favouring the autonomy of the executive in shaping foreign policy can override institutional structures that may otherwise constrain executive foreign policy-making prerogatives.

By operationalising these three variables, Ripsman established the structural autonomy of the American and British foreign policy executives, in contrast to their much less autonomous French counterparts. He then related the independent and dependent variables by examining how the three executives reacted to German rearmament after the Second World War. Demonstrating their policy independence, the structurally autonomous foreign policy executives of the United States and Great Britain supported German rearmament despite objections from their domestic public. Conversely, the French foreign policy executive, much less autonomous than its Anglo-American counterparts, could not defy domestic opinion and support Germany's rearmament, although it deemed this a paramount security issue. Building on these observations, Ripsman concludes that 'the impact of domestic opinion on foreign security policy is not comparable across democratic states, as traditional theories posit.' Rather, 'it varies across democracies, depending on the degree of structural autonomy afforded by each state's domestic decision-making environments.' Moreover, and against neorealist expectations, the foreign policies of democracies do not always reflect systemic pressures. Whether or not they do so depends on the level of structural autonomy of the foreign-policy executive: 'Highly autonomous democracies should be able to adapt to the international environment as neorealists expect; weaker democracies should display little policy independence, as traditional theorists claim.'[58]

Ripsman's autonomy model allows for a richer conception of the relationship between systemic pressures, domestic constraints, and foreign policy choices than Zakaria's first-cut theory. By unpacking the institutional, procedural, and normative determinants of structural autonomy, it allows for a better conception of the effects of the independent variable on foreign security policies among democracies. Yet the determinants of structural autonomy used in Ripsman's model become overdetermined when applied to the (mainly) non-democratic political systems of the Arab Middle East. After all, in the Middle East, institutional structures and decision-making procedures tend to concentrate foreign policy-taking in the hands of a number of regime insiders. Similarly, and with the exception of Lebanon and post-1991 Kuwait, procedural norms in Middle Eastern states militate towards concentrating the process of foreign policy-shaping and -taking among the members of the ruling regime. Nevertheless, this convergence among institutional structures, decision-making procedures, and procedural norms does not explain the differences among Arab states in terms of the effects of regime autonomy on foreign policy independence and the domestic uses of foreign policy choices. Consequently, we should search for an alternative method of unpacking the structural autonomy of Arab regimes than the one deployed in Ripsman's model.

Regime Autonomy and the Organization of State-Society Relations in the Middle East

Insights from historical institutionalism allow for an analysis of the determinants of regime autonomy in non-democratic political systems. Historical institutionalism underscores the varying impacts different 'configurations' in the organization of state-society relations have on political outcomes.[59] Institutions structure the constellations of constraints and incentives faced by political actors in different contexts, thus defining the relations of power not only among different socio-political groups, but also between them and ruling regimes.[60] Configurations in the institutional organization of state-society relations produce different levels of regime autonomy in the Middle East, which in turn affects foreign policy independence and the domestic use of foreign policy and alignment choices. What then are the determinants of regime autonomy in the Arab Middle East?

In the Arab Middle East, regime autonomy is best evaluated by looking at the strategies regimes deploy to organize state-society relations. Corporatism is one such strategy, deployed in both liberal democratic and authoritarian settings.[61] Philippe Schmitter has provided one of the earliest, and often-cited, generic definitions of corporatism:

> Corporatism can be defined as a system of interest representation in which the constituent units are organized into a limited number of singular, compulsory, noncompetitive, hierarchically ordered and functionally differentiated categories, recognized or licensed (if not created) by the state and granted a deliberate

representational monopoly within their respective categories in exchange for observing certain controls on their selection of leaders and articulation of demands and support.[62]

Schmitter distinguishes between 'state corporatism' (or corporatism from above) and 'societal corporatism' (or corporatism from below), reserving the latter label for the analysis of different patterns of governability and interest intermediation in advanced capitalist countries.[63] In the Arab Middle East, corporatism is an authoritarian theme for organizing state-society relations with heterogeneous manifestations, assuming different forms in different political contexts, and a continuous dimension along which various cases may be arranged.[64]

Nazih Ayubi gathers most Arab regimes under two broad labels. 'Populist-corporatist' regimes are those that attempted various strategies of social engineering from above, resulting in significant mobilizational and redistributional changes in society. Egypt, Iraq, Syria, Algeria, Tunisia, and sometimes Sudan and Libya belong (or once belonged) to this group. They are inclusionary, but not participatory, mobilizing and organizing strategic sectors of society into state-controlled corporatist institutions.[65] The regimes of the Gulf region, and also Morocco and Jordan, are referred to as 'conservative-corporatist.' These regimes opted to reproduce patriarchy, tribalism and ethnic control, mainly through wealth circulation, in a manner conducive to the preservation of regime control. In this case regimes satisfy their coalition partners through neopatrimonial policies, such as lavish public expenditures, employment in bloated public bureaucracies, economic subsidies, and land allocations.[66] In both cases, regimes seek to control the active sectors of the population through various corporatist strategies.

Conversely, in his study of corporatist arrangements of state-society relations in Egypt, Robert Bianchi argues that the heterogeneous systems of interest representation in the Middle East and Asia are neither the 'state corporatism' of Latin America nor the 'societal corporatism' of Western European political systems. Instead they are eclectic systems of interest organization, combining a mixture of corporatist, pluralist, and hybrid structures depending on specific contextual characteristics.[67] Bianchi disaggregates from his Egyptian case study three types of sectoral organization, each corresponding to a distinctive pattern of associational evolution: First are the 'corporatist sectors,' where corporatism has always been the typical mode of sectoral and interest representation and organization. These sectors include most of the middle-class professional syndicates. Second are the 'corporatized sectors,' such as the labour movement and the agricultural cooperatives. Originating as spontaneous and voluntary social movements, they gradually come under state regulation or are supplanted by corporatist organizations. Finally, there are the 'hybrid sectors' where 'pluralist and corporatist structures continue to coexist and compete for predominance, sometimes producing a highly conflictual chain reaction of group organization and counter-organization.'[68] The business community and the religious associations belong to this latter sector.

The aim of attempts at organizing state-society relations, populist-corporatist or otherwise, is to blur, if not eliminate, 'the horizon of options' available to opposition groups, and to ensure, in the words of Adam Przeworski, the 'absence of preferable [or, more accurately, viable] alternatives' to existing ruling regimes.[69] This process usually entails an attack on the organizational autonomy of opposition groups, primarily among labour unions and professional syndicates.[70]

Evaluating regime autonomy a priori in the Arab Middle East entails unpacking the strategies deployed by regimes to organize state-society relations. This amounts to operationalising the independent variable (regime autonomy) in different contexts, tracing how regimes organize their relations with the active sectors of society. This involves examining whether or not a regime penetrates society and organizes labour unions, professional and peasant syndicates, popular organizations, and other associational interests, stripping them from their organizational resources and autonomy; how it pursues these objectives, whether through corporatist, corporatized, or hybrid strategies; whether or not it mobilizes the active sectors of society into corporatist state or party institutions to control them; whether or not it creates pseudo-popular organizations to occupy social space which may otherwise be filled by forces beyond the regime's control; how it organizes or reorganizes representational ties; and how it organizes alliances, populist or otherwise, with strategic coalitions to ensure political control and inhibit the emergence of viable alternatives. The operationalization of the independent variable, then, requires unpacking the peculiar ensemble of interest organization and representation adopted or sanctioned by the ruling regime from above, whether it is of the neopatrimonial or corporatist, corporatized, or hybrid subtypes. Unpacking this ensemble allows us to examine how the organization of state-society relations in a specific context allows for regime autonomy. This in turn explains why certain regimes enjoy foreign policy independence while others do not.

Two hypotheses follow from this model:

Hypothesis 1 (H1) The closer regime strategies of organizing state-society relations are to the state corporatism type, the greater the level of regime autonomy. Consequently, we should expect these regimes to enjoy foreign policy independence, and their foreign policy and alignment choices to follow neorealist predictions.

Hypothesis 2 (H2) The further the organization of state-society relations from corporatist types, the less the level of regime autonomy. Consequently, the regime does not enjoy foreign policy independence; its foreign policy and alignment choices have domestic origins and uses.

In H1, foreign policy and alignment choices reflect a preoccupation with mainly external shifts in the regional balance of power. This holds even when these choices are deeply unpopular with a majority of the population. Alternatively, in H2 foreign policy and alignment choices may have domestic origins and uses. Operationalising this model creates a continuum along which Arab states may be arranged, with Lebanon, the most H2, occupying one pole and Saddam's Iraq, the most H1, the other. The next section uses the model developed above to examine regime autonomy and foreign policy independence in Jordan and Syria.

Deploying the Model: Toward a First-Cut Theory of Middle East State Behaviour

Comparing Jordan and Syria on both the independent and dependent variables operationalizes the model presented in this chapter.[71] Jordan and Syria are Arab states, inhabited by Arab Muslim majorities, sharing the same cultural-historical background. In both states, the regime is faced with roughly similar domestic dynamics: a society segmented along sectarian, nationalist, and/or class lines; the allegiance of significant sectors of the population is not always fully guaranteed; the political domination of minority social segments; a highly permeable regional environment; scarcities in the economic resource base; and a regime that has not shied away from deploying ruthless force at times of open confrontation. Moreover, and as front line states in the Arab-Israeli conflict, with large military expenditures, Syria and Jordan have relied on external, mainly Arab, budgetary assistance. Despite these similarities, they vary considerably, especially on the independent and dependent variables.

Jordan and Syria have different levels of regime autonomy. Unlike its Ba'thi counterpart, the Hashemite regime did not organize the active sectors of society into compulsory, non-competitive, functionally differentiated corporatist institutions. It rather employed a neopatrimonial system of populist rentierism to organize a mainly Hashemite-Transjordanian ruling coalition, one that includes strategic Palestinian segments. This system has maintained the Hashemite monarchy in power for many decades, but failed to shield it from domestic constraints when taking a number of foreign policy and alignment choices. To be sure, the regime did assemble a powerful political-legal edifice and coercive apparatus, organized its relationship with strategic sectors of the East Bank population in a manner that inhibited the emergence of a viable alternative to Hashemite rule, and deployed its loyal Bedouin troops to crush domestic threats at times of open confrontation. Nevertheless, and with the exception of the corporatized labour unions, substantial sectors of the politically active population remain beyond regime control. Consequently, the organization of state-society relations in Jordan, before and after the political liberalization initiated on the morrow of the 1989 *habat nisan*, denied the regime foreign policy independence.

By contrast, in Syria the Ba'th installed a populist authoritarian system of rule based on the organization of state-society relations along strict corporatist channels. The ensemble of corporatist institutions organizing and controlling the active sectors of the population stretched throughout society. Labour, peasants, students, youth, women, teachers, the different business chambers, and a host of other associational interests were organized into Ba'thi-dominated compulsory, non-competitive, functionally differentiated corporatist institutions. Moreover, this institutional infrastructure of corporatist control was linked to the Ba'th Party through the Regional Command's respective specialized bureaus, ensuring regime control over the active sectors of society. This corporatist ensemble of populist authoritarianism proved durable under Hafiz al-Asad, enduring a long trial of strength with the Muslim Brotherhood and an alarming fiscal crisis. It has hitherto inhibited the emergence of a viable alternative to Ba'thi rule, and has allowed the regime a substantial degree of control over, and autonomy from, society. It also contributed to the smooth transition of power from Hafiz to Bashar al-Asad. Consequently, and in contrast to his Hashemite counterpart, the corporatist institutional organization of state-society relations in Ba'thi Syria has ensured a high measure of foreign policy independence.

This variation in the respective regime's foreign policy independence can be examined by looking at the origins of a number of important foreign policy and alignment choices in Jordan and Syria. In Jordan, the lack of foreign policy independence is evident on at least three occasions, the first of which appears in the use of foreign policy and alignment choices for state-building and regime survival objectives in the 1950s and 1960s. In this period of acute regional permeability, foreign policy and alignment choices were deployed for domestic political uses: namely, to insulate the domestic political arena from external interferences and thus to allow the regime's integrative state-building policies some time to take effect. Alternatively, foreign policy and alignment choices were deployed to shield the regime from its domestic opponents, and, subsequently, to pave the way for a domestic crackdown by the army and the *mukhabarat*. The second is Jordan's disengagement from the West Bank in July 1988, a choice rooted in strictly domestic motivations, namely to insulate the East Bank from any detrimental reverberations originating in the Palestinian *intifada*. Disengagement was also deployed for domestic political uses, specifically, as a cover for a series of restructuring initiatives aimed at fortifying the Hashemite regime's East Bank base. Finally, Jordan's alignment choice during the 1990-91 Gulf War runs counter to neorealist predictions—according to which Jordan should have joined the American-led coalition—and is rooted in domestic political pressures and constraints, namely the country-wide opposition to the war against Iraq, a stance the regime could oppose only at the risk of internal strife.

In Syria, on the other hand, the ensemble of corporatist institutions organizing the populist authoritarian system of rule has guaranteed regime autonomy. Consequently, the Asad regime enjoys a high level of foreign policy independence, reflected in its preoccupation with geopolitical balance of power considerations. On a number of crucial occasions, and when faced with shifts in the regional balance of power, the Asad regime responded by taking foreign policy and alignment choices aimed at restoring the regional balance, hence safeguarding

Syria's geopolitical and security interests. This was done even when these choices were deeply unpopular with a majority of the Syrian population. This was the case during Syria's intervention in Lebanon in June 1976 against an alliance of Muslim and Palestinian forces; the alliance with Iran against Iraq throughout the Iran-Iraq war from 1980 to 1988; and Syria's alignment with the American-led coalition against Iraq during the 1990-91 Gulf War. Indeed, Asad's foreign policy career is veritably an uninterrupted geopolitical contest with Israel for the domination of both countries' immediate security environments, a contest punctuated by episodic conflicts with Iraq, Syria's other geopolitical competitor.

The implications of the model developed in this chapter to any projected neoclassical realist first-cut theory of Middle East state behaviour are not difficult to discern. Neoclassical realist attempts to trace how systemic incentives are translated into foreign policy choices would benefit most from a unit-level analysis of the specific organization of state-society relations in any national context. Whether or not states can pursue their geopolitical interests through straightforward balance of power considerations hinges on the domestic organization of state-society relations. Only when this organization ensures a regime considerable autonomy from domestic pressures and constraints will the foreign policy and alignment choices of a state adhere to defensive or offensive realist expectations. Given that the determinants of the independent variable are elastic enough to travel across cases, a unit-level analysis of the impact of regime autonomy on foreign policy independence and the domestic uses of foreign policy in the Middle East may expand the explanatory scope of neoclassical realist theories beyond the democracies of the developed world, thus generating a first-cut neoclassical realist theory of Middle East state behaviour. In turn, this may bridge not only comparative politics and international relations theorizing, but also international relations research across different regions of the world.

Notes

[1] See James A. Caporaso, 'Across the Great Divide: Integrating Comparative and International Politics,' *International Studies Quarterly* vol. 41, no. 4 (December 1997), pp. 563-592; and Bruce Bueno de Mesquita, 'Domestic Politics and International Relations,' *International Studies Quarterly* vol. 46, no. 1 (March 2002), pp. 1-9.

[2] See the relevant literature cited in section four of this chapter.

[3] A regime is defined as 'that nexus of alliances within and without the formal bureaucratic and public sectors that the leader forms in order to gain power and to keep it.' At its core is the leader, flanked by a coterie of rotating officials who are strategically placed throughout the executive, army, and intelligence establishments. Membership in this coterie is not static. One time members may be ejected from it, and new elements may be incorporated into it. Nor are regimes monolithic entities. They include liberal and conservative elements, the latter often found in the bureaucracy and the intelligence services. For the quote see John Waterbury, *The Egypt of Nasser and Sadat: The Political Economy of Two Regimes* (Princeton: Princeton University Press, 1983), p. xiii.

[4] See Michael Brecher, *Decisions in Israel's Foreign Policy* (London: Oxford University Press, 1974); Brecher, 'Towards a Theory of International Crisis Behavior,' *International Studies Quarterly* vol. 21, no. 1 (March 1977), pp. 39-74; and Brecher, *Decisions in Crisis: Israel, 1967 and 1973* (Berkeley: University of California Press, 1980).

[5] See Brecher, *Decisions in Israel's Foreign Policy*; Brecher, *Decisions in Crisis*; Adeed Dawisha, *Syria and the Lebanese Crisis* (New York: St. Martin's Press, 1980); Bahgat Korany, 'When and How Do Personality Factors Influence Foreign Policy?: A Comparative Analysis of Egypt and India,' *Journal of South Asian and Middle Eastern Studies* vol. 9, no. 3 (Spring 1986), pp. 35-59; Jamal A. Zahraan, *al-Siyaasa al-Kharijiyya li-Misr: 1970-1981* [Egypt's Foreign Policy] (Cairo: Maktabat Madbouli, 1987); Moshe Ma'oz, *Asad: The Sphinx of Damascus* (London: Weidenfeld and Nicolson, 1988); James Lunt, *Hussein of Jordan: A Political Biography* (London: Macmillan, 1989); Abdelfattah A. Rashdan, 'Foreign Policy-Making in Jordan: The Role of King Hussein's Leadership in Decision-Making,' Ph.D. dissertation, (University of North Texas, 1989); Uriel Dann, *King Hussein and the Challenge of Arab Radicalism: Jordan, 1955-1967* (New York: Oxford University Press, 1989); Sa'd Abu-Diyye, *'Amaliyyat Ittikhaz al-Qarar fi Siyasat al-Urdun al-Kharijiyya* [The Decision-Taking Process in Jordanian Foreign Policy] (Beirut: Markaz Dirasat al-Wihda al-'Arabiyya, 1990); Dann, *King Hussein's Strategy of Survival*, Policy Papers No. 29 (Washington, D.C.: The Washington Institute for Near East Policy, 1992); Zeev Maoz and Allison Astorino, 'Waging War, Waging Peace: Decision Making and Bargaining in the Arab-Israeli Conflict, 1970-1973,' *International Studies Quarterly* vol. 36, no. 4 (December 1992), pp. 373-399; and Yaacov Y.I. Vertzberger, *Risk Taking and Decisionmaking: Foreign Military Intervention Decisions* (Stanford: Stanford University Press, 1998), pp. 325-386.

[6] Korany, 'Biased Science or Dismal Art? A Critical Evaluation of the State of the Art of Arab Foreign Policies' Analysis,' in Earl L. Sullivan and Jacqueline S. Ismael, eds., *The Contemporary Study of the Arab World* (Edmonton: University of Alberta Press, 1991), p. 191. See also Korany, 'The Take-Off of Third World Studies? The Case of Foreign Policy,' *World Politics* vol. 35, no. 3 (April 1983), p. 469; and Ibrahim A. Karawan, 'Sadat and the Egyptian-Israeli Peace Revisited,' *International Journal of Middle East Studies* vol. 26, no. 2 (May 1994), pp. 249-266.

[7] Dawisha, *Syria and the Lebanese Crisis*.

[8] Dawisha, *Syria and the Lebanese Crisis*, p. 60.

[9] For realism see Itamar Rabinovich, 'The Limits of Military Power: Syria's Role,' in P. Edward Haley and Lewis W. Snider, eds., *Lebanon in Crisis: Participants and Issues* (Syracuse: Syracuse University Press, 1979), pp. 55-73; Avner Yaniv and Robert J. Lieber, 'Personal Whim or Strategic Imperative?' *International Security* vol. 8, no. 2 (Fall 1983), pp. 117-142; Rabinovich, 'The Changing Prism: Syrian Policy in Lebanon as a Mirror, an Issue and an Instrument,' in Moshe Ma'oz and Avner Yaniv, eds., *Syria Under Assad: Domestic Constraints and Regional Risks* (London: Croom Helm, 1986), pp. 179-190; Raymond A. Hinnebusch, Jr., 'Syrian Policy in Lebanon and the Palestinians,' *Arab Studies Quarterly* vol. 8, no. 1 (Winter 1986), pp. 1-20; and Avner Yaniv, *Dilemmas of Security: Politics, Strategy, and the Israeli Experience in Lebanon* (Oxford: Oxford University Press, 1987). For neorealism see Yair Evron and Yaacov Bar Simantov, 'Coalitions in the Arab World,' *Jerusalem Journal of International Relations* vol. 1, no. 2 (Winter 1975), pp. 71-107; Alan R. Taylor, *The Arab Balance of Power* (Syracuse: Syracuse University Press, 1982); Yehoshua Porath, *In Search of Arab Unity, 1930-1945* (London: Frank Cass, 1986); Stephen Walt, *The Origins of Alliances* (Ithaca: Cornell University Press, 1987); Shibley Telhami, *Power and Leadership in International Bargaining: The Path to the Camp David Accords* (New York: Columbia University Press, 1990); and David Garnham, 'Explaining

Middle Eastern Alignments During the Gulf War,' *Jerusalem Journal of International Relations* vol. 13, no. 3 (September 1991), pp. 63-83.

[10] This is especially true of Walt's analysis of pan-Arab unionism and of Jordan's foreign policy choices, both between 1955 and 1967. For correctives see Malik Mufti, *Sovereign Creations: Pan-Arabism and Political Order in Syria and Iraq* (Ithaca: Cornell University Press, 1996); and Bassel F. Salloukh, 'State Strength, Permeability, and Foreign Policy Behavior: Jordan in Theoretical Perspective,' *Arab Studies Quarterly* vol. 18, no. 2 (Spring 1996), pp. 39-65.

[11] On malleability see Fareed Zakaria, *From Wealth to Power: The Unusual Origins of America's World Role* (Princeton: Princeton University Press, 1998), p. 27. See also F. Gregory Gause, III, 'Balancing What? Threat Typology and Alignment Decisions in the Gulf, 1971-1991,' Paper presented at the Middle East Studies Association of North America 29th Annual Meeting (Washington, DC, December 1995), p. 21; and Laurie A. Brand, 'Economics and Shifting Alliances: Jordan's Relations with Syria and Iraq, 1975-81,' *International Journal of Middle East Studies* vol. 26, no. 3 (August 1994), p. 393.

[12] Michael N. Barnett, 'Sovereignty, Nationalism, and Regional Order in the Arab States System,' *International Organization* vol. 49, no. 3 (Summer 1995), p. 490; and Gause, 'Sovereignty, Statecraft and Stability in the Middle East,' *Journal of International Affairs* vol. 45, no. 2 (Winter 1992), p. 452, respectively.

[13] See Steven R. David, *Choosing Sides: Alignment and Realignment in the Third World* (Baltimore: The Johns Hopkins University Press, 1991); David, 'Explaining Third World Alignment,' *World Politics* vol. 43, no. 2 (January 1991), pp. 233-56.

[14] Jack S. Levy and Michael M. Barnett, 'Alliance Formation, Domestic Political Economy, and Third World Security,' *Jerusalem Journal of International Relations* vol. 14, no. 4 (December 1992), p. 23.

[15] See Tareq Y. Ismael, *International Relations of the Contemporary Middle East: A Study in World Politics* (Syracuse: Syracuse University Press, 1986), pp. 17-40; Korany and Ali E. Hillal Dessouki, eds., *The Foreign Policies of Arab States: The Challenge of Change*, 2nd ed., (Boulder: Westview Press, 1991); and Nasir Muhammad Tahbub, *Al-Siyasa al-Kharijiyya al-Urduniyya wa-l-Bahth 'an al-Salaam* [Jordanian Foreign Policy and the Search for Peace] (Amman: Matba'at al-Quds, 1994).

[16] See Levy and Barnett, 'Alliance Formation, Domestic Political Economy, and Third World Security;' Brand, 'Economics and Shifting Alliances: Jordan's Relations with Syria and Iraq, 1975-81,' *International Journal of Middle East Studies* vol. 26, no. 3 (August 1994), pp. 393-413; and Brand, *Jordan's Inter-Arab Relations: The Political Economy of Alliance Making* (New York: Columbia University Press, 1994).

[17] See Gause, *Saudi-Yemeni Relations: Domestic Structures and Foreign Influence* (New York: Columbia University Press, 1990).

[18] See Daniel Pipes, *Greater Syria: The History of an Ambition* (Oxford: Oxford University Press, 1990). Among other factors, the impact of sectarian considerations on foreign policy is also discussed in Peter B. Heller, 'The Syrian Factor in the Lebanese Civil War,' *Journal of South Asian and Middle Eastern Studies* vol. 4, no. 1 (Fall 1980), pp. 56-76; Mahmud A. Faksh, 'Syria's Role in Lebanon,' *Journal of South Asian and Middle Eastern Studies* vol. 9, no. 4 (Summer 1986), pp. 10-25; and As'ad Aboukhalil, 'Syria and the Shiites: Al-Asad's Policy in Lebanon,' *Third World Quarterly* vol. 12, no. 2 (April 1990), pp. 1-20.

[19] See Yaacov Bar-Simon-Tov, *Linkage Politics in the Middle East: Syria Between Domestic and External Conflict, 1961-1970* (Boulder: Westview Press, 1983); Valerie Yorke, *Domestic Politics and Regional Security: Jordan, Syria, and Israel: The End of an Era?* (Aldershot: Gower, 1988); Fred H. Lawson, *The Social Origins of Egyptian Expansionism During the Muhammad 'Ali Period* (New York: Columbia University Press,

1992); Amatzia Baram, 'The Iraqi Invasion of Kuwait: Decision-making in Baghdad,' in Amatzia Baram and Barry Rubin, eds., *Iraq's Road to War* (New York: St. Martin's Press, 1993), pp. 5-36; Mufti, *Sovereign Creations*; and Gause, 'Iraq's Decisions to Go to War, 1980 and 1990,' *Middle East Journal* vol. 56, no. 1 (Winter 2002), pp. 48-70.

[20] See Brand, 'Liberalization and Changing Political Coalitions: The Bases of Jordan's 1990-1991 Gulf Crisis Policy,' *Jerusalem Journal of International Relations* vol. 13, no. 4 (1991), pp. 1-46; Lisa Anderson, 'Democratization and Foreign Policy in the Arab World: The Domestic Origins of the Jordanian and Algerian Alliances in the 1991 Gulf War,' in Miles Kahler, ed., *Liberalization and Foreign Policy* (New York: Columbia University Press, 1997), pp. 121-142.

[21] See Michael C. Hudson, 'Democracy and Foreign Policy in the Arab World,' in David Garnham and Mark Tessler, eds., *Democracy, War, and Peace in the Middle East* (Bloomington: Indiana University Press, 1995), pp. 195-220.

[22] See Lawson, 'Syrian Intervention in the Lebanese Civil War, 1976: A Domestic Conflict Explanation,' *International Organization* vol. 38, no. 3 (Summer 1984), pp. 451-480; and Lawson, *Why Syria Goes to War: Thirty Years of Confrontation* (Ithaca, NY: Cornell University Press, 1996).

[23] See Salloukh, 'State Strength, Permeability, and Foreign Policy Behavior;' and Mohammad-Mahmoud Mohamedou, 'State-Building and Regime Security: A Study of Iraq's Foreign Policy Making During the Second Gulf War,' Ph.D. dissertation (City University of New York, 1996).

[24] See Mohammad I. Faddah, *The Middle East in Transition: A Study of Jordan's Foreign Policy* (New York: Asia Publishing House, 1974); Barnett and Levy, 'Domestic Sources of Alliances and Alignments: The Case of Egypt, 1962-73,' *International Organization* vol. 45, no. 3 (Summer 1991), pp. 369-395; Curtis R. Ryan, 'Shifting Arab Alignments: Jordan in Inter-Arab Politics, 1971-1991,' Ph.D. dissertation (University of North Carolina, 1995); Richard J. Harknett and Jeffrey A. VanDenBerg, 'Alignment Theory and Interrelated Threats: Jordan and the Persian Gulf Crisis,' *Security Studies* vol. 6, no. 3 (Spring 1997), pp. 112-153; and Michael J. Gilligan and W. Ben Hunt, 'The Domestic and International Sources of Foreign Policy: Alliance Formation in the Middle East, 1948-78,' in Randolph M. Siverson, ed., *Strategic Politicians, Institutions, and Foreign Policy* (Ann Arbor: University of Michigan Press, 1998), pp. 143-168.

[25] For a critique of the term 'domestic structure' see John Kurt Jacobsen, 'Are All Politics Domestic? Perspectives on the Integration of Comparative Politics and International Relation Theories,' *Comparative Politics* vol. 29, no. 1 (October 1996), p. 108.

[26] Lawson, *Why Syria Goes to War*, pp. 169 and 157, respectively.

[27] Lawson, *Why Syria Goes to War*, p. 180.

[28] Antonio Gramsci, *Selections from the Prison Notebooks*, in Quintin Hoare and Goeffrey Nowell Smith, ed. and tr. respectively, (New York: International Publishers, 1971), p. 178.

[29] Muhammad al-'Imadi (Former Minister of Economy and Foreign Trade and Former Minister of Planning), personal interview by the author (Damascus, 27 October 1998).

[30] See Alexander E. Wendt, 'The Agent-Structure Problem in International Relations Theory,' *International Organization* vol. 41, no. 3 (Summer 1987), pp. 335-372; David Dessler, 'What's at Stake in the Agent-Structure Debate?' *International Organization* vol. 43, no. 3 (Summer 1989), pp. 441-473; Wendt, 'Anarchy is What States Make of it,' *International* Organization, vol. 46, no. 2 (Spring 1992), pp. 391-425; Peter J. Katzenstein, ed., *The Culture of National Security: Norms and Identity in World Politics* (New York: Columbia University Press, 1996); and Jeffrey T. Checkel, 'The Constructivist Turn in International Relations Theory,' *World Politics* vol. 50, no. 2 (January 1998), pp. 324-348.

[31] See Barnett, *Dialogues in Arab Politics: Negotiations in Regional Order* (New York: Columbia University Press, 1998); Barnett, 'Identity and Alliances in the Middle East,' in Katzenstein, ed., *The Culture of National Security*, pp. 400-447; Marc Lynch, *State Interests and Public Spheres: The International Politics of Jordan's Identity* (New York: Columbia University Press, 1999); Dalia Dassa Kaye, *Multilateralism in the Middle East* (New York: Columbia University Press, 2001); and Telhami and Barnett, *Identity and Foreign Policy in the Middle East* (Ithaca: Cornell University Press, 2002).

[32] Unlike, for example, studies by Fouad Ajami, *The Arab Predicament: Arab Political Thought and Practice Since 1967*, Updated ed. (Cambridge: Cambridge University Press, 1992); and Paul Salem, *Bitter Legacy: Ideology and Politics in the Arab World* (Syracuse: Syracuse University Press, 1994). In a recent work, Ajami also speaks of fragmentation, but it is of the Arab cultural and moral order; its causes are rooted in the 'ailments' and 'atavisms' of Arab culture. See Ajami, *The Dream Palace of the Arabs: A Generation's Odyssey* (New York: Pantheon Books, 1998).

[33] Gause, 'Systemic Approaches to Middle East International Relations,' *International Studies Review* vol. 1, no. 1 (Spring 1999), p. 21.

[34] See Waterbury, *The Egypt of Nasser and Sadat*, pp. 307-353; Hinnebusch, *Egyptian Politics Under Sadat: The Post-Populist Development of an Authoritarian-Modernizing State*, Updated ed. (Boulder: Lynne Rienner, 1988), pp. 11-39; and Marsha Pripstein Posusney, *Labor and the State in Egypt: Workers, Unions, and Economic Restructuring* (New York: Columbia University Press, 1997), pp. 40-79.

[35] Barnett, *Dialogues in Arab Politics*, p. 45.

[36] Kjell Goldmann, 'International Relations: An Overview,' in Robert E. Goodin and Hans-Dieter Klingemann, eds., *A New Handbook of Political Science* (Oxford: Oxford University Press, 1996), pp. 416-417.

[37] Franklin B. Weinstein, 'The Uses of Foreign Policy in Indonesia: An Approach to the Analysis of Foreign Policy in the Less Developed Countries,' *World Politics* vol. 24, no. 3 (April 1972), p. 371. See also Rex Brynen, 'Between Parsimony and Parochialism: Comparative Politics, International Relations, and the Study of Middle East Foreign Policy,' Paper Presented at the Annual Conference of the American Political Science Association (Washington, DC, September 1993).

[38] These are 'forced accommodation,' which refers to making concessions to an external actor wielding influence over the domestic arena without resolving the state's domestic crisis, either to avoid an escalation of internal conflict, to enact a new consensus, or to prepare for a crack down against the domestic opposition; and 'active preventive accommodation,' which is characterized by a *rapprochement* with the regional power wielding the most influence over the domestic arena. This latter foreign policy choice allows the domestic regime to consolidate national consensus and regime survival through state-building. See Nassif Hitti, *The Foreign Policy of Lebanon: Lessons and Prospects for the Forgotten Dimension,* Papers on Lebanon No. 9 (Oxford: Centre for Lebanese Studies, 1989), pp. 12-13 and 20.

[39] See Gause, 'Sovereignty, Statecraft and Stability in the Middle East;' Brynen, 'Palestine and the Arab State System: Permeability, State Consolidation and the *Intifada*,' *Canadian Journal of Political Science* vol. 24, no. 3 (September 1991), pp. 595-621; Joel S. Migdal, 'Internal Structure and External Behaviour: Explaining Foreign Policies of Third World States,' *International Relations* vol. 4, no. 5 (1974), p. 523; Mohamedou, 'State-Building and Regime Security;' and Salloukh, 'State Strength, Permeability, and Foreign Policy Behavior.'

[40] See Barnett, *Dialogues in Arab Politics*, p. 68; Hudson, *Arab Politics: The Search for Legitimacy* (New Haven: Yale University Press, 1977); Dawisha, 'Arab Regimes:

Legitimacy and Foreign Policy,' in Giacomo Luciani, ed., *The Arab State* (Berkeley: University of California Press, 1990), pp. 284-299; and Muhammad Hasanayn Heikal, *Khareef al-Ghadab: Qisat Bidayat wa Nihayat 'Asr Anwar al-Sadat* [Autumn of Fury: The Story of the Beginning and End of Anwar Sadat's Age] (Beirut: Sharikat al-Matbo'at lil-Tawzi' wa-l-Nashr, 1983), p. 146.

[41] See Joe D. Hagan, 'Regimes, Political Oppositions, and the Comparative Analysis of Foreign Policy,' in Charles F. Hermann, Charles W. Kegley Jr., and James N. Rosenau, eds., *New Directions in the Study of Foreign Policy* (Boston: Allen & Unwin, 1987), p. 349.

[42] See Anderson, 'Peace and Democracy in the Middle East: The Constraints of Soft Budgets,' *Journal of International Affairs* vol. 49, no. 1 (Summer 1996), pp. 25-43.

[43] This corresponds to Hitti's 'active preventive accommodation' foreign policy choice. See also Robert D. Putnam, 'Diplomacy and Domestic Politics: The Logic of Two-Level Games,' *International Organization* vol. 42, no. 3 (Summer 1988), pp. 427-460; David, *Choosing Sides*.

[44] See Randolph M. Siverson, 'Introduction,' in Siverson, ed., *Strategic Politicians, Institutions, and Foreign Policy*, p. 2. For other examples see also Robert Burrowes and Gerald DeMaio, 'Domestic/External Linkages: Syria, 1961-1967,' *Comparative Political Studies* vol. 7, no. 4 (January 1975), pp. 478-507; Barnett and Levy, 'Domestic Sources of Alliances and Alignments;' Levy and Barnett, 'Alliance Formation, Domestic Political Economy, and Third World Security;' Mohammed Ayoob, *The Third World Security Predicament: State Making, Regional Conflict, and the International System* (Boulder: Lynne Rienner, 1995); Ryan, 'Shifting Arab Alignments;' Mufti, *Sovereign Creations*; Christopher Clapham, *Africa and the International System: The Politics of State Survival* (New York: Cambridge University Press, 1996), pp. 62-74; and Gilligan and Hunt, 'The Domestic and International Sources of Foreign Policy.' Michael Barnett's constructivist analysis of inter-state Arab politics also begins with the same assumption about Arab leaders' concern with regime survival, see Barnett, *Dialogues in Arab Politics*, p. 34.

[45] For a philosophical critique see R.B.J. Walker, *Inside/Outside: International Relations as Political Theory* (Cambridge: Cambridge University Press, 1993), especially pp. 125-140.

[46] Gideon Rose, 'Neoclassical Realism and Theories of Foreign Policy,' *World Politics* vol. 51, no. 1 (October 1998), p. 146. For works operating simultaneously on both systemic and domestic levels of analysis see Putnam, 'Diplomacy and Domestic Politics;' Randall L. Schweller, 'Domestic Structure and Preventive War: Are Democracies More Pacific?' *World Politics* vol. 44, no. 2 (January 1992), pp. 235-269; Zakaria, 'Realism and Domestic Politics: A Review Essay,' *International Security* vol. 17, no. 1 (Summer 1992), pp. 177-198; and Schweller and David Priess, 'A Tale of Two Realisms: Expanding the Institutions Debate,' *Mershon International Studies Review* vol. 41, no. 1 (May 1997), pp. 1-32.

[47] See Zakaria, *From Wealth to Power*. On p. 9, Zakaria defines state power as 'that portion of national power the government can extract for its purposes and reflects the ease with which central decision-makers can achieve their ends.' Another intervening variable, the perceptions of decision-makers, is operationalized in Schweller, *Deadly Imbalances: Tripolarity and Hitler's Strategy of World Conquest* (New York: Columbia University Press, 1998).

[48] Zakaria, *From Wealth to Power*, pp. 54 and 184 respectively.

[49] Zakaria, *From Wealth to Power*, p. 9.

[50] For general statements see David Skidmore and Valerie M. Hudson, eds., *The Limits of State Autonomy: Social Groups and Foreign Policy Formulation* (Boulder: Westview Press, 1993); Richard Rosecrance and Arthur A. Stein, 'Beyond Realism: The Study of Grand Strategy,' in Richard Rosecrance and Arthur A. Stein, eds., *The Domestic Bases of Grand Strategy* (Ithaca: Cornell University Press, 1993), pp. 3-21; and Hagan, 'Domestic Political

Explanations in the Analysis of Foreign Policy,' in Laura Neack et al., eds., *Foreign Policy Analysis: Continuity and Change in Its Second Generation* (Eaglewood Cliffs, N.J.: Prentice Hall, 1995), pp. 117-143. On domestic structures and state-society relations see Katzenstein, 'International Relations and Domestic Structures: Foreign Economic Policies of Advanced Industrial States,' *International Organization* vol. 30, no. 1 (Winter 1976), pp. 1-45; Katzenstein, ed., *Between Power and Plenty: Foreign Economic Policies of Advanced Industrial States* (Madison: University of Wisconsin Press, 1978); T. Clifton Morgan and Sally Howard Campbell, 'Domestic Structure, Decisional Constraints, and War,' *Journal of Conflict Resolution* vol. 35, no. 2 (June 1991), pp. 187-211; and Andrew Moravesik, 'Taking Preference Seriously: A Liberal Theory of International Politics,' *International Organization* vol. 51, no. 4 (Autumn 1997), pp. 513-553. On domestic coalitions see Lawson, 'Domestic Conflict and Foreign Policy: The Contribution of some Undeservedly Neglected Historical Studies,' *Review of International Studies* vol. 11, no. 4 (October 1985), pp. 275-299; and T. Clifton Morgan and Kenneth N. Bickers, 'Domestic Discontent and the External Use of Force,' *Journal of Conflict Resolution* vol. 36, no. 1 (March 1992), pp. 25-52. On domestic political and economic institutions see John G. Ikenberry, 'Conclusion: An Institutional Approach to American Foreign Economic Policy,' *International Organization* vol. 42, no. 1 (Winter 1988), pp. 219-243; and Ikenberry, David A. Lake, and Michael Mastanduno, 'Introduction: Approaches to Explaining American Foreign Economic Policy,' *International Organization* vol. 42, no. 1 (Winter 1988), pp. 1-14. See also the review essay by Ethan B. Kapstein, 'Is Realism Dead? The Domestic Sources of International Politics,' *International Organization* vol. 49, no. 4 (Autumn 1995), pp. 751-774.

[51] For an early example of this analysis see Migdal, 'Internal Structure and External Behaviour.' For more recent studies see Walter Carlsnaes, 'The Agency-Structure Problem in Foreign Policy Analysis,' *International Studies Quarterly* vol. 36, no. 3 (September 1992), pp. 245-270; Suzanne Werner and Douglas Lemke, 'Opposites Do Not Attract: The Impact of Domestic Institutions, Power, and Prior Commitments on Alignment Choices,' *International Studies Quarterly* vol. 41, no. 3 (September 1997), pp. 529-546; and Siverson, ed., *Strategic Politicians, Institutions, and Foreign Policy.*

[52] See David A. Lake, 'Powerful Pacifists: Democratic States and War,' *American Political Science Review* vol. 86, no. 1 (March 1992), pp. 24-37; and Bruce Russett, *Grasping the Democratic Peace* (Princeton, NJ: Princeton University Press, 1993).

[53] See Bueno de Mesquita, 'Domestic Politics and International Relations,' p. 6; and Kenneth A. Schultz, *Democracy and Coercive Diplomacy* (Cambridge: Cambridge University Press, 2001).

[54] See Kahler, 'Liberalization and Foreign Policy,' in Kahler, *Liberalization and Foreign Policy*, p. 9; and Mark R. Brawley, *Turning Points: Decisions Shaping the Evolution of the International Political Economy* (New York: Broadview Press, 1998), pp. 88-89.

[55] See Thomas Risse-Kappen, 'Public Opinion, Domestic Structure, and Foreign Policy in Liberal Democracies,' *World Politics* vol. 43, no. 4 (July 1991), pp. 479-512; Susan Peterson, 'How Democracies Differ: Public Opinion, State Structures, and the Lessons of the Fashoda Crisis,' *Security Studies* vol. 5, no. 1 (Autumn 1995), pp. 3-37; and Miriam Fendius Elman, 'Unpacking Democracy: Presidentialism, Parliamentarism, and Theories of Democratic Peace,' *Security Studies* vol. 9, no. 4 (Summer 2000), pp. 97-135.

[56] See Norrin M. Ripsman, 'The Curious Case of German Rearmament: Democracy, Structural Autonomy, and Foreign Security Policy,' *Security Studies* vol. 10, no. 2 (Winter 2000/1), pp. 1-47.

[57] Ripsman, p. 3.

[58] Ripsman, p. 47.

[59] For a general statement see Ira Katznelson, 'Structure and Configuration in Comparative Politics,' in Mark Irving Lichbach and Alan S. Zuckerman, eds., *Comparative Politics: Rationality, Culture, and Structure* (Cambridge: Cambridge University Press, 1997), pp. 81-112. See also Theda Skocpol, 'Bringing the State Back In: Strategies of Analysis in Current Research,' in Peter B. Evans, Dietrich Rueschemeyer, and Theda Skocpol, eds., *Bringing the State Back In* (Cambridge: Cambridge University Press, 1985), p. 21; Kathleen Thelen and Sven Steinmo, 'Historical Institutionalism in Comparative Politics,' in Sven Steinmo, Kathleen Thelen, and Frank Longstreth, eds., *Structuring Politics: Historical Institutionalism in Comparative Analysis* (Cambridge: Cambridge University Press, 1992), pp. 6-7; and Karen L. Remmer, 'Theoretical Decay and Theoretical Development: The Resurgence of Institutional Analysis,' *World Politics* vol. 50, no. 1 (October 1997), pp. 34-61.

[60] See Thelen and Steinmo, 'Historical Institutionalism in Comparative Politics,' p. 13.

[61] See David Collier, 'Trajectory of a Concept: Corporatism in the Study of Latin American Politics,' in Peter H. Smith, ed., *Latin America in Comparative Perspective: New Approaches to Methods and Analysis* (Boulder: Westview Press, 1995), p. 136. See also Ilja Scholten, 'Introduction: Corporatist and Consociational Arrangements,' in Ilja Scholten, ed., *Political Stability and Neo-Corporatism: Corporatist Integration and Societal Cleavages in Western Europe* (London: Sage Publications, 1987), pp. 1-38.

[62] Philippe C. Schmitter, 'Still the Century of Corporatism?' *The Review of Politics* vol. 36, no. 1 (January 1974), pp. 93-94.

[63] See Schmitter, 'Interest Intermediation and Regime Governability in Contemporary Western Europe and North America,' in Suzanne Berger, ed., *Organizing Interests in Western Europe: Pluralism, Corporatism, and the Transformation of Politics* (Cambridge: Cambridge University Press, 1981), pp. 285-327.

[64] See Collier, 'Trajectory of a Concept,' pp. 142-143; James M. Malloy, 'Authoritarianism, Corporatism and Mobilization in Peru,' *Review of Politics* vol. 36, no. 1 (January 1974), pp. 52-84; Malloy, 'Authoritarianism and Corporatism in Latin America: The Modal Pattern,' in Malloy, ed., *Authoritarianism and Corporatism in Latin America* (Pittsburgh: University of Pittsburgh Press, 1977), p. 4; and Collier and Ruth Berins Collier, 'Who Does What, to Whom, and How: Toward a Comparative Analysis of Latin American Corporatism,' in Malloy, ed., *Authoritarianism and Corporatism in Latin America*, p. 493.

[65] See Nazih N. Ayubi, *Over-stating the Arab State: Politics and Society in the Middle East* (London: I.B. Tauris, 1995), pp. 196-223.

[66] See Ayubi, pp. 224-255. See also Khaldun Hasan al-Naqeeb, *al-Mujtama' wa-l-Dawla fi-l-Khalij wa-l-Jazira al-'Arabiya: Min Manzur Mukhtalif* [Society and State in the Gulf and Arabian Peninsula: A Different Perspective] (Beirut: Markaz Dirasat al-Wihda al-'Arabiyya, 1987), pp. 149-161; and Gause, *Oil Monarchies: Domestic and Security Challenges in the Arab Gulf States* (New York: Council on Foreign Relations Press, 1994), pp. 42-118.

[67] See Robert Bianchi, *Unruly Corporatism: Associational Life in Twentieth Century Egypt* (New York: Oxford University Press, 1989).

[68] Bianchi, *Unruly Corporatism*, p. 21.

[69] Robert Fatton Jr., *The Making of a Liberal Democracy: Senegal's Passive Revolution, 1975-1985* (Boulder: Lynne Rienner, 1987), p. 166; and Adam Przeworski, 'Some Problems in the Study of the Transition to Democracy,' in Guillermo O'Donnell, Philippe C. Schmitter, and Laurence Whitehead., eds., *Transitions from Authoritarian Rule: Comparative Perspectives* (Baltimore: The Johns Hopkins University Press, 1986), p. 52 respectively.

[70] See Alfred Stepan, 'State Power and the Strength of Civil Society in the Southern Cone of Latin America,' in Evans, Rueschemeyer, and Skocpol, eds., *Bringing the State Back In*, p. 323.

[71] For the full analysis and supporting evidence see Salloukh, 'Organizing Politics in the Arab World: State-Society Relations and Foreign Policy Choices in Jordan and Syria,' Ph.D. dissertation (McGill University, 2000).

Chapter 6

Regional Dynamics of Refugee Flows:
The Case of Iran

Asya El-Meehy

The question of state permeability in the contemporary Middle East has been approached predominantly from the ideational perspective, typically emphasizing the roles of pan-Arabism and pan-Islamism in undermining the dual processes of nation formation and modern state consolidation. A less explored component of regional permeability, however, is that represented by the cross-border movements of people in the form of refugee flows. At times of political turbulence, the latter often constitute a fundamental challenge to state authorities whose limited capacities to monitor, regulate and respond to the influx of asylum seekers constrain their range of policy choices. Indeed, the case of Iran, host to roughly two million refugees, highlights both the importance of examining the dynamics behind refugee policy formulation as well as the dilemmas of state border permeability more generally. The United States Commission on Refugees (USCR) estimates that during the 1990s, Iran 'sheltered a staggering 4.5 million exiles from Afghanistan and Iraq, the largest refugee caseload any single country has handled in modern times.'[1] The state's response to such massive influxes of people has varied considerably over the last couple of decades, ranging from 'open' strategies oriented towards the local integration of asylum seekers, to 'preventive' ones involving the involuntary repatriation of refugees, the closure of borders and the extension of relief beyond its territories.

This chapter explores the underlying dynamics behind variations in host state policies towards refugee populations in the Middle East and Central Asia. It comparatively examines Iranian policies towards two sets of displaced populations, delineating the causal factors behind Iran's contrasting treatment of these refugee groups, and inferring the reasons behind the overall restrictive evolution of the country's refugee policies. The first set is the 200,000 Azerbaijani refugees displaced in the wake of the 1993 conflict in Nagorno Karabakh and denied entry to Iran, and the two million Afghan refugees whose status has changed considerably as the state's policies largely shifted from integration in the 1980s to prevention in the 1990s.

The following begins with a brief discussion of theoretical perspectives on refugee policy-making and their relevance to the Iranian case. Based on an overview of the country's policies, the analysis next focuses on the role of state capacity as an explanatory factor.   Finally, the chapter concludes with an assessment of the driving dynamics behind host state policy formulation in the region.

Theoretical Perspectives on Refugee Policy-making

A series of contending global, regional and local forces can be seen at work in the process of refugee policy-making. At the global level, the causal impacts of ideational factors and the international refugee regime are considered by many to be enormously significant. Constructivists argue that the political discourse surrounding asylum seekers not only influences the perceptions and responses of governments, but also contributes to the reproduction of national and racial ideologies in societies.[2] For liberal institutionalists, the international refugee regime influences state policies at the practical level, due to the need for burden sharing, and, more normatively, through the threat of bad international publicity.[3] By building a constituency supportive of its agenda within the state, the United Nations High Commission for Refugees (UNHCR) not only provides institutional support to the host but also encourages 'policymakers to pursue existing interests in security, stability and international legitimacy through refugee protection.'[4] Yet international influences represented by the international refugee regime are not particularly useful in explaining the variations in Iranian policies. UN assistance began as late as 1983 at the modest scale of a $2.5 million program of emergency assistance,[5] and the organization's operation in Iran under the umbrella of the recently launched voluntary repatriation program remains limited due to heavy restrictions on the operations of its implementing partners in the NGO sector.[6]

Regional security considerations typically come into play in refugee policy formulation whenever there is a potential risk of violence spilling into the host state.[7] In these cases, 'the location of refugee warriors on the border makes their presence especially salient'[8] and invites retaliation, thereby threatening regional stability and complicating relations between host and origin states. In addition, refugee warriors or armed exile groups may intentionally attempt to drag the host state into an ongoing conflict through conducting raids and guerrilla activity,[9] thus constituting a direct security burden to their hosts, whose policies are driven by the degree of security risk they face.[10]

In contrast to these claims, however, evidence from the Iranian case indicates that regional security considerations were not salient in the formulation of Tehran's refugee policies, since neither Afghan nor Azerbaijani refugees posed a direct threat to state security. With less than five per cent of the refugees in camps and the great majority assimilated in the population centers of the eastern provinces, there has been little potential for 'a major Afghan refugee resistance complex in Iran.'[11] In addition, although the potential destabilizing effects of hosting armed refugees in the northern Azeri-populated territories of Iran may have been a reason behind Iran's adoption of a preventive refugee strategy, there is no proof to substantiate this line of argument. Indeed, while there are some references in news reports of Azeri Iranians crossing to fight alongside the Azerbaijanis,[12] there is no evidence of armed Azerbaijanis taking refuge in Iran. Rather, the most direct link between refugees and state insecurity in Iran seems to relate to the problem of drug-trafficking along the border with Afghanistan, where the drug war has claimed the lives of more than 3,000 Iranian soldiers and policemen since the early 1980s.[13] In fact, the Head of Iran's Parliamentary Commission for National Security and Foreign Affairs contends that 'insecurity on the eastern borders and drug trafficking have [a] direct relationship with immigration of Afghans to Iran' since in many cases 'the trip of Afghan refugees from Iran and their return are mainly being made for drug deal[s] and [for] transporting drugs.'[14] Furthermore, some of the anti-drug trafficking policies seem to have explicitly targeted Afghan refugees inside Iran. For example, in January 2001, Afghan refugees residing in the Northeastern province of Khorasan were ordered to evacuate five towns close to the border with Afghanistan and restrictions were placed on their movement in certain areas.[15]

At the domestic level, refugees are said to trigger *indirect* security risks if their presence accentuates *already* existing ethnic strife within the host state.[16] Collective action opportunities, according to theories of social movements, emerge when groups hold an advantage in the area of resources, alignments, elite support or potential allies, which leads to the belief that their chance of success is greater. Building on this logic, refugees are typically conceptualized as having the potential to trigger opportunities for collective action in two key ways. One is when a refugee presence results in changes in the country's ethnic composition, which in turn encourages pre-existing challenger groups to act.[17] The other is when the diversion of state security resources, as a result of a refugee influx, creates a window of opportunity for a marginalized group elsewhere in the country to engage in collective action.[18]

Some argue that the question of refugee presence is particularly sensitive in Iran due to the country's multiethnic composition.[19] Others are apprehensive that domestic unrest in Iran may trigger new refugee flows.[20] However, there is little evidence to support the notion that there is a trigger effect between refugee presence and challenges to the Iranian state by the Sunni and Azeri minorities, who constitute 15% and 25% of the Iranian population, respectively. In fact, incidences of ethnic strife in Iran seem to be correlated with periods of decline in central state control in Tehran and do not correspond with periods of refugee influxes.[21] Although the peak phase of violent conflict between the central government and the Sunni communities coincided with the beginning of the Afghan refugee influx, nevertheless, given that an increased refugee flow in the 1980s did not cause an escalation of violence suggests that other variables affecting the opportunity structure are responsible for the decision of the minorities to engage in collective action.[22] Similarly, Azerbaijani refugees did not pose a significant opportunity threat to the Iranian regime. Since the collapse of the autonomous Republic of Azerbaijan in 1947, the establishment of which owed much to external actors, 'there has been no conflict in the region which might raise ethnic sentiments.'[23] In fact, the Azeris were part of the movement that led to the collapse of the Shah's regime in 1979, which increased their representation among the political elite. Furthermore, according to Abdollah Ramezanzadeh, the 'religious ideology of the post-revolutionary state and the lifting of the ban on ethnic languages and cultures after the revolution caused the full integration of the community and made it a part of the "dominant coalition."'[24]

Local perceptions of 'unfair distribution' and relative deprivation are considered to be another significant dynamic' whereby refugees may trigger security risks to their hosts. Indeed, grievances may be generated by the perception that refugees are benefiting from preferential treatment or may be associated with changes in domestic conditions, such as environmental deterioration, declining food security, rising unemployment or intense competition for scarce resources.[25] While there is no clear evidence of grievances stemming from perception of preferential treatment of refugees, the initial flow of Afghan refugees into Iran during the early 1980s seems to have triggered indirect grievance threats focused on issues of health and social stability. In fact, according to a 1986 report, the poor health conditions of Afghan refugees were a major concern for Iranian authorities[26] because the arrival of refugees was associated with the costly re-introduction of diseases, such as malaria, tuberculosis and cholera, which had virtually disappeared from Iran.[27]

The level of grievances has escalated since the beginning of the 1990s, however. The bombing in 2001 of UNHCR's Zahedan office signalled local frustration over perceived preferential treatment of Afghan refugees. Grievances over the question of drug-trafficking and crime have become more manifest, especially when local villagers in Khorasan held demonstrations over a series of kidnappings and blamed the Afghan refugees for the lack of security in the province.[28] Economic grievances also emerged as a major issue in the public discourse over the last decade: members of parliament, and most recently the Minister of Labour, argued that only a fraction of Afghan migrant workers pay taxes, and should leave the country to give young Iranians greater job opportunities.[29] This trend may be attributed to a variety of factors, including the need to free up resources for post-war reconstruction, the rise in unemployment levels due to the doubling of Iran's population size since 1980, and the demobilization of the Iranian army.

Aside from security-related local dynamics, analysts point to national identity traits as another key influence on refugee policy formulation. The thrust of the argument is that the 'unique history of each country, its conceptions of citizenship and nationality, as well as debates over national identity and social conflicts within it, shape immigration policies.'[30] Variations in migration control policies are thus attributed to basic differences in national identities—settler societies or ethnic states; homogeneous or heterogeneous countries—and to citizenship laws tending towards *jus sanguinis* (by place of birth) versus those approximating *jus soli* (by parentage).[31] While admittedly migration policy-making does not take place in a cultural vacuum, a major shortcoming of this approach is its inability to account for the dynamic policy choices of a state like Iran using variables that are rather static at least on the short run.[32]

The state capacity hypothesis adopted in this study suggests that variations in the refugee policies pursued by Iran are rooted in the development of its institutional strength in the areas of refugee prediction, regulation and control. The basic premise is not necessarily that refugee presence is unwanted, but rather that the state's ability to control its borders, regulate the movement of refugees inside its territories or conduct repatriation programs cannot be readily assumed. Unlike the security framework, which assumes that a state can rationally 'choose' to pursue an open, closed, or preventive refugee policy, this approach emphasizes the degree of institutional strength in the area of refugee control as the primary determinant of refugee policies.

Refugee policy-making is thus conceptualized as largely a product of state autonomy and prior legal bureaucratic decisions, reflecting the prevailing societal demands and the political will of the elite in power. More specifically, this model's explanatory potential focuses on two sets of variables: the character of institutions and their degree of autonomy from international actors.[33] Karen Jacobsen contends that refugee agencies linked to the military are associated with restrictive policies, while those with civilian hierarchies, usually located within the Ministry of Interior or Social Welfare, tend to be associated with more open policies. This is the case as there is a greater likelihood for allotting resources to refugees once a civilian agency is established. Furthermore, 'since refugees are the means for bureaucratic survival and career advancement, the personnel in these agencies have a vested interest in refugee matters.'[34] The character and level of international involvement is another key determinant of refugee policies, because the degree of autonomy maintained by refugee agencies from international actors influences both the character and future development of its refugee policies. State autonomy—reflected by the degree of institutional control over asylum-screening procedures, camps administration and, most importantly, whether international assistance is channeled through the official administrative structure or the NGO sector—shapes future host government policies.

The puzzle of Iran's contrasting treatment of the Afghan and Azerbaijani refugees is thus attributed to the development of the state's ability to deal with refugees over the last twenty years. The state capacity hypothesis would be validated in this study if two conditions are met: that we can trace significant development in the state's institutional capacity to manage refugee influxes and, second, that Afghan refugees seeking asylum in Iran during roughly the same time as the Azerbaijani displaced were treated in a broadly similar manner.

Iran's Refugee Policies: Admission and Treatment of Afghan and Azerbaijani Refugees

With the appearance of displaced people at its borders, a state must decide on a range of refugee policy issues. This section compares the policy responses of the Iranian state to the Afghan and Azerbaijani refugees along six main parameters: admission, screening, location, rights and restrictions, safety, and repatriation.[35]

Admission

The initial decision to admit asylum seekers or to deny them entry sets up the foundation of the refugee policy and determines its overall orientation. In the early 1980s, Afghans who attempted to cross the border into Iran or took detours through Pakistan were admitted into the country. Iran's policy of open-borders continued throughout the decade, yet by the late 1990s, the state altered its stance on Afghan refugee admission. In order to deter drug traffickers and stop the flow of Afghans, the government 'built a "Maginot Line" of vast concrete barriers across mountain valleys and hundreds of miles of deep trenches to stop all-terrain vehicles crossing the border, as well as a network of watchtowers along the frontier.'[36] Systematic large scale 'push-backs' were also conducted as part of a preventive strategy, involving the interception of refugees at or just inside the border and sending them back to Afghanistan.[37] However, despite the sealing of borders, thousands of asylum seekers crossed into Iran, especially during periods of heightened insecurity, such as during the renewal of fighting following the Taliban's rise to power.[38] By 2000, the state's preventive policies also involved the construction of camps inside Afghanistan, a trend that was continued with the massive displacement of Afghans following the bombing by the United States.

Iran's admission policy towards the Azerbaijani asylum seekers stands in sharp contrast to its strategy towards the early waves of Afghan refugees a decade earlier. In 1993, the conflict over Nagorno-Karabakh, which created an unregulated, chaotic and often bloody exchange of populations among Armenia, Azerbaijan and Nagorno-Karabakh since 1988, forced the expulsion of the biggest wave of Azerbaijani displaced persons from Armenian occupied territories.[39] Faced with a mass of 200,000 would-be refugees pressing against its northern border—an area largely populated by ethnic Azeris—Iran responded by setting up eight camps in Azerbaijan with a combined capacity of 100,000 persons.[40] Commenting on Iran's policy in that regard, President Rafsanjani stated that 'we regard the refugees [from Azerbaijan] in the same way as our own refugees [who were displaced as a result of the Iraqi invasion], but we prefer them to remain on the territory of Azerbaijan so that they can achieve their aims sooner.'[41] In fact, as more territory fell to the ethnic Armenians in the latter part of 1993, Iran opted to transport those who entered the countryIran by crossing the Aras River to safer Azerbaijani territory around Imishli where Iranian refugee camps were set up, instead of allowing them to apply for asylum.[42] Unwilling to admit asylum seekers and fearful of a potential backlash among its ethnic Azeri population, Tehran took the risk of mobilizing elements of its armed forces to extend assistance to refugees outside its territories.

Screening Asylum Seekers

The screening of asylum seekers requires substantial state capacity and institutional development, yet during the first years of the Afghan refugees influx, the Iranian authorities did not seem to have effective asylum-screening procedures.

In fact, the chairman of the Council for Afghan Refugees, which is part of the Ministry of Interior, was quoted in the middle 1980s stating that there is no policy distinction between economic migrants and refugees. According to him, 'the Afghans leave their country because of the war...if there is a small number who come to Iran to look for a job, the war is the main reason for their departure. We do not have a phenomenon of emigration provoked only by the quest for jobs.'[43]

By the middle 1990s, the Iranian state had developed asylum screening mechanisms linked to the Ministry of Interior, coinciding with an official distinction between Afghan refugees who fled to Iran before the Soviet withdrawal from Afghanistan and those fleeing the inter-factional fighting or the Taliban's rule over the 1990s (considered 'illegal immigrants following the traditional pattern of job migration between the countries').[44] Yet the screening procedure has been the subject of much criticism in refugee circles, with noted problems such as deterring or excluding uneducated applicants from rural backgrounds, whose claims for persecution are based on religion (being Shi'a) or ethnic background (being Hazaras).[45] Tehran's insistence on limiting the UNHCR's involvement with the screening procedures of Iran's Bureau of Aliens and Foreign Immigrant Affairs (BAFIA), which lasted only briefly during the 1999-2000 joint repatriation programs, has also added to concerns over the consistency and transparency of the procedures.

Location of Refugees

Iran's policies on refugee location have changed considerably since the beginning of the Afghan refugee influx in the late 1970s, recently leaning towards the physical containment of refugees. This is perhaps manifested by the decision to build camps for Azerbaijani and (more recently) Afghan refugees across the borders, and a growing trend towards relocating those inside Iran to camps and designated residential areas.

One of the outcomes of the state's weak capacity in the area of refugee control in the early 1980s was the limited number of refugees in the camps. According to USCR statistics, only five per cent of Iran's total refugee population resided in camps as of late 2002.[46] Afghan refugees have until recently been integrated into Iran's major cities, with a higher concentration in the eastern provinces of the country. Although this trend proved to be a cost effective mechanism for handling the refugee burden, and quite beneficial to the Iranian economy throughout the war with Iraq, it does not seem to have been an intended state policy. In fact, as early as 1986 the Iranian press periodically reported on the rounding up of Afghans and their forcible return to camps.[47]

According to Roger Zetter, host states typically seek to contain the penetration of refugees to regulate entry into politically-sensitive urban areas as well as to minimize their impact on the developed and more intensely populated areas.[48] Statements by Iranian officials indicate that the desire to relocate Afghans to camps has been driven by the need to ease strains within the local population, particularly regarding competition for jobs in the cities.[49] Furthermore, the state's efforts at relocating Afghan refugees into designated areas in Mashad and newly expanded camps is linked to its repatriation efforts.

Rights and Restrictions

Although Iran is a signatory to the 1951 Refugee Convention, the absence of a national law on refugees in that country left the rights and responsibilities of refugees vaguely defined, with assistance largely provided on an ad-hoc basis.[50] On the whole, Afghan refugees have enjoyed more de facto rights than their Azerbaijani counterparts, including residency, employment, education and access to state subsidies. Until recently, the rights accorded to Afghan refugees differed considerably depending on the legal category of their registration or the lack thereof. Yet the passage by Iran of an act called 'Article 48' in 2000 represented a paradigm shift in the legal status of Afghan refugees.[51] Citing high unemployment, the Ministry of Interior was empowered to 'expel all foreigners without work permits whose lives would not be threatened upon return to their country of origin.'[52] This step was in turn followed by a major registration exercise by BAFIA in 2001, whereby all refugees were required to report to one of its 250 centers and have their status standardized through the issuing of new certificates, superseding all previous documents. The shift in Iran's policies towards a more restrictive orientation began in the middle 1990s with the withdrawal of the subsidies on food and health care estimated by the authorities to amount to $27 per refugee per day.[53] In addition, stricter implementation of labour laws since early 1999 and the 2001 introduction of legal sanctions against Afghan-hiring employers have resulted in limited employment opportunities for refugees, and coincided with the state's attempt to limiting their freedom of movement.

Refugee Protection

With the shift towards closed and preventive policies, Iran's mixed record on refugee safety has become an issue of significant concern in international refugee circles. Though the transfer of Azerbaijani refugees trapped after the closure of the Jibrail-Fizuli to Imishli escape route appears to have reflected Iran's strong commitment to refugee protection, its recent 'voluntary' repatriation schemes and the sealing of its Afghan border raise questions about refugee safety. Since the 1990s, questions pertaining to rising discontent among the local host community and the safety of both international workers and refugees have been raised. Mob attacks on Afghan refugees, following the murders of Iranian diplomats in Mazar-i Sharif in late 1999, in addition to the bomb blast in front of the UNHCR office in Zahedan and the violent backlash to refugees' protests against their deteriorating conditions, all seem to point to an increasingly hostile environment inside Iran.[54] Finally, the extension of relief in camps based in Afghanistan has compromised the security of refugees. In November 2001, according to Human Rights Watch (HRW), the Makiki camp was caught in the fighting between Taliban troops and Northern Alliance troops, forcing the withdrawal of aid workers.[55]

Repatriation

Iran's early attempts to repatriate members of its resident Afghan refugee population began in the early 1990s and gained considerable momentum towards the end of the decade, with the government setting several deadlines in recent years for refugees to leave the country. The formation of a Tripartite Commission (comprised of Afghanistan, Iran and UNHCR) in late 1992 marked the beginning of systematic attempts at repatriation.[56] The commission was charged with the implementation of various logistical aspects of Afghan repatriation including transportation as well as assistance to returnees in their own country.[57] Although the renewal of fighting in Afghanistan in the middle 1990s halted broad-based repatriation efforts, Iranian authorities nevertheless attest that by 1997 '1.3 million displaced Afghans voluntarily returned to their country, 566,000 of whom were processed through the commission's facilities.'[58] A repatriation package consisting of 50 kg of wheat, blankets, and the equivalent of roughly $50 in cash was extended to repatriating refugees.

Iran and the UNHCR resumed formal activities for voluntary repatriation in November 1998, targeting the recent wave of unregistered Afghan refugees. However, the program was suspended a month later primarily due to UNHCR objections over the deportation of refugees.[59] In fact, the USCR estimates that at least 34,000 of the returnees to Afghanistan in 1998 alone were involuntary repatriated and 'that the true number of involuntary returns is likely much higher.'[60] Despite continuing differences over the ongoing deportation policy, the UNHCR and the Iranian government agreed in June 1999 to launch a joint program of support for voluntary repatriation intended to repatriate 104,000 Afghans over a period of six months.[61] The main components of the new program were financial incentives to refugees, a joint UNHCR and BAFIA refugee-screening mechanism for persons claiming a continued need for protection, and an information campaign describing the program and the available options.[62] Several issues, however, remained unresolved, including Iranian insistence on relocating Afghan refugees to designated areas, a policy that the UNHCR perceived as 'tipping the balance for refugees from reasonable self-sufficiency to dependence.'[63] As well, despite promises by the Iranian authorities to end refugee deportation, forcible repatriations remained a serious concern, as UNHCR figures for 1999 showed that there were 107,000 forcible repatriations to Afghanistan, compared to only 20,000 voluntary repatriations by the agency.[64] Indeed, according to USCR statistics, Iran's rate of involuntary expulsions in 1999 was the highest worldwide.[65]

Despite concerns regarding drought, cholera outbreaks and renewed fighting in northern Afghanistan, over 150,000 refugees returned under the 2000 joint voluntary repatriation effort.[66] In drafting the repatriation agreement, 'the UNHCR sought to avoid a program of "voluntary" repatriation accompanied by a parallel program of forced repatriation.'[67] Thus, under this joint repatriation scheme, the UNHCR instituted its own screening procedures in order to ascertain the voluntary nature of refugee return. Furthermore, and for the first time since the UNHCR's involvement in Iran's repatriation schemes, those without proper documentation were given six months to register their presence, as well as a choice between returning to Afghanistan and seeking permission to stay in Iran (through a process of government/UNHCR adjudication).[68] By October 2000, 10,064 applicants were given temporary residence in Iran 'until solutions are found to their situation,' while the cases of 18,183 have been rejected.[69]

Although UNHCR did not continue its participation in the voluntary repatriation program in 2001, the USCR reported that 'the Iranian government facilitated the "spontaneous return" of 143,501 Afghans during the year, of whom some 111,000 returned during the second half of the year,' and deported at least 120,000 refugees.[70] Following the change of regime in Afghanistan, a refugee repatriation agreement was signed between the governments of Iran, Afghanistan and UNHCR in April 2002 to facilitate the anticipated repatriation of 400,000 in an 'orderly way.'[71] Within four months of the agreement's implementation, close to 150,000 people returned to Afghanistan, a rate that raised concerns about 'induced' pressures by Iranian authorities.[72] The repatriation program, which allowed the UNHCR access to Afghan detainees and participation in the screening of their asylum claims, was also accompanied by a series of government deadlines for undocumented Afghans to register and obtain exit permits from the country by the end of the summer.[73]

To sum up, Tehran pursued a 'preventive' strategy towards displaced Azerbaijanis that stands in contrast to its integration policies vis-à-vis Afghans who sought refuge in Iran since the late 1970s. In fact, the overall trend in Iran's refugee policy has been one of increasing restrictiveness with the state's treatment of Afghan refugees undergoing fundamental changes since the early 1990s. Furthermore, and in line with the state capacity's first contention, the shift towards a more exclusionary orientation was, to a large extent, similarily evident in Iran's responses to the Azerbaijani and later Afghan refugees, who sought its asylum during the roughly the same period.[74] Iran's move away from open door refugee policies coincided with a scaling back of refugee rights in the areas of subsidized food, health, employment and education. In addition, as the state opted increasingly for the repatriation rather than integration of Afghans, their safety emerged as a major concern in international refugee circles.

The Role of State Capacity

Several dimensions of the above outlined policies seem to suggest significant development in the state's capacity in the area of managing refugee influxes. First, Iran's treatment of the displaced in Azerbaijan and more recently Afghanistan reflects both an ability to predict the outbreak of refugee flows as well as to adopt a preventive strategy. Second, the tendency towards the physical containment of refugees through relocating them to camps and 'designated areas' indicates a growing will and capacity to manage refugees inside the country. Third, despite the fact that the newly-institutionalized asylum screening procedures may not be uniformly enforced or consistent with UNHCR guidelines, their introduction corresponds with an upgrading of the state's ability to regulate refugee influxes. Finally, although the porous nature of Iran's borders with Afghanistan continue to allow for the influx of refugees, thereby deeply complicating the state's efforts at repatriation, Iran's attempts at enhancing border control underline its increasing preparedness for refugee flows.

According to the state capacity hypothesis, developments at the level of the state structure hold the key to explaining differences in refugee policies, and hence groups that seek asylum at roughly the same time tend to be treated in a broadly similar manner. As shown in the previous discussion of Iran's policies towards the latter waves of refugees from Afghanistan and the displaced from Azerbaijan, the second part of the hypothesis is to a large extent true. The state adopted similar sets of policies oriented towards the prevention of admission, physical containment and restriction of rights for both sets of refugees that sought asylum in the 1990s. The next section explores the hypothesis's first contention: that refugee policy outcomes are a function of a state's capacity to realize its policy goals as influenced by the institutional structures responsible for refugee issues and their degree of autonomy from international actors.

BAFIA: Between Autonomy and Burden-sharing

Unlike many countries in the Third World, Iran has developed a relatively sophisticated and centralized refugee administrative structure centred around BAFIA, which falls under the auspices of the Ministry of Interior.[75] The Bureau, which cooperates with other relevant cabinet departments such as the Ministry of Foreign Affairs and the Ministry of Labor, is subdivided into the Council for the Coordination of Refugee Affairs and the Council for the Coordination of Affairs of the Displaced. The establishment of BAFIA, considered one of the largest refugee-specialized structures worldwide, enhanced the Iranian state's ability to manage the refugee agenda.[76] In fact, according to the director of the bureau, BAFIA's mandate encompasses policy setting, program coordination, and implementation.[77] This, in turn, has limited the scope for the typical problems of a multi-agency aid environment: bureaucratic inertia, paucity of information, and poor coordination. With a total of about 1000 personnel and 250 provincial level offices, BAFIA monopolizes the implementation of refugee assistance programs and administers 48 refugee camps.[78]

Although there is little information on the bureaucratic evolution of the bureau, evidence suggests that the institutionalization of BAFIA was a gradual process that transpired in response to the influx of Afghan refugees and reflected growing state capacity. Indeed, according to a UNHCR report, centralized refugee-specialized institutions typically emerge in contexts where there is a lack of capacity to meet refugee needs through line ministries, a restrictive environment towards NGO activity and a large refugee influx.[79] Moreover, the director of BAFIA commented in a 1995 interview on the lack of Iranian institutional capacity in the area of refugee regulation during the late 1970s:

We have experienced...different policies in the past 15 years and have corrected our weak points. In the first stage we had the influx of Afghan refugees to the country. Unfortunately at that time we did not have a formulated plan to receive such a large number of refugees and settle them in special places. Therefore, the Afghans were scattered everywhere to the extent that today they have become part of our society. However, despite all the difficulties, their return is underway.[80]

On this basis, one could argue that the institutionalization of BAFIA as a centralized professional refugee-specialized agency evolved in response to regional crises that forced the state to deal with refugee inflows, and that its establishment reflected rising state capacity to regulate refugees.

Aside from the character of the institutional structures in charge of the refugee agenda, their degree of autonomy from external actors constitutes an important determinant of state capacity. The issue of state capacity could, to a large extent, be conceptualized within the dialectic tension between the need for 'burden sharing' and international assistance on the one hand, and the state's drive for preserving its autonomy and integrity on the other. Refugees represent a significant financial burden for host countries like Iran. Its records put the expenditure on refugees at around $20 billion over the last 16 years, and the cost of maintaining the 2 million refugees currently residing in the country at $10 million per day.[81] In refugee policy-making, the desire for international assistance is indeed complicated by the potential associated effects of 'institutional destruction,' which have emerged as a major concern for host governments in recent years.[82]

Despite the fact that building state capacity has been formally recognized in international refugee circles as both the most efficient and cost-effective mechanism for assisting governments in dealing with their refugee populations, the internationalization of refugee assistance continues to represent a potential threat to state structures. UNHCR has shown preference for direct implementation of its assistance programs or forging strategic alliances with international NGOs as implementing partners, both of which involve creating administrative structures parallel to those of the host government. Hence, between 1983 and 1995 the percentage of UNHCR expenditure through international NGOs increased from 25 per cent to 40 per cent, while the percentage channeled through government agencies declined from 55 per cent to 26 per cent over the same period.[83] Moreover, the proportion of overall budget spent through implementing partners declined from 46 per cent to 39 per cent between 1991 and 1993.[84] In fact, according to a recent UNHCR evaluation report, the organization has remained ambivalent in its commitment to defining and supporting capacity-building activities, which may involve considerable delay in the provision of assistance to refugees and has a longer-term orientation.[85]

Although fiercely proud of its handling of repeated refugee influxes, Iran appealed for international help in the middle 1980s and stepped up its appeals in the early 1990s. With the UNHCR's 1999 budget for operation in Iran amounting to $18 million which amounts to a small fraction of the costs involved for the Iranian state, officials have made the case that the country's humanitarian efforts have not been appreciated.[86] For instance, Ahmed Hosseini, the director of BAFIA, called for burden-sharing by the international community, adding that the alternative would be a costly increase in the numbers of asylum seekers to the West.[87] Nevertheless, parallel to these calls for assistance, the Iranian state has sought to mitigate the potential risk of institutional destruction through two main strategies: maintaining the autonomy of its refugee administrative structures, and preserving institutional control over the refugee agenda through placing restrictions on the NGO sector (largely confining the activities of the UNHCR to state administered camps).

The Iranian state's concern with the autonomy of its refugee-specialized institutions is clearly manifested in its handling of international funding. The authorities require the UNHCR, which finances all administrative costs incurred by BAFIA, to pay a lump sum to the government, which then decides on its allocation. While this system guarantees the autonomy of the state in deciding on refugee-related expenditures, it has been criticized for the lack of accountability to the donor agency.[88] Iran's attempt to monopolize control over the refugee agenda has also been evident in the prevalent implementation mode of refugee operations. Together with China, Iran falls at the high end of the spectrum in terms of government involvement in the implementation of UNHCR assistance programs, with Egypt and Honduras at the other end.[89] According to the World Food Programme, all refugee operations are implemented by the state through BAFIA, and 'the government provides the administration and management services for all activities in the refugee camps.'[90] Furthermore, a major point of contention between the UNHCR and the Iranian authorities has been the lack of non-governmental implementing partners, due to the unclear legal status of NGOs in Iran. 'NGOs complain of difficulties in opening bank accounts and delays in the issuance of visas and government approval of NGO project proposals, as well as internal travel restrictions.'[91] Although an NGO law was drafted after President Khatami's 1997 election, a formal legal framework defining the conditions under which NGOs can operate remains lacking.[92] The recent trend has been for centralized control by the Iranian state and marginalization of the NGO sector. Under the prevailing regulations, NGOs have been barred from joining formal cooperation agreements with UNHCR. The state has limited the role of the NGO sector by blocking UNHCR funding of international NGOs and by requiring national NGOs to cover partial costs of proposed projects.[93] Secondly, NGOs are required to register with a government agency, 'the consortium of non-governmental charity organizations,' and sign an agreement with the authorities specifying the field and timeline of their activities.[94]

UNHCR activities have been largely restricted to assisting refugees residing in camps, estimated at around 5 per cent of the total Afghan refugees in the country. In 1999, the organization expanded its activities for non-camp refugees, with funds allocated for that purpose doubling from 20 per cent of their budget allocation for Iran in 1998 to 40 per cent in 1999.[95] However, given the limited scope of operational partnership with the NGO sector, UNHCR faced significant challenges in program delivery and the diversification of its activities.[96]

Furthermore, UNHCR staff faced repeated problems of impeded access to refugees and centralized government control over project management.[97]

Conclusion

This study explored the underlying dynamics determining the orientation of host state policies towards refugee populations in the Middle East and Central Asia. By comparatively examining Iranian policies towards two sets of displaced populations that sought asylum, it unpacked the causal factors behind the state's contrasting treatment of these refugee groups. The analysis pointed to state capacity as the primary influence on refugee policy formulation. The character of Iran's institutions and their autonomy from international actors were found to have contributed to the state's ability to regulate refugee influxes. Furthermore, the state's similar patterns of treatment of the latter waves of Afghan and Azerbaijani refugees validated the second component of the state capacity hypothesis.

While the state capacity hypothesis is premised on the notion of autonomy and ascribes institutional factors significant weight in explaining policy-making, agency and politics have also played central roles in the development of the state's ability to regulate refugee influxes. A number of social and economic factors influenced the leadership's decision to develop the state's refugee management capacity: the rise of grievances driven by a societal backlash against refugees, pressures for job creation, and the need for reconstruction after the end of the war with Iraq. Moreover, in the case of Iran, two sets of factors seem to have been particularly conducive to the development of the state's ability to regulate refugee influxes. First, the country's international isolation forced it to single-handedly deal with its refugee burden and shielded the state from the potential development of a parallel administrative structure. Second, the fact that the state faced a large refugee influx and did not encourage an active role for the NGO sector created an urgent need to develop capacity in the areas of refugee regulation and assistance.

While the main propositions of the state capacity hypothesis were found to be consistent with evidence from the Iranian case, the above analysis raises questions about the presumed relationship between the character of refugee-specialized institutions and the orientations of the state's policies. Contrary to the common assumption that refugee-specialized agencies operating within a civilian hierarchy tend to foster a positive attitude towards refugees, the case of BAFIA showed that the civilian nature of the institution did not guarantee more open-oriented refugee policies, especially since its creation in the early 1990s. Furthermore, on the issue of state capacity, the case of Iran indicates that the critical question pertaining to refugee policies is the *type* of capacity the host develops in response to refugee influxes. In fact, Iran's success in developing the capacity to manage refugee flows—through preserving BAFIA's autonomy, marginalizing the NGO sector and restricting the operations of UNHCR—resulted in the adoption of preventive and progressively exclusive policies in the 1990s. This trend highlights the need for international actors, such as UNHCR, to adopt strategies aimed at promoting the development of host state capacity along patterns consistent with humanitarian norms and refugee rights.

The findings of this study also suggest that while the current trend in refugee studies—focusing on issues of security—may fall short of explaining host state policies, it rightly focuses the spotlight on the state as the appropriate level of analysis. Nevertheless, a critical flaw in the security approach to refugee policy-making is its implicit assumption that the state is a rational actor capable of reaching its policy goals. As demonstrated by the Iranian case, state capacity cannot be assumed, and its influence on the character of refugee policies is enormous. In fact, the key to understanding a developing state's refugee policy lies not in the ethnic or cultural character of the refugee population, nor the degree of threats they may trigger, but rather in the prevailing institutional state structure.

Notes

A more detailed version of this paper was presented at the Middle East Studies Association 2001 conference in San Francisco. I thank Rex Brynen and Nihad El-Ghamry for their valuable comments.

[1] Ray Wilkinson, 'An Iranian Surprise,' *Refugees Magazine* no. 108 (1997), United Nations High Commission for Refugees (UNHCR), 21 November 2000 <http://www.unhcr.ch/pubs/rm108/rm10806.htm>.

[2] See Helga Leitner, 'International Migration and the Politics of Admission and Exclusion in Post-War Europe,' *Political Geography* vol. 14, no. 3 (1995), pp. 262-263.

[3] Karen Jacobsen, 'Factors Influencing the Policy Response of Host Governments to Mass Exodus,' *International Migration Review* vol. XXX, no. 3 (Autumn 1996), p. 662.

[4] Kevin Hartigan, 'Matching Humanitarian Norms with Cold, Hard Interests: The Making of Refugee Policies in Mexico and Honduras, 1980-89,' *International Organization* vol. 46, no. 3 (Summer 1992), p. 720.

[5] Chris Kutschera, 'Forgotten Refugees: Afghans in Iran' *The Middle East* no.142 (August 1986), p. 44.

[6] There are signs of some changes on this front post-11 September 2001. See UNHCR, *Global Appeal 2002 (Addendum)* December 2001, p. 18, 6 January 2002. <http://www.unhcr.ch/cgibin/texis/vtx/home/opendoc.pdfid=3e1a9fbf18&tbl=MEDIA>.

[7] In these situations, many argue that refugees constitute a cause for, rather than just a consequence of, state insecurity. For more on this perspective see, Myron Weiner, 'Security, Stability and International Migration,' *International Security* vol. 17, no. 3 (Winter 1992).

[8] James Milner, *Sharing the Security Burden: Towards the Convergence of Refugee Protection and State Security* (Oxford: Refugee Studies Centre, Queen Elizabeth House, 2000), p. 13.

[9] Alan Dowty and Gil Loescher, 'Refugee Flows as Grounds for International Action,' *International Security* vol. 21, no. 1 (Summer 1996), p. 49, cited in Milner, *Sharing The Security Burden*, p. 13.

[10] Milner, *Sharing the Security Burden*.

[11] Ewan W. Anderson, 'Afghan Refugees: Geopolitical Context,' in Ewan W. Anderson and Nancy Hatch Dupree, eds., *The Cultural Basis of Afghan Nationalism* (Oxford: Refugee Studies Programme, Oxford University Press, 1990), p. 244.

[12] Abdollah Ramezanzadeh, 'Iran's Role as Mediator in the Nagorno-Karabakh Crisis,' in Bruno Coppieters, ed., *Contested Borders in the Caucasus* (Brussels: Vrije Universiteit Brussels Press, 1996), p. 7.

[13] Andrew North, 'Iran's Drug Wars,' *The Middle East* no. 314 (November 2000), p. 8.

[14] 'Iran: Majles to Debate Strategy To Deal with Afghan Refugees,' *Islamic Republic News Agency* (Tehran), 2 December 2000, found in Foreign Broadcast Information Service, Near East and South Asia (FBIS-NES-2000-1202).

[15] Ali Reza Davanlu, 'Passage and Living of Foreign Nationals Forbidden in Five Northern Towns of Khorasan Province,' *Mashhad Khorasan* (Khorasan), 17 Jan 2001, found in Foreign Broadcast Information Service, Near East and South Asia (FBIS-NES-2001-0204), p. P13.

[16] Milner, *Sharing the Security Burden*, p. 17.

[17] Milner, *Sharing the Security Burden*, p. 20.

[18] Milner, *Sharing the Security Burden*, pp. 20-21.

[19] See for instance Ahmed Hashim, 'The Crisis of the Iranian State,' *Adelphi Paper* no. 296 (Oxford: Oxford University Press, 1995).

[20] See Laurent Lamote, 'Iran's Foreign Policy and Internal Crises,' in Patrick Clawson, ed., *Iran's Strategic Intentions and Capabilities* (Washington: Institute for National Strategic Studies, National Defense University, 1994), pp. 21-22.

[21] Abdollah Ramezanzadeh, *Internal and International Dynamics of Ethnic Conflict: The Case of Iran*, no. 25, (Katholieke Universiteit Leuven: Faculteit der Sociale Wetenschappen, Departement Politieke Wetenschappen, 1996), p. 229.

[22] Ramezanzadeh, *Internal and International Dynamics of Ethnic Conflict*, p. 229.

[23] Ramezanzadeh, *Internal and International Dynamics of Ethnic Conflict*, p. 216.

[24] Ramezanzadeh, *Internal and International Dynamics of Ethnic Conflict*.

[25] Ramezanzadeh, *Internal and International Dynamics of Ethnic Conflict*, p. 19.

[26] Kutschera, 'Forgotten Refugees,' p. 44.

[27] Kutschera, 'Forgotten Refugees,' p. 44.

[28] Chris Recknagel and William Samii, 'Afghanistan: UN, Host Nations Push for Repatriation of Refugees,' Part 1, 28 September 2000, Radio Free Europe, 14 December 2000 <http://www.rferl.org/nea/features/2000/09/200014403>.

[29] United Nations Office for the Coordination of Humanitarian Affairs Integrated Regional Information Network for Central Asia (UN OCHA IRIN-CA) 'Iran: Afghan Refugee Programme "proceeding positively,"' 12 October 2000, *ReliefWeb*, 14 October 2000 <http://www.reliefweb.int/w/rwb.nsf/s/A70EB6FD835A8ED08525697600625D32>, p. 1.

[30] Eytan Meyers, 'Theories of International Migration Policy: A Comparative Analysis,' *International Migration Review* vol. 34, no. 4 (Winter 2000), p. 1249.

[31] Meyers, 'Theories of International Migration Policy.'

[32] In fact, Iran's mixed context of history, race and culture has led to the emergence, over the last century, of ill-defined as well as deeply contested conceptualisations of the political community, in addition to radically different imaginations of ethnic and national identity. See Mostafa Vaziri, *Iran as Imagined Nation* (New York: Paragon House, 1993).

[33] While the author acknowledges that state capacity involves more than institutional characteristics, and would be more adequately defined in terms of the state's engagement with social forces and its degree of penetration of society, this study has opted to narrowly focus on autonomy and the characteristics of the institutions due to lack of sufficient sources on the subject.

[34] Jacobsen, 'Factors,' p. 661.

[35] The choice of the variables is based on Jacobsen's categorization of policy types and responses. See Jacobsen, 'Factors,' p. 659.

[36] North, 'Iran's Drug Wars,' p. 8.

[37] Human Rights Watch (HRW), 'Closed Door Policy: Afghan Refugees in Pakistan and Iran,' *Human Rights Watch* vol. 14, no.2 (February 2002), p. 5.

[38] Bahram Rajaee, 'The Politics of Refugee Policy in Revolutionary Iran,' *Middle East Journal* vol. 54, no. 1 (Winter 2000), p. 57. The refugees seem to have turned to smugglers to sneak illegally into Iran.

[39] HRW Helsinki, *Azerbaijan: Seven Years of Conflict in Nagorno –Karabakh* (New York: HRW, 1994), p. 58.

[40] HRW Helsinki, *Azerbaijan*, p. 36. In fact there are reports that thousands of Azerbaijani refugees fled across the border to Iran before the Iranian authorities set up on the Azerbaijani side of the border.

[41] Ramezanzadeh, 'Iran's Role,' p. 9.

[42] United States Commission on Refugees (USCR), *Fault Lines of Nationality Conflict: Refugees and Displaced Persons From Armenia and Azerbaijan Issue Paper* (Washington, DC: USCR, 1994), p. 35.

[43] Kutschera, 'Forgotten Refugees,' p. 45.

[44] Recknagel and Samii, 'Afghanistan.'

[45] USCR, 'Country Reports: Iran, 2002,' *World Refugee Survey Country Reports*, 2 January 2003 <http://www.refugees.org/world/countryrpt/mideast/2002/iran.cfm>, p. 4.

[46] USCR, 'Country Reports: Iran, 2002,' p. 4.

[47] Central Intelligence Agency (CIA), 'Iran,' *The World Fact Book 2000*, CIA, 20 January 2000 <http://www.odci.gov/cia/publications/factbook/geos/ir.html>. These appear to be cases of Afghans that had no work permit allowing them residence in cities.

[48] Roger Zetter, 'International Perspectives on Refugee Assistance,' in Ed Alastair Ager, ed., *Refugees: Perspectives on the Experience of Forced Migration* (London: Pinter, 1999), pp. 68-69.

[49] USCR, 'Country Reports: Iran, 2000,' *World Refugee Survey Country Reports*, 10 February 2001 <http://www.refugees.org/world/countryrpt/mideast/2000/iran.htm>, p. 2.

[50] UNHCR, 'The Islamic Republic of Iran in Short,' *Global Appeal 2000*, December 1999, 14 December 2000 <http://www.unhcr.ch/cgi-bin/texis/vtx/home/opendoc.pdf?id=3e2ebc1c0&tbl=MEDIA>, p. 139.

[51] HRW, 'Closed Door Policy,' p. 15.

[52] USCR, 'Country Reports: Iran, 2002,' p. 2.

[53] World Food Programme (WFP), 'Protracted Refugee and Displaced Persons: Project Iran 5950' *First Regular Session of the Executive Board* (Rome, 4-6 Feburary 1998), 25 December 2000 <http://www.wep.org/eb_public/EB.1_98_English/eitem8_2.html>.

[54] UNHCR, 'Country Operation: Islamic Republic of Iran', *UNHCR Global Report 1999*, June 2000, 14 December 2000 <http://www.unhcr.ch/cgi-bin/texis/vtx/publ/opendoc.pdf?id=3e2d4d5e0&tbl=MEDIA>, p 207; and HRW, 'Closed Door Policy.'

[55] See HRW, 'Closed Door Policy.'

[56] Rajaee, 'The Politics of Refugee Policy in Revolutionary Iran,' p. 56.

[57] Islamic Republic of Iran, 'A statement by the Permanent Representative of the Islamic Republic of Iran on Agenda Term No.99,' *Report of the UNHCR: Questions relating to refugees, returnees and displaced persons and humanitarian questions at the Third Committee of the 49th Session of the UN General Assembly* (New York: UNHCR, 1994).

[58] Rajaee, 'The Politics of Refugee Policy in Revolutionary Iran,' p. 56.

[59] Rajaee, 'The Politics of Refugee Policy in Revolutionary Iran,' p. 58.

[60] Bill Frelick, 'Refugees in Iran: Who Should Go? Who Should Stay?,' *Refugee Reports* vol. 20, no. 6 (June 1999), p. 4.

[61] Frelick, 'Refugees in Iran,' p. 2.

[62] Frelick, 'Refugees in Iran,' p. 2. In fact, the UNHCR's goal was to administer pre-screening interviews prior to joint adjudication. The Iranian authorities opposed this, however. See Frelick, 'Refugees in Iran,' pp. 2-4.

[63] Frelick, 'Refugees in Iran,' p. 5.

[64] UN OCHA IRIN-CA, 'Iran.'

[65] See USCR, *World Refugee Survey 2000*, 10 February 2001 <http://www.refugees.org/world/statistics/wrs00_returns.html>.

[66] This program offers the same package of repatriation to refugees as the earlier ones. However, it is not clear if the UNHCR has reached arrangements with the Iranian authorities whereby self-sufficient refugees would not be returned to camps.

[67] USCR, 'Country Reports: Iran, 2000,' p. 4.

[68] Agence France-Presse, 'Iran Bows to Complaints Over Afghan Refugee Deportations,' 16 March 2000, *ReliefWeb*, 14 December 2000 <http://www.reliefweb.int/w/rwb.nsf/s/6FBAF11B67D6229BC12568A500409A11>.

[69] UN OCHA IRIN-CA, 'Iran.'

[70] USCR, 'Country Reports: Iran, 2002,' p. 3.

[71] UNHCR, 'Key Repatriation Agreement Signed between Iran, Afghanistan and UNHCR,' 3 April 2002, *UNHCR News Stories*, 14 January 2003 <http://www.unhcr.ch/cgi-bin/texis/vtx/print?tbl=NEWS&id=3cab30fd4>.

[72] UNHCR, 'Iran: number of repatriating Afghans continues to rise,' 20 August 2002, *UNHCR News Stories*, 14 January 2003 <http://www.unhcr.ch/cgi-bin/texis/vtx/print?tbl=NEWS&id=3d6215e91>.

[73] UNHCR, 'Iran grants UNHCR access to detained Afghans and right to review Asylum claims,' 9 August 2002, *UNHCR News Stories*, 14 January 2003 <http://www.unhcr.ch/cgi-bin/texis/vtx/print?tbl=NEWS&id=3d6215e91>.

[74] While largely similar, Iran's preventive strategy towards the displaced from Afghanistan in the nineties has been less consistently implemented compared to its treatment of the Azerbaijani counterparts. Most notably, in 1998, Iran briefly interrupted its closed-door policy to allow Afghans into the country while refraining from registering them in order to facilitate their future repatriation. This incident points to the potential influence of factors, other than state capacity, on the host state's policy-making. While further research is needed on this issue, relevant factors may include the scale of the humanitarian crisis, the number of refugees involved, or the level of pressure by the international community (all of which were considerably much more significant in the case of later Afghan refugees).

[75] Ahmad Hosseini, 'Refugees in the Islamic Republic of Iran,' published interview with newspaper staff, 15 May 1995, *Payam-e-Safeer* (Tehran) vol. 1, no. 1 (May-June 1995), 13 December 2000 <http://www.netiran.com/htdocs/clippings/Fpolitics/950515xxFP04.html>, p. 2.

[76] Fabrizio Hochschild, Lowell Martin and Robert White, 'Review of UNHCR Implementing Arrangements and Implementing Partner Selection Procedures,' November 1997, *Evaluation Reports*, UNHCR, Document number EVAL/08/97, 16 March 2001 <http://www.unhcr.ch/evaluate/reprots/97implem.htm>, p. 11.

[77] Hosseini, 'Refugees in the Islamic Republic of Iran,' p. 2.

[78] Hochschild *et al.*, 'Review of UNHCR,' p. 14.

[79] Hochschild *et al.*, 'Review of UNHCR,' p. 3.

[80] Hosseini, 'Refugees in the Islamic Republic of Iran,' p. 3.

[81] Rajaee, 'The Politics of Refugee Policy in Revolutionary Iran,' p. 59.

[82] Zetter, 'International Perspectives on Refugee Assistance,' p. 69.

[83] Hochschild *et al.*, 'Review of UNHCR,' p. 11.

[84] Hochschild *et al.*, 'Review of UNHCR,' p. 11.

[85] Hochschild *et al.*, 'Review of UNHCR,' p. 11.

[86] Rajaee, 'The Politics of Refugee Policy in Revolutionary Iran,' p. 59.

[87] He stated that 'the international community should provide Iran with the requested assistance and if they fail, for political or inhuman reasons, from now on we should not be responsible for the movement of the refugees towards the West and it is the West which should pay the cost for it.' See Hosseini, 'Refugees in the Islamic Republic of Iran,' p. 5.

[88] For instance, an Iranian Red Crescent Society (IRCS)-administered refugee camp in Shoushtar was financed by UNHCR and the Canadian Red Cross Society, yet the assistance was channelled indirectly through BAFIA. See International Federation of Red Cross and Red Crescent Societies, 'Country Assistance Strategy Islamic Republic of Iran 2000 – 2001,' 1 January 2000, *Where We Work: Country Assistance Strategies*, 16 March 2001 <http://www.ifrc.org/docs/rascas/irrascas.asp>.

[89] Hochschild *et al.*, 'Review of UNHCR,' p. 14.

[90] WFP, 'Protracted Refugee and Displaced Persons.'

[91] Frelick, 'Refugees in Iran,' p. 9.

[92] Frelick, 'Refugees in Iran,' p. 9.

[93] UNHCR, 'Country Operation: Islamic Republic of Iran,' September 2000, *UNHCR Mid-Year Report 2000*, 14 December 2000 <http://www.unhcr.ch/cgi-bin/texis/vtx/home/+pwwBmekRkFKwwwwrwwwwwwwhFqhT0yfEtFqnp1xcAFqhT0yfEcFq1Mome2lxxwGaGnpdGBa+XXXMzmZwwwwwwwDzmxwwwwwww/opendoc.pdf>, p. 146.

[94] Based on Hosseini, 'Refugees in the Islamic Republic of Iran.'

[95] UNHCR, 'Country Operation: Islamic Republic of Iran,' June 2000, *UNHCR Global Report 1999*, 14 December 2000 <http://www.netiran.com/htdocs/clippings/Fpolitics/950515xxFP04.html >, p. 207.

[96] UNHCR, 'Country Operation: Islamic Republic of Iran,' *UNHCR Mid-Year Report 2000*.

[97] UNHCR, 'Country Operation: Islamic Republic of Iran," *UNHCR Global Report 1999*.

Chapter 7

Permeability Revisited: Reflections on the Regional Repercussions of the al-Aqsa *Intifada*

Rex Brynen

In his seminal analysis of the Arab regional system, Paul Noble emphasized that communications and the flow of ideas had to be set alongside more traditional military and economic determinants of influence. Intraregional transnational linkages, he noted, had always been an important part of Arab politics. The relative salience of this, however, was changing. Writing in the wake of the Gulf War, he suggested in 1991 that there had been a 'decline in the permeability of Arab societies and political systems,' such that 'the intensity of popular concern for larger Arab causes had declined.'[1] Others too have noted the apparent decline of Arabism, and the rise of 'statism,' in the region.[2]

A decade ago I argued, as these others have done, that Arab responses to the first Palestinian *intifada* demonstrated the increasing 'stateness' of the Arab system and the slowly declining permeability of the territorial state to transnational ideological influences. Specifically, I suggested that 'state consolidation has, by enhancing the autonomy of Arab states relative to both other states and civil society, created conditions under which state resources can be used increasingly to insulate (if only partially) inter- and intra-state politics from the transnational repercussions of the Palestine issue.'[3] With the 1990-91 Gulf War, the regional passions generated by coalition military action against Iraq seemed to briefly suggest that transnational political appeals could continue to reverberate through, and even threaten to overwhelm, Arab politics. These echoes soon faded, however: Saddam Hussein's calls did not prevent substantial Arab military participation in the coalition, and despite widespread sympathy for the Iraqi people and opposition to the UN sanctions regime, the cause never seemed to coalesce as a powerful rallying cry for regional movements.

In late September 2000, a new *intifada*—the 'al-Aqsa *intifada*'—erupted in the occupied Palestinian territories. By the end of 2002, almost 2000 Palestinians (and over 600 Israelis) were dead.[4] A World Bank assessment of the first twenty-seven months of the uprising put the costs at $930 million in damage to Palestinian infrastructure as a result of Israeli military action; $3.2 billion in lost investment; and $5.2 billion in lost national income (mainly due to curfews and closures).

Unemployment rates stood at 37 per cent, and around 60 per cent of the population had sunk into poverty (defined as less than $2 per day).[5]

With the *intifada*, the Palestinian-Israeli peace process collapsed. Hard-line Likud leader Ariel Sharon was elected as Prime Minister of Israel in February 2001, and again in January 2003. Palestinian suicide attacks and Israeli military strikes became frequent occurrences. In the spring of 2002, Israeli forces reoccupied almost all areas of the West Bank. While the human and physical costs of the conflict paled in comparison to the 1982 Israeli invasion of Lebanon or any of the regular Arab-Israeli wars, the *intifada* nonetheless represented the most intense assault against the Palestinians, in Palestine, since the Israeli military occupation of the West Bank and Gaza in June 1967.

What has been the reaction of Arab populations to this? In particular, to what extent has the intensification of the conflict generated pressures on Arab regimes to take specific actions, and if so, what kinds of pressures and reactions have resulted? Most importantly, what does all of this tell us about trends in transnationalism, permeability, and state consolidation in the Arab world?

In trying to answer these questions, one is faced with a number of serious methodological challenges. First, how can the scope of popular reaction to Palestinian events be gauged in the context of authoritarian Arab regimes where the public expression of political views (especially critical ones) may be suppressed? Second, how can Arab foreign policies resulting from 'pressures from below' be distinguished from policy calculations that reflect more realist, political-diplomatic calculations by elites? Third, is it possible to establish trends, to say that popular reaction is 'more' or 'less' than expected, or to even objectively compare it to reactions to the first *intifada*? In all of these regards, the evidence can only be weighed impressionistically.

In addition to these analytical challenges, there exists another: how can popular political expressions, spurred by the *intifada*, be divorced from overlapping sentiments generated by other stimuli, or from broader trends? Could Arab reactions to the *intifada* be the product of cumulative irritations—war in Iraq, Western support for authoritarian regimes, and other issues—of which the Palestine issue is only one. This possibility assumes particular importance in the wake of the 11 September 2001 terrorist attacks against Washington and New York, the US-led 'war on terrorism' in Afghanistan and elsewhere, and especially the US occupation of Iraq. All of these issues have, not surprisingly, increased perceptions of threat and alienation in much of the Arab and Islamic worlds.

Put simply—and with a tongue-in-cheek nod to quantitative methods, rational choice, and hopes of publication in the *American Political Science Review*—both the processes at work and the methodological challenges involved in understanding them can be expressed in a formula of sorts:

$$\text{observed effect} =$$

$$\text{permeability} \times \text{stimulus (Palestine, Iraq, other issues...)} \times \text{freedom of expression}$$

The argument presented in this chapter is that the permeability of Arab politics to transnational political influences has not grown in recent years, but that its long-term decline since the 1970s (a decline due to the territorialization and consolidation of Arab states) has now halted. This situation is not due, as some would suggest, to the reassertion of politicized ethnic identity in the face of globalization, or a corresponding defence of culture in the face of Westernizing pressures. Rather, it is largely due to the effects of new information and communication technologies (notably direct broadcast satellite television). Changes in the regional media have had technical effects both on permeability (that is, the extent to which ideas, events, and ideologies have transnational appeal) and on freedom of expression, enabling critical ideas to be more easily voiced than once was the case.

The chapter will also argue that the observed effects of the *intifada* in the Arab world are not merely the product of the Palestinian-Israeli conflict, but of a confluence of foreign policy grievances. Put simply, the collapse of the peace process and continued Israeli occupation of the Palestinian territories have become one aspect of a multi-faceted popular critique of Western (especially US) policy in the Middle East, as well as of most pro-Western regimes.

Throughout this chapter, extensive use will be made of major public opinion polls conducted in the Middle East by the Gallup Organization in early 2002, by Zogby International in 2001, and March-April 2002, and by the Pew Global Attitudes Project in 2002 and 2003. While all of these surveys contain only imperfect indicators of the sorts of issues raised here (and many suffer from a number of methodological weaknesses besides), they nonetheless offer an interesting and unusual perspective on attitudes in a region where public opinion is still only rarely measured.

Popular and Official Reactions to the al-Aqsa *Intifada*

The eruption of the second Palestinian *intifada* started with a provocative visit by then opposition member Ariel Sharon to the Haram al-Sharif (Temple Mount) in Jerusalem on 28 September 2000. Heavy clashes between Israeli security forces and protesters the next day left seven Palestinians dead and more than 200 injured. Confrontations quickly escalated.

Taking place in Arab Palestine, and originating at the site of the al-Aqsa mosque, the violence touched upon Arab, nationalist, and Islamic symbolism. However, the reverberation of the issue in the ideologically permeable Arab world has been much different than among non-Arab Muslims. According to one Gallup survey conducted in early 2002, Arabs were far more likely than non-Arab Muslims to watch television reports on events in Palestine (Figure 7.1).[6]

A 2001 survey conducted by Zogby International seems to confirm (although perhaps exaggerate) the salience of the Palestinian issue in the Arab world. It found Arab respondents overwhelmingly rating Palestine as the most important issue to them personally.[7] Respondents also indicated in a 2002 poll, by overwhelming

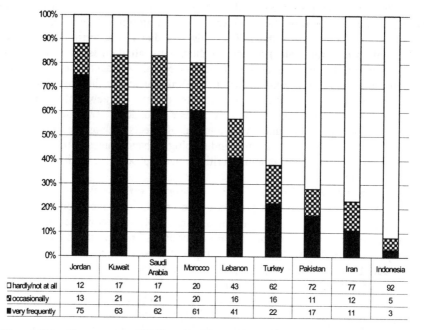

	Jordan	Kuwait	Saudi Arabia	Morocco	Lebanon	Turkey	Pakistan	Iran	Indonesia
☐ hardly/not at all	12	17	17	20	43	62	72	77	92
▨ occasionally	13	21	21	20	16	16	11	12	5
■ very frequently	75	63	62	61	41	22	17	11	3

Figure 7.1   Frequency of Following News About Palestine
Source: Gallup Organization

margins, that they saw the Palestine issue as a very important issue facing the Arab world as a whole.[8]

Given the extent to which the issue reverberates in the Arab political consciousness, it is not surprising that the eruption of the *intifada* generated a wave of public solidarity. Demonstrations took place across the Arab world in the fall of 2000, in immediate reaction to the violence. Pictures of Muhammad al-Dura, a young boy shot by Israeli troops in Gaza in late September, could be seen throughout the region. Public protests continued on a smaller scale through 2001, and were stepped up again in the spring of 2002 following the Israeli reoccupation of most of the West Bank.

Perhaps the largest demonstrations were in distant Morocco, where 500,000 marched in support of the Palestinians in Rabat on 9 October 2000. A demonstration of similar size took place again on 7 April 2002. Demonstrations took place in the Gulf, despite the general infrequency of public protests in these countries. In Egypt, student demonstrations took place in Alexandria, Cairo and elsewhere. Unusually, even in tightly controlled Syria an angry crowd got out of control, threatening the US embassy on one occasion.[9] More generally, the *intifada* spurred aid initiatives, telethons (raising tens of millions of dollars for relief assistance and Palestinian 'martyrs'), and boycott campaigns (aimed at companies with perceived Israeli and/or American links) throughout much of the Arab world.

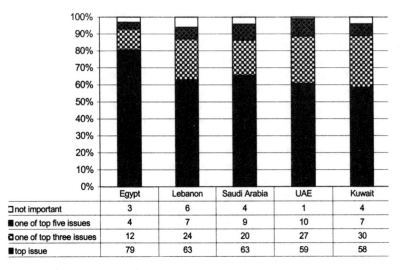

	Egypt	Lebanon	Saudi Arabia	UAE	Kuwait
▢ not important	3	6	4	1	4
▮ one of top five issues	4	7	9	10	7
▨ one of top three issues	12	24	20	27	30
▮ top issue	79	63	63	59	58

Figure 7.2 Personal Importance of Palestine Issue
Source: Zogby International

Not surprisingly, Jordan—adjacent to the territories, with a large Palestinian population, a peace treaty with Israel, and warm relations with the US—was most affected by the regional repercussions of the al-Aqsa *intifada*. Shortly after violence erupted in Palestine, a protest by tens of thousands on 5 October 2000 led to some rioting and clashes with police. On October 7, a protester was shot dead by police during a smaller demonstration, and 97 persons arrested. On October 24 water cannons and arrests were used to break up marches by thousands of Palestinian refugees on the bridges into the West Bank.

The government quickly responded to the second *intifada* (as it had to the first in 1987) by limiting all public protests, a ban that was later renewed in April 2001. When protesters attempted to demonstrate, they were confronted by the security forces.[10] Following the dissolution of parliament in July 2001 (in preparation for elections, later postponed until June 2003) the government decreed a new, restrictive 'temporary' law on public assembly. In April 2002, when the opposition threatened to proceed with an unlicensed demonstration near the Israeli embassy, King Abdullah personally met with opposition leaders to warn that protests could 'destabilize national unity and security' and that there were 'irresponsible groups that aim to disrupt stability and destroy public and private property.'[11] Perhaps most telling of all, Abdullah unveiled a major domestic public relations campaign around the slogan 'Jordan First.' According to the King, 'we want to establish this principle as a working approach and a daily practice for each Jordanian man and woman who believes in this country as a cradle of security and stability, and as one which has a promising future; those who seek self-fulfilment through their native land, *and not via external loyalties whatever the goals and objectives are*' (emphasis added).[12] In announcing the program, the King noted that '[the] opposition can exercise its role and convictions with regard to government policies and programs, but it cannot be opposed to the state's system and established principles.' Moreover, '*opposition should be exercised in the service of the causes and interests of the Jordanian people and the building up of Jordan, before any other interests and goals*' (emphasis added). Clearly, the threat of transnationalism—especially arising from events in neighbouring Palestine and Iraq—was perceived as substantial.

Since September 2000, the Arab League has held multiple meetings devoted to the Palestinian issue, and in March 2002 endorsed a Saudi peace proposal (the so-called 'Beirut Declaration') holding out to Israel the prospect of full normalization in the region in exchange for an end to the occupation of Arab lands.[13] In many cases, Arab leaders have made efforts in order to been seen at the forefront of public concern: Gulf leaders have made highly publicized financial contributions to the Palestinian cause; King Abdullah of Jordan helped load relief supplies onto waiting helicopters and his wife marched in a peaceful solidarity demonstration; the mass rallies in Morocco and Tunisia enjoyed official sanction. In Egypt, the security services have (by the standards of the past) been relatively muted in their response to protests, clearly not wanting to be seen as somehow defending Israeli actions and US policy. Perhaps most importantly, Saudi Arabia, Jordan, and Egypt have pressed hard for both diplomatic initiatives that might resuscitate the peace process, and for greater American engagement.

It is, as noted earlier, impossible to fully determine what motivated these initiatives: pressure from below (thus demonstrating both the permeability of the Arab system and the foreign policy significance of that permeability); genuine support for the Palestinian cause among elites; more *realpolitik* foreign policy calculations; or (most likely) a combination of all three. Confusing the analytical picture still further, Arab regimes have an incentive both to downplay public anger (so as not to allow it to acquire excessive momentum that might be directed against themselves) and to exaggerate it (so as to use it as a bargaining tool with Washington).

Certainly, Arab diplomatic efforts have left the impression (probably accurate) in Washington that regime security—that is, leadership concern with the destabilizing effects of public anger at the US and dissatisfaction with Arab actions—has been the primary motivating force behind such initiatives.[14] King Abdullah of Jordan noted that 'People are angry—the rage is on.' He warned that 'although there seems to be a relative calm now, that is only temporary.... If we don't articulate a vision in the next couple of weeks, that rage is going to come back, and it's going to be twice as strong.'[15] Jordanian foreign minister Marwan Muasher added that '[the] demonstrations are getting stronger by the day.... the street is literally boiling.' He noted, moreover, that '[we] are being forced to take steps we don't want to take... because people are angry and public opinion in the Arab world cannot be ignored.'[16] Similarly, a Saudi foreign policy advisor, on the eve of the important meeting between President Bush and Crown Prince Abdullah in April 2002, observed that Arab governments were increasingly being forced to respond to public anger: '[it] is a mistake to think that our people will not do what is necessary to survive, and if that means we move to the right of bin Laden, so be it; to the left of Qaddafi, so be it; or fly to Baghdad and embrace Saddam like a brother, so be it. It's damned lonely in our part of the world, and we can no longer defend our relationship [with the US] to our people.'[17]

In addition to what Arab regimes have said and done, is what they have *not* said and *not* done. Neither Egypt nor Jordan severed official relations with Israel, although some lesser symbolic diplomatic actions were taken to signal their displeasure at Israeli policy. In response to appeals from Islamists and others to use military pressure against Israel, the Egyptian government, and even President Mubarak himself have flatly ruled out military force as an option. Virtually no Arab country has downgraded relations with the US or seriously threatened bilateral relations as a consequence of US support for Israel. The only partial exception to this is Saudi Arabia. On 24 August 2001 Crown Prince Abdullah sent a blunt personal letter to George Bush threatening a major reorientation of bilateral relations if the US failed to show more concern for resolving the Palestinian issue. The letter had some effect on administration policy, but was largely overshadowed by the subsequent fallout from the terrorist attacks of 11 September 2001 (and their Saudi connections).

This sort of reaction—contained popular protests, symbolic official actions, appeals to Washington to 'do something,' yet no fundamental reorientations in regional or global foreign policy—are strikingly similar to Arab reactions to Israel's 1982 invasion of Lebanon or the first *intifada*. They indicate regimes under pressure, but not regimes whose stability is fundamentally threatened by events in Palestine, and associated Arab nationalist or Islamist transnationalism. Thus, the Arab system remains less permeable than it once was, especially contrasted with the 1950s and 1960s, but more permeable to transnational political influences than other regional systems.

What is also striking about current reactions to the crisis in Palestine is the apparent vulnerability of Gulf regimes. In the past, oil rents have helped Gulf states stave off transnational political pressures, such as those associated with the Iranian revolution.[18] As oil rents stagnate and demographic pressures grow, the power of rentierism appears to have weakened somewhat. In this context, the Palestinian issue becomes yet another element of popular discontent, in addition to concern over economic mismanagement, corruption, authoritarianism, close ties to the US, and a range of other issues. This is not to suggest that the Gulf states have become strikingly unstable. Rather, it is to suggest that these states may become more like other Arab countries in the extent to which they are affected by transnational issues.

Permeability and the Changing Regional Media Environment

One key change in the context of Arab transnationalism has been the changing regional media environment. Traditionally, the media environment in the Arab world has been tightly controlled, through a combination of state ownership, formal and informal censorship, patronage, and political intimidation. In the past decade, however, this has changed, in large part due to the effect of new information and communication technologies (ICT).[19]

The most important aspect of this has been the rapid spread of direct broadcast satellite (DBS) television in the Middle East. Of much lesser (but perhaps growing) importance is the slow growth of internet connectivity in the region. These 'new media' have played a significant role in shaping local attitudes to the collapse of the Arab-Israeli peace process, as well as the conflict in Iraq, and other Western policies towards the Arab and Muslim world, and will have important repercussions for the way public diplomacy is conducted in the region in the future.

Satellites, News, and Public Opinion: The al-Jazira Effect

As noted above, the most important aspect of the changing regional media environment has been the rapid spread of direct broadcast satellite television in the Middle East. DBS TV has circumvented traditional state censorship to provide a substantial proportion of the population with access to more timely and diverse opinions and information. Because of the declining size and cost of satellite dishes, and because most stations are broadcast 'free-to-air' and hence do not require subscriptions or decoders, access has grown rapidly in recent years. Moreover, the Arab world represents a relatively compact geographic region of 270 million people, almost all of them Arabic-speaking: a situation ideal for DBS broadcasts.

According to World Bank data, the Middle East and North Africa (MENA) averages 172 televisions sets per 1,000 people, compared to 185 for low and middle income countries as a whole. Television possession is higher than Africa or South Asia, but lower than East Asia or Latin America. Given average family sizes of six to seven persons per household, the data suggests that a large majority in most countries have access to a television set. As for television access to satellite broadcasts, public opinion surveys put this at 26 per cent in Egypt, 64 per cent in Lebanon, 88 per cent in Saudi Arabia, 90 per cent in the UAE, and 98 per cent in Kuwait. In Indonesia—a country with a GNP/capita similar to that of Egypt—the comparable rate of satellite TV access is only two per cent.

Starting in the 1990s, a number of commercial satellite television stations were established to offer entertainment and current affairs programming to the Middle East. These included Middle East Broadcasting Centre (MBC), the Arab Radio and Television Network (ART), and the *al-Jazira* news channel. Also, a number of conventional state and private television broadcasters—notably in Lebanon and the Gulf—broadened their reach by adding satellite broadcasts.

Increased demand for non-Western news coverage spurred the growth of these services, especially during and after the 1990-91 Gulf War.

Studies indicate that such services are widely watched for their pluralism, diversity, and because they offer exposure to a wider world. In the Gulf, 70 per cent rely on satellite channels for their news. Moreover, even in the saturated media environment of the West Bank and Gaza (with access to Palestinian, Israeli, Jordanian and sometimes even Syrian or Lebanese conventional broadcast channels), respondents indicate that satellite stations are the most watched and trusted source of news and information.

The Arabic satellite television news channel *al-Jazira* has been the most important (but not the only) aspect of this media revolution. *al-Jazira* was established in Qatar in 1996 with a five year, $150 million government grant that expired in November 2001. The station grew out of the wreckage of an earlier, failed effort by the BBC to produce a new regional consortium with a Saudi station, Orbit. Because of its willingness to air a range of competing and controversial viewpoints, *al-Jazira* has reshaped Arab news coverage, and won a regular audience of up to 35 million viewers in the region. Some of its broadcasting tends to the sensational, and the content of its news reports show a tilt towards general attitudes in the Arab street (support for the Palestinian cause, sympathy for the Iraqi people, and suspicion of Western policies in the region). Nevertheless, it remains generally committed to good journalistic standards and airing a range of opinions, from radical Islamist to secular and pro-Western. It has also broadcast interviews with Israeli politicians. Because of its independence and diversity, the station has been criticized, at one time or another, by virtually every government in the region. In one Gallup survey, 56 per cent of Kuwaitis identified *al-Jazira* as their preferred television news station, as did 47 per cent of Saudis, 44 per cent of Jordanians, 37 per cent of Lebanese, and 20 per cent of Moroccans. In most countries, this was far ahead of any competitor. For its part, CNN only scored one to seven per cent popularity. The same survey showed that viewers generally regarded *al-Jazira* as timely, daring, comprehensive, and objective.[20]

Reporting by *al-Jazira* and other television stations has dramatically amplified the political impact on Arab populations of violence in the Palestinian territories. Newscasts are filled with detailed reports of civilian casualties, and sometimes live coverage of clashes between Palestinians and Israeli troops. The broadcasts, not surprisingly, tend to emphasize Israeli aggression, Palestinian victimization, and the failure of the international community to end Israeli occupation and secure Palestinian self-determination. Satellite news has thus brought the Palestinian issue home to Arabs in a much greater way than before. As one reporter has noted:

> With the majority of the Arab satellite stations having correspondents in Palestine, and with the widespread availability of mobile phones to those besieged in Palestinian towns and refugee camps, enabling eyewitnesses to recount what is going on live, the war has entered the living room of virtually every Arab family outside Palestine. Such coverage has played a major role in pushing people to act

in the best way they know how to express solidarity: taking to the streets, donating money and blood, and calling on the Arab governments to take action to stop the Israelis.

Live call-in shows have also given people an opportunity to express views (often critical of Arab inaction) that could not or would not have been expressed in the more traditional media. [21]

This effect, it should be noted, has not been limited to Arab publics, but has affected Arab elites too. According to the *Washington Post*:

> In a series of letters to Bush and in other messages to Washington, [Saudi Crown Prince] Abdullah made his frustrations clear. "Don't they see what is happening to Palestinian children, women and the elderly?" Abdullah asked in an interview with the *Financial Times* in June. He was seeing this himself, his associates said, on television almost every night. Official Saudi television showed extensive film clips of the fighting and of Israel's forceful military actions in nearly every news broadcast.
>
> On the night of August 23 [2001], Israeli tanks made their deepest incursion yet into the West Bank, into the town of Hebron, marking a new escalation of the fighting. On the same day, according to two Saudi officials, Abdullah saw news footage from the West Bank of an Israeli soldier holding a Palestinian woman to the ground by putting his boot on her head. "Abdullah saw that and he went berserk," one senior Saudi recounted. "A woman being beaten by a man - he just felt this is the ultimate insult."
>
> The result was Abdullah's stern message to Bush on 24 August, threatening a fundamental downgrading of Saudi-American relations if the administration didn't step up its peacemaking efforts.[22]

Television has also provided extensive coverage of other issues of Arab and Islamic concern, such as the civilian costs of the wars in Afghanistan and Iraq. In doing so, the new media appears to have contributed to growing discontent with US foreign policy in the area. This discontent, as will be argued below, is not caused by a sense of cultural alienation due to greater exposure to the wider world. One Gallup survey found that *al-Jazira* viewers were, in fact, more concerned about improving relations between Islamic countries and the West, and were more likely to enjoy Western cultural imports (film, music). At the same time, however, they tended to be more critical of Western leaders, and to hold more unfavourable opinions regarding the United States.[23] Moreover, the closer viewers follow news about Palestine (or Afghanistan), the more unfavourable these opinions were likely to be.[24]

It is also important to note that, as seminal as the effects of satellite television are, they tend to be reinforcing and publicizing policy attitudes rather than creating (or, as Israel has sometimes charged, 'inciting') them. As Shibley Telhami has noted of the Zogby International poll findings:

> What explains this amazing ranking of the Palestinian issue in such places as upper Egypt and the Arabian desert? It is not the new satellite media, such as

Qatari al-Jazira TV, as has been so widely speculated. The results were robust even among those who don't watch such media, including in Egypt, where satellite receivers are scarce. These media may be a factor in getting the public to the streets, but not so much in setting its preferences.

Two factors explain the importance of the Palestinian issue that cannot be ignored. First, the Palestinian issue remains an 'identity' issue for most Arabs, regardless of what they think of Yasser Arafat or the Palestinian Authority. Most Arabs are shamed by their inability to help the Palestinians and feel personally insulted when the Palestinians seem slighted. The way the United States behaves toward the Palestinians is taken as a message to all Arabs.

Second, the Arab narrative about the failure of the Camp David negotiations and the eruption of violence is the mirror image of the Israeli narrative: Arabs blame Israel for what happened and continues to happen, in the same way that Israelis place the blame on Arafat. Whereas Israelis understandably focus on the innocent casualties of horrifying suicide bombings, Arabs focus on daily pictures of dead Arab civilians, helicopter gunships attacking Palestinian targets and demolitions of homes of ordinary people who look like their cousins.[25]

Virtual Permeability?

As noted earlier, the second major aspect of new information and communication technologies in the Arab world is the internet. One difficulty in gauging the impact of the internet on the Arab world, however, is knowing the actual extent of internet penetration. Public opinion surveys reveal quite high levels of access inside or outside the home: 35 per cent in Kuwait, 30 per cent in Lebanon, 27 per cent in Saudi Arabia, 26 per cent in Jordan, 19 per cent in Morocco.[26] However, these figures probably indicate persons with any access, not regular users. Data based on network traffic and ISP accounts shows a very much smaller proportion of users. One source estimates 2.7 million internet users in the Arab world as of February 2002 (up from 1.9 million in March 2000).[27] This data is both more comparable and probably more accurate. Such internet user data reveals three aspects of what the *Arab Human Development Report* has termed the 'digital divide' in the Arab world.[28]

The first aspect of this 'digital divide' is the gap between Arab countries and others. Populations in Arab countries have similar (or better) access to telephone lines and personal computers than do populations in other comparable developing countries. In the Middle East North Africa region, there were 92 telephone mainlines and 31 personal computers per 1,000 persons in the year 2000. This compares to 148 telephone mainlines and 44 computers in Latin America, 101 telephone mainlines and 22 computers in East Asia, 27 telephone mainlines and four computers in South Asia, and 14 telephone mainlines and four computers in sub-Saharan Africa. However, Arab countries lag behind in terms of internet users, websites, and similar indicators of connectivity. World Bank data, for example, shows in the year 2000 that only six per thousand of the population in the MENA region are internet users, a level comparable to the less developed regions of South Asia (four per thousand) and sub-Saharan Africa (six per thousand). By contrast, it is estimated that 28 per thousand East Asians, 37 per thousand Latin Americans, and 301 per thousand persons in high income/OECD countries are internet users (see Table 7.1).[29]

Table 7.1 Communications Connectivity

Region	telephone mainlines per 1,000 persons	personal computers per 1,000 persons	internet users per 1,000 persons
MENA	92	31	6
sub-Saharan Africa	14	4	4
South Asia	27	4	6
East Asia	101	22	28
Latin America	148	44	37
OECD high income	610	401	301

Source: World Bank Data

Historically, the growth of the internet has been hampered by government controls and censorship, as well as telecommunications practices and policies (such as monopolies, high-metered local call costs, poor line quality, waiting lists for landlines, the absence of high-speed internet backbones, and the absence of suitable regulatory/legislative frameworks) that are unsupportive of greater connectivity.[30]

There is some evidence that the region is catching up. Between 1997 and 2000, the number of estimated internet users in the MENA region increased 782 per cent, compared to 743 per cent for lower and middle income countries. This rate of growth was higher than Africa, South Asia, or Latin America, but well behind that of East Asia. The MENA region—with 4.8 per cent of the world's population—now contains 0.51 per cent of global internet users, up from 0.22 per cent in 1997. However, the number of internet hosts in the MENA region grew by only 140 per cent, compared to 245 per cent for low and middle income countries as a whole.[31] This may suggest that the MENA region is much more a consumer, than producer, of internet-based knowledge.

A second aspect of the 'digital divide' is the gap between Arab countries. As can be seen in Figure 7.3, net access is concentrated in a few wealthy Gulf states and Lebanon. The UAE, for example, has only one-tenth of the population of the Sudan, but 25 times as many internet users.

A third aspect of the 'digital divide,' and one of particular relevance to the possible impact of the internet in influencing political change, is the profound socio-economic and gender gaps that exist within Arab countries with regard to internet access. The small proportion with net access are generally those elites rich enough to afford computers and ISP accounts, and educated enough to utilize them.

Users also tend to be male. The domination of Western languages (especially English) on the internet further limits accessibility.

The internet provides an opportunity for political groups to exchange information and to network. A daily flood of emails from the West Bank and Gaza by both organizations and individuals detail Israeli curfews, human rights violations, Israeli military actions, and other developments. Palestinian refugees have mobilized in support of their 'right of return' in unparalleled ways, for example, by using the internet to link diaspora communities and their supporters. Outside Palestine, human rights groups have used the net to publicize abuses. Radical Islamists have mobilized and organized using the internet, for both peaceful and violent purposes. The internet allows news to disseminate relatively uncontrolled by the authorities, and for rumours to circulate rapidly across the region and the world. Internet rumours that no Jews were present in the World Trade Center on September 11—and hence that the attack was a Jewish-Israeli plot—circulated widely across the Middle East and South Asia via email, and from there into regular media outlets. Many of these reports were accepted as truth, with up to half of all Palestinians believing that the attack on the World Trade Center was such a conspiracy. Another survey found that most Lebanese, Kuwaitis, and Moroccans did not believe that Arabs were responsible for the attacks, with the largest proportion blaming Israel instead.[32]

The New Communication Technologies and Arab Identities

But what are the effects of all this for Arab identity, and identity-based transnationalism? As noted at the outset of this chapter, since the 1970s scholars of the Middle East have pointed to the decline of active pan-Arab sentiment and the increasing 'stateness' of the Arab world, as post-colonial political systems have been consolidated and as political loyalties or attentions have increasingly been focused within state boundaries.[33] Might new information and communications technologies—whether by facilitating transnational networks (via the internet) or providing uncensored news, in Arabic, of issues of regional concern—have reversed this long-term erosion of pan-Arabism?

The available evidence does suggest that DBS television has been an effective purveyor to Arab populations of news touching upon key Arab (nationalist) concerns, such as the Palestinian-Israeli conflict or the situation in Iraq. Indeed, as noted earlier, surveys show that not only do most Arabs have a strong interest in, for example, Arabic news programming on Palestine, but also that this is a particularly Arab concern (Figure 7.1). Survey evidence from Egypt suggests that those with satellite TV access tend to be more critical of US policy towards Palestine, and also more critical of US policy toward Iraq (although popular opinion is strongly negative among other Egyptians too).[34]

But has this generated a new regional sense of Arabism? In some Zogby International polling, respondents generally indicated that satellite television coverage made them feel 'more sympathy toward fellow Arabs.'[35] However, there

Persistent Permeability?

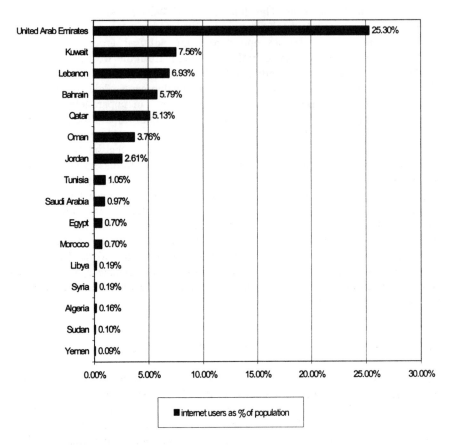

Figure 7.3 Internet Usage in Arab Countries
Source: World Bank Data

seems to be little evidence that this has served to transform regional identities: polling results also show that while a substantial minority of Arabs feel that inter-Arab differences have declined in the past five years, a much larger proportion feel that such differences have remained the same or have even become larger (Figure 7.4).[36] Thus, it would appear that while new ICTs may have slowed or even halted the decline of politically salient Arab nationalism, they have not put in place new, overwhelming dynamics of identity or integration. Given the substantial economic, class, and geopolitical differences among Arab states, this is hardly surprising. To the extent that ICT may promote transnational identities, there are simultaneously many contending forces that also counterweigh and fragment these. Indeed, just as television broadcasts or the internet can contain content that promotes greater pan-Arab identity, it can also disseminate ideas and information that reinforces state-centred, ethnic, class, or other identities.[37]

One clear example of the latter effect can be seen in the case of the Kurds, where new ICT has played an important role in circumventing geographic dispersal and limits on free expression (especially in Turkey) and facilitating the development of national/ethnic identity. Commenting on the impact of the European-based Kurdish satellite television station MED-TV, David Romano notes that 'MED-TV, probably more than any other factor, is promoting ethnic consciousness amongst Kurds in the twenty-first century. Its broadcasts are the most popular programmes in the Kurdish world.' According to Romano, Turkish estimates suggest that around 90 per cent of the Kurdish population in eastern Turkey watch the station.[38] Kurds have also been effective in using the internet to disseminate ethnic and nationalist materials, and to use it to support transnational networks of nationalist activism.

Another example would be the use of new information and communications technologies by diaspora-based Coptic activists to highlight issues of relevance to the Coptic community in Egypt. By the use of new ICT, such (relatively small) groups can have substantial impact. As Paul Rowe notes, 'the external Coptic lobby has presented a challenge to the limitations of domestic political institutions by externalizing protest and communication.... [The] ability to garner public consideration at the domestic and international level has challenged earlier forms of integration into the Egyptian polity. Its future will invariably hinge upon the continued development of diaspora communities, new communications fora, and transnational political organization.'[39]

ICT, Globalization, and Westernization: A Clash of Civilizations?

Both the internet and even more so DBS TV have accelerated the exposure of Arab populations to globalized, especially Western, cultural messages. A quick check of the entertainment programming offered by the popular MBC satellite channel shows the extent to which this is so: Arabic movies, live prayers from Mecca, Middle East sporting events and news programming are interspersed with 'The Bold and the Beautiful,' 'Digimon,' and 'Buffy the Vampire Slayer.' What might be the socio-political effects of this?

For Benjamin Barber, for example, the alienating effects of globalization are accompanied by an opposite retribalization of local politics, a dialectic that he referred to as 'Jihad versus McWorld.'[40] In another well-known prediction, Samuel Huntington suggested that the post-Cold War period has seen a reassertion of civilizational difference as the fault lines of international identity and conflict.[41]

Certainly, there is a profound sense of threat on the part of many in the Arab (and Islamic) world. According to a Gallup survey, 72 per cent of Jordanians saw the West as having a negative effect on local cultural values (six per cent saw it as positive), as did 67 per cent of Moroccans (nine per cent positive), 62 per cent of Lebanese (16 per cent positive), 53 per cent of Saudis (20 per cent positive), and 48 per cent of Kuwaitis (26 per cent positive).[42] Large proportions felt that 'economic, social and cultural modernity' (which Gallup defined as 'as

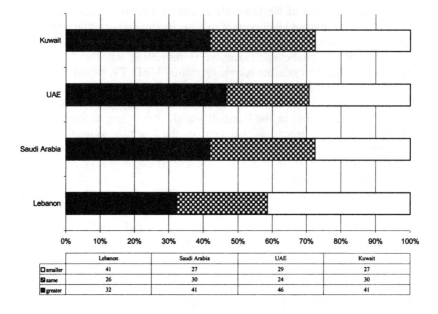

	Lebanon	Saudi Arabia	UAE	Kuwait
☐ smaller	41	27	29	27
▨ same	26	30	24	30
■ greater	32	41	46	41

Figure 7.4 Are Differences Among Arabs Greater or Smaller?
Source: Zogby International

experienced in Western societies') is 'in contradiction to our value system.' In Jordan, 84 per cent of respondents agreed, as did 73 per cent of Lebanese, 71 per cent of Moroccans, 57 per cent of Saudis, and 45 per cent of Kuwaitis.[43] Other findings suggested a significant correlation between the strength of Muslim religiosity and negative evaluations of the United States, suggesting possible religio-cultural fault lines.[44]

In general, those with little education are least likely to see positive things in the West. There is little difference by gender or age, although younger persons were more likely to appreciate Western entertainment.[45] Gallup's overall summary of its findings painted the following picture of a cultural gap:

> First, it is evident that these respondents simply don't think that the United States and the nations of the West have respect for Arabs or for Islamic culture or religion. The people of these Islamic cultures say that the West pays little attention to their situation, does not attempt to help these countries, and makes few attempts to communicate or to create cross-cultural bridges.
>
> Second, these respondents have deep-seated disrespect for what they see as the undisciplined and immoral lifestyles of people in Western nations. These sharply disapproving perceptions are evident at numerous points within the survey context. The disapproval extends not just to the sexual and violent content in movies and music, but respondents also hold the view that the West embodies the

concept of an inappropriately relaxed culture, and that the West has lost respect for its own traditions and religion, extending even to a lack of respect for its elders.

Again, it is not that the people interviewed in this project don't have a keen awareness of what the West has that many Islamic nations don't: economic success, technological knowledge, and even personal freedoms. But there is a strong feeling that the United States and the West have little interest in helping spread this success and know-how to other nations. There is also the overwhelming view that the decadent and undisciplined and irreligious lifestyle that they believe has accompanied the West's success in many ways overwhelms the positives.[46]

Certainly, it seems reasonable to believe that such sense of alienation and threat might generate an inward-looking cultural defensiveness in the Arab (and/or Islamic) worlds. Radical Islamist movements, which frequently rail about the dangers of imported Western culture, are a case in point.

However, there is also evidence that suggests a more complex picture. Contrary to the 'defensive retribalization' thesis, polls show that greater exposure to the West (in the form of internet access, or contact through the emigration of friends and relatives) somewhat improves general attitudes to the Western world, although the effects are often small.[47] Other data shows that those with access to the internet or satellite TV are generally more likely to have a positive view of Western (US) democracy.[48] Polls also suggest that large majorities of Arabs believe that "Western-style democracy can work well" in their own countries.[49]

Survey data also indicates that majorities or near majorities in most Arab countries (60 per cent of Moroccans, 56 per cent of Lebanese, 49 per cent of Kuwaitis, 45 per cent of Saudis, and 44 per cent of Jordanians) express concern with improving the degree of understanding between the West and the Arab and Islamic world. Few are unconcerned with the issue.[50] Perhaps most significant, however, is strong evidence that negative attitudes to the West tend to be rooted in political/policy differences, rather than a civilizational *kulturkampf* born of globalization.

According to a recent report by the Pew Research Center, it is 'policy, not culture' that generates anti-American feeling, both inside and outside the Middle East:

> Why do so many people in the Middle East and elsewhere dislike the United States? One surprise from the recent surveys is that anti-American sentiment is not driven by hostility toward US culture or resentment of American multinationals. The Pew Research Center's survey last November of influential political, cultural and business leaders in 24 countries showed that most viewed American culture as at most a minor reason for this hostility. The main sources of friction are unrivaled American power and policies that have widened divisions between rich and poor. Zogby International's 10-nation survey in March contained similar findings: majorities in eight predominantly Muslim nations and 75% of those in Iran had favorable impressions of American movies and television. More than seven-in-ten

respondents in those nations took an unfavorable view of US policies toward Arab nations.[51]

Another Pew survey, of public attitudes, found that most respondents in the Middle East attributed differences with the US to differences in policies rather than values. Indeed, Arabs were no more likely than Canadians or Britons to see a fundamental value divide at the root of such differences (Figure 7.5).[52]

Permeability and Provocation: The Effects of US Policy

According to Gallup, its recent surveys show that 'only a handful of people living in most of these nations believe that the West acts fairly in its stance on the Palestinian issue.'[53] Moreover, after a review of its findings, Gallup concluded that 'the Palestinian issue is an important driver of negative attitudes towards the United States.' Similarly, polling by Zogby International found:

> Incredibly low marks are given everywhere for United States policy toward the Arab nations and toward the Palestinians. The United States is only given single-digit favorable ratings on its dealings with the Arab nations by every Arab nation (except UAE where it is 15%, driven mostly by the large numbers of non-U.A.E. citizens included in the poll). In all countries, more than nine out of ten are unfavorable.
>
> On US policy toward the Palestinians, the numbers are even lower. Notably, the negative ratings are at least nine out of ten in every Arab nation.
>
> In every country, the "Palestinian issue" is viewed as "the most" or "a very important" issue facing the Arab world today. The range on this is from two in three in Saudi Arabia up to four in five in Lebanon and Egypt.
>
> Those polled in every country indicate that they would overwhelmingly react more favorably toward the US if it "were to apply pressure to ensure the creation of an independent Palestinian state". This includes 69% in Egypt, 79% in Saudi Arabia, 87% in Kuwait (91% of Kuwaiti nationals), 59% in Lebanon, and 67% in UAE (76% of Emiratis).[54]

Palestine is not the only issue, however. Instead, it is simply one of the most salient of a series of foreign policy grievances. The Gallup surveys found, for example, that 63 per cent of Jordanians saw the West as showing 'little' or 'no' concern for the Arab/Islamic worlds (15 per cent saw 'some' or 'a lot' of concern), as did 53 per cent of Lebanese (27 per cent), 48 per cent of Kuwaitis (21 per cent), 43 per cent of Saudis (28 per cent), and 39 per cent of Moroccans (22 per cent).[55]

> The residents of many of the nine countries included in this project—Lebanon, Kuwait, Saudi Arabia, Jordan, Turkey, Pakistan, Iran, Morocco, and Indonesia—have strongly unfavorable opinions of the United States and US President George W. Bush. At almost every opportunity within the survey, respondents overwhelmingly agree that the United States is aptly described by such negative labels as ruthless, aggressive, conceited, arrogant, easily provoked, biased. There

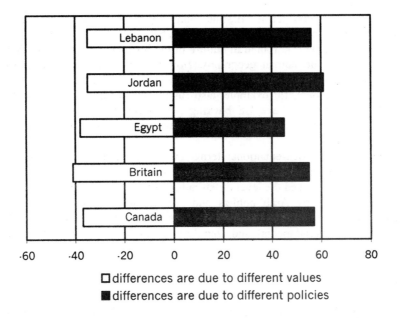

differences are due to different values

differences are due to different policies

Figure 7.5 Accounting for Differences with US Policy
Source: Pew Global Attitudes Project

is overwhelming disagreement with statements that the West and the United States are trustworthy, are friendly, care about poorer nations, or are willing to share technology.

The people of Islamic nations also believe that Western nations do not respect Arab or Islamic values, do not support Arab causes, and do not exhibit fairness toward Arabs, Muslims, or in particular, the situation in Palestine.[56]

In other words, the Palestinian issue is acting as a lightning rod for a broad array of grievances against the West, and the United States in particular. Today, as a consequence of the crisis in Palestine, the 'war against terrorism,' US intervention in and occupation of Iraq, and US support for repressive Arab regimes, these effects have become particularly strong. That this discontent is focused on perceived policy biases is confirmed, moreover, by substantial variation in attitudes towards other Western countries. Britain (closely allied with the US on many of these issues) generally shares the same negative evaluation. By contrast, attitudes towards France (which is seen as having a very different Middle East policy) are more favourable.[57]

It should be noted that Arab dismay with US policy in the Middle East need not be explained through some culturalist lens. Certainly, what Arab citizens may value (that is, why conflict in Palestine counts for more than conflict in the south Sudan, or why the occupation of Jerusalem is more contentious than the occupation of the Western Sahara) is rooted in culture in the broadest sense: history, religion, social networks, and human geography. However, it is striking that for almost everywhere else in the world there are broadly similar criticisms. Pew's survey of global opinion leaders, for example, also found that in Latin America and Asia, 'roughly eight-in-ten believe US backing [for Israel] has been excessive.'[58] In France, 74 per cent of the public has an unfavourable view of US policy on the Palestinian issue.[59]

Put into the mock-equational terms mentioned in the introduction to the chapter, the argument here is simple: US policies have (especially under the Bush administration) increased the level of 'stimulus' (or provocation) considerably. The observed response by Arab publics and regimes to the *intifada* thus reflects generally stable levels of permeability, increased freedom of expression (due to changes in the regional media), and, frankly, an awful lot to be annoyed about.[60]

Conclusion

This chapter has argued that the Arab world remains permeable to transnational political influences, and that the extent of that permeability has remained relatively stable in the past decade or two. The al-Aqsa *intifada* has certainly reverberated across the region, generating public protests at Israeli actions, US policy, and perceived Arab inaction. While such discontent is significant, however, and is certainly worrying to Arab leaders, it is not fundamentally regime-threatening. In the Gulf (and especially Saudi Arabia), however, it appears to have compounded broader frustrations resulting from authoritarian/monarchical politics, demographic pressures, and declining rentierism.

Changes in the regional media environment, and the consequent freer flow of news, images, and information across Arab state boundaries, has played an important role in maintaining a permeability that has traditionally been rooted in common language, ethnic and religious identity, and history. Shibley Telhami and Michael Barnett have suggested, in discussing the importance of (Arab and/or Islamic) identity in Middle Eastern foreign policy, that media trends are possibly 'creating an increasingly common world view in the Arab world, especially on foreign policy questions.'[61] This study concurs.

This chapter has also briefly examined the question of whether there has been a (re)emergence of stronger Arab identities by virtue of a growing salience of civilizational conflict or a defensive retribalization of ethnic politics in the face of the cultural threat of (Westernizing) globalization. By contrast, there is much stronger evidence that a range of specific foreign policy grievances against the US are sparking growing grassroots (and occasionally, official) anger. The al-Aqsa *intifada* is a lightening rod for this, an exemplar for much that ordinary citizens perceive wrong, unjust, or unfair in their societies, and the frustrations they have about the slow pace of change.

Such findings have a number of implications for the study of foreign policy and international relations in the Middle East. It underscores the continued importance of examining the domestic-foreign policy nexus, the influence of even suppressed public opinion in authoritarian states, and the extent to which regime security may figure prominently in foreign policy decision-making. A realist perspective (of almost any variety) would tell us little about how or why Arab leaders have responded the way that they have, and certainly would have fundamental difficulties explaining the apparent genuine willingness of the Saudis to restructure (and downgrade) their relations with their US ally/patron as a result of Washington's Arab-Israeli policies.

This chapter also points to the importance of addressing issues of identity in foreign policy. This is not to say that an exclusively culturalist thrust is best or even desired: on the contrary, responses to the al-Aqsa *intifada* highlight the complex interaction between events, actions, attitudes, technology, political economy, and institutions. It may also be useful—although not explored in this chapter—to devote more attention to issues of fairness and justice in our analyses. Work by psychologists, sociologists, and others certainly suggest that perceptions of 'unfairness' are a powerful motivator for human action, regardless of cultural setting.

Notes

[1] Paul Noble, 'The Arab System: Pressures, Constraints, and Opportunities,' in Bahgat Korany, Ali Dessouki, *et al.*, *The Foreign Policies of Arab States: the Challenge of Change* 2nd ed. (Boulder: Westview Press, 1991), p. 59.

[2] See, for example, Avraham Sela, *The Decline of the Arab-Israeli Conflict: Middle East Politics and the Quest for Regional Order* (Albany: State University of New York Press, 1998), p. 350; Michael Barnett, *Dialogues in Arab Politics: Negotiations in Regional Order* (New York: Columbia University Press, 1998), pp. 256-270; Shibley Telhami and Michael Barnett, 'Identity and Foreign Policy in the Middle East,' in Telhami and Barnett, eds., *Identity and Foreign Policy in the Middle East* (Ithaca: Cornell University Press, 2002), p. 20.

[3] Rex Brynen, 'Palestine and the Arab State System: Permeability, State Consolidation, and the *Intifada*,' *Canadian Journal of Political Science* vol. 24, no. 3 (September 1991), p. 619. On the impact of the first *intifada* on the region, see Brynen, ed., *Echoes of the Intifada: Regional Repercussions of the Palestinian-Israeli Conflict* (Boulder: Westview Press, 1991).

[4] *Conflict Statistics*, Middle East Policy Council, 17 January 2003 <http://www.mepc.org/public_asp/resources/mrates.asp>.

[5] World Bank, *Twenty-Seven Months: Intifada, Closures, and Palestinian Economic Crisis—An Assessment* (Washington, DC: World Bank, 2003), pp. xi-xiv, 7-8.

[6] Gallup Organization, 'Islamic Views of the US: The Palestine Factor,' Gallup Organization, 15 June 2002 <http://www.gallup.com/poll/tb/goverPubli/200020402.asp>.

[7] James Zogby, 'Measuring Arab Public Opinion,' 30 July 2001, *Washington Watch*, 15 June 2002 <http://www.aaiusa.org/wwatch/o73001.htm>.

[8] 80 per cent of Egyptians, 64 per cent of Saudis, 76 per cent of Kuwaitis, 78 per cent of Lebanese, and 64 per cent of the UAE rated Palestine as 'very important' or 'most important.' Zogby International, 'The Ten Nations Impressions of America Poll,' 11 April 2002 <http://www.zogby.com/features/features.dbm?ID=141>.

[9] For an overview of initial reactions, see 'Arab Reactions,' *Middle East International* vol. 635 (13 October 2000), pp. 12-15.

[10]   Sana Kamal, 'Violent Crackdown,' *Middle East International* vol. 650 (18 May 2001), p. 11.

[11] Kamal, 'Public Anger,' *Middle East International* vol. 673 (19 April 2002), p. 18.

[12] *Middle East Newsline*, 4 November 2002 < http://www.menewsline.com>.

[13] Council of the League of Arab States, 'The Beirut Declaration,' Council of the League of Arab States, 15 June 2002 <http://www.arts.mcgill.ca/MEPP/PRRN/docs/beirut_ declaration.html>.

[14] *Ha'aretz*'s well-informed diplomatic correspondent, Aluf Benn, noted in June 2002 that 'The [US] administration's recent round of consultations with Saudi Arabian, Egyptian, and Jordanian leaders convinced it that the Arab nations are primarily concerned about the stability of their own regimes and are willing to wait for a final-status agreement, which the Americans believe is currently unobtainable. *Ha'aretz – English*, 14 June 2002 <http://www.haaretzdaily.com>.

[15] 'Jordanian King Warns Of Growing Arab Rage,' *Washington Post*, (13 May 2002), p. A8. See also 'Popular Arab Anger: A Long-Term Threat to the Foundations of Peace,' *New York Times* (8 April 2002).

[16] 'Anger in the Streets Is Exerting Pressure On Arab Moderates,' *New York Times* (3 April 2002).

[17] 'Saudi to Warn Bush of Rupture Over Israel Policy,' *New York Times* (25 April 2002).

[18] See, for example, F. Gregory Gause, III, 'Domestic Structures and the "Export" of Revolution in the Middle East,' *Journal of South Asian and Middle Eastern Studies* vol. 14, no. 3 (Spring 1991).

[19] For useful discussions, see the special issue on 'The Information Revolution,' *Middle East Journal* vol. 54, no. 3 (Summer 2000).

[20] Gallup Organization, 'Al-Jazira: Arabs Rate its Objectivity,' 23 April 2002, Gallup Organization, 15 June 2002 <http://www.gallup.com/poll/tb/goverPubli/20020423.asp>. The perceived reliability of *al-Jazira* took some damage, however, during the 2003 Gulf War. Some viewers, astonished at the rapid fall of Saddam Hussein, blamed *al-Jazira* for not showing the regime's weakness more clearly.

[21] Kamal, 'The Power of Satellite TV,' *Middle East International* vol. 673 (19 April 2002).

[22] Robert G. Kaiser and David B. Ottaway, 'Saudi Leader's Anger Revealed Shaky Ties— Bush's Response Eased a Deep Rift On Mideast Policy; Then Came Sept. 11,' *Washington Post* (10 February 2002), p. A1.

[23] Gallup Organization, '*Al-Jazira* Viewers Perceive West Differently,' 23 April 2002 <http://www.gallup.com/poll/tb/goverPubli/20020423b.asp>. The Gallup survey does not analyze how much of this effect may be due to social class: presumably, those who have access to DBS TV and hence view *al-Jazira* are generally of higher socioeconomic class than those who do not have such access.

[24] Gallup Organization, 'Islamic Views of the US: The Palestine Factor.'

[25] Shibley Telhami, 'Sympathy for the Palestinians,' *Washington Post* (25 July 2001), p. A21.

[26] Gallup Organization, 'Does Western Contact Affect Islamic Opinions?' 7 May 2002, Gallup Organization, 15 June 2002 <http://www.gallup.com/poll/tb/goverPubli/ 200220507/asp>. Data from the Zogby International polls shows still higher levels of internet access. Access, however, is not the same as usage: one might have 'access' by having an internet café in the neighbourhood, while never in fact accessing it.

[27] NUA.ie, 'How Many Online?' *Nua.ie*, 12 June 2002 <http://www.nua.ie/surveys/how_ many_online/index.html>. See also Marcus Franda, *Launching Into Cyberspace: Internet*

Development and Politics in Five World Regions (Boulder: Lynne Rienner Publishers, 2002), p. 42.

[28] United Nations Development Programme and the Arab Fund for Economic and Social Development, *Arab Human Development Report 2002* (New York: UNDP, 2002), p. 73.

[29] Data derived from World Bank, *World Development Indicators*, May 2002, World Bank, 5 August 2003 <http://devdata.worldbank.org/dataonline/ >.

[30] For discussions, see Joshia Teitelbaum, 'Dueling for Da'wa: State versus Society on the Saudi Internet,' and Karla J. Cunningham, 'Jordan's Information Revolution: Implications for Democracy,' both in *Middle East Journal* vol. 56, no. 2 (Spring 2002).

[31] Toby E. Huff, 'Globalization and the Internet: Comparing the Middle Eastern and Malaysian Experiences,' *Middle East Journal* vol. 55, no. 3 (Summer 2001), pp. 442-442.

[32] Gallup Organization, 'Blame for September 11 Attacks Unclear for Many in Islamic World,' Gallup Organization, 15 June 2002 <http://www.gallup.com/tb/goverPubli/20020301.asp>.

[33] See, for example, Gabriel Ben-Dor, *State and Conflict in the Middle East: The Emergence of the Postcolonial State* (New York: Praeger, 1983); Brynen, 'Palestine and the Arab State System: Permeability, State Consolidation, and the *Intifada*;' Sela, *The Decline of the Arab-Israeli Conflict*; Barnett, *Dialogues in Arab Politics*.

[34] Zogby International, 'The Ten Nations Impressions of America Poll.'

[35] Shilbey Telhami, 'Survey of Public Opinion on the Middle East,' 15 June 2002 <http://www.bsos.umd.edu/sadat/middle_east_survey.htm>.

[36] Zogby International, 'The Ten Nations Impressions of America Poll.'

[37] On the complex effects of new ICTs in Kuwait, for example, see Deborah Wheeler, 'New Media, Globalization, and Kuwaiti National Identity,' *Middle East Journal* vol. 54, no. 3 (Summer 2000).

[38] David Romano, 'Modern Communications Technology in Ethnic Nationalist Hands: The Case of the Kurds,' *Canadian Journal of Political Science* vol. 35, no. 1 (March 2002), pp. 140-141.

[39] Paul Rowe, 'Four Guys and a Fax Machine?: Diasporas, New Information Technologies, and the Internationalization of Religion in Egypt,' *Journal of Church and State* vol. 43, no. 1 (Winter 2001), 1 August 2002 <http://www.copts.com/journal_of_church_and_state.htm>.

[40] Benjamin Barber, *Jihad Versus McWorld* (New York: Times Books, 1995).

[41] Samual Huntington, *The Clash of Civilizations and the Remaking of World Order* (New York: Touchstone Books, 1998).

[42] Gallup Organization, 'Poll of the Islamic World: Perceptions of Western Culture,' Gallup Organization, 15 June 2002 <http://www.gallup.org/poll/tb/goverPubli/20020312.asp>.

[43] Gallup Organization, 'Does Modernity Challenge Islamic Values?' Gallup Organization, 15 June 2002 <http://www.gallup.org/poll/tb/religValue/20020312b.asp>.

[44] Gallup Organization, 'Most Religious in Predominantly Islamic Countries Are Most Negative Toward the United States,' Gallup Organization, 15 June 2002 <http://www.gallup.org/poll/tb/religValue/20020423b.asp>.

[45] Gallup Organization, 'What do Islamic World Residents Like About the West?' Gallup Organization, 15 June 2002 <http://www.gallup.org/poll/tb/goverPubli/20020528.asp>.

[46] Gallup Organization, 'Gallup Poll of the Islamic World,' Gallup Organization, 15 June 2002 <http://www.gallup.com/poll/tb/goverpubli/20020226.asp>.

[47] Gallup Organization, 'Does Western Contact Affect Islamic Opinions? The Zogby polls show the same effect.

[48] The data for Figures 4 and 5 is drawn from Zogby International, 'The Ten Nations Impressions of America Poll.' The apparent anomalous data for Kuwait and the UAE is probably explained by the near-universal access to satellite TV in these countries, and hence the small cell size (and peculiarities) of the 'no satellite' group in these countries.

[49] Pew Global Attitudes Project, *Views of a Changing World* (Washington DC: Pew Research Center for the People and the Press, June 2003), p. 7.

[50] Gallup Organization, 'Many in the Islamic World Express Concern About Understanding,' 1 August 2002 <http://www.gallup.com/poll/tb/religvalue/20020305b.asp>. Iran and Pakistan show much less concern with improving relations with the West.

[51] Pew Research Center, 'International Surveys: What We Are Finding,' 29 April 2002, Pew Research Center, 30 April 2002 <http://people-press.org/commentary/display.php3?AnalysisID=46>.

[52] Pew Global Attitudes Project, *What the World Thinks in 2002* (Washington DC: Pew Research Center for the People and the Press, 2002), p. 141.

[53] Gallup Organization, 'Islamic Views of the US: The Palestine Factor.'

[54] James Zogby, 'It's the Policy, Stupid!' 15 April 2002, *Washington Watch*, 15 June 2002 <http://www.aaiusa.org/wwatch/041502.htm>.

[55] Gallup Organization, 'Poll of the Islamic World: Perceptions of Western Culture.'

[56] Gallup Organization, 'Gallup Poll of the Islamic World.'

[57] Gallup Organization, 'Poll of Islamic World: Favorability Toward US, Britain,' Gallup Organization, 15 June 2002 <http://www.gallup.com/poll/tb/goverpubli/20020226c.asp>.

[58] Pew Research Centre, 'America Admired, Yet its Vulnerability Seen as a Good Thing, Say Opinion Leaders,' Pew Global Attitudes Project, 15 June 2002 <http://208.240.91.18/1219011.htm>.

[59] Zogby International, 'The Ten Nations Impressions of America Poll.'

[60] In fairness, it should also be noted that the US has consistently failed to get credit where it *has* acted on behalf of Muslim populations. According to the Zogby 2002 poll, only Kuwaitis had a strongly positive view of the US liberation of Kuwait, while Egyptians (52 per cent), Saudis (59 per cent), and Lebanese (52 per cent) had a generally unfavourable impression. Less than a third had favourable impressions of US efforts to halt ethnic cleansing (of Bosnian and Kosovar Muslims) in the Balkans. Zogby International, 'The Ten Nations Impressions of America Poll.'

[61] Telhami and Barnett, 'Identity and Foreign Policy in the Middle East,' p. 21.

Chapter 8

Globalization of a Torn State: Turkey from the Middle East to European Integration

Ersel Aydinli

This chapter advances the thesis that Turkey is, and has long been, a key example of the contending dynamics in the Middle East of regionalism, localism, and globalization. Turkey is the bordering state between the Middle East and Europe, the latter being a leading 'producer' of globalization. It has felt the attractions of European (and Western) trade, exported labour to Europe, been exposed to Western media and cultural exports, contended with the difficult dynamics of democratization, and aspired to membership in the European Union. After highlighting Turkey's modern relations with the Middle East, the chapter will examine its aspiration to join the EU, a unique phenomenon in this region. It will then analyse the contending forces of globalization and security in Turkish foreign and domestic policy, situating EU accession within the context of globalist arguments about Turkey's future.

Turkey and the Middle East

Until the 1990s, Turkish policy towards the Middle East could largely be summed up by the following principles: non-interference in Middle Eastern countries' domestic affairs; non-interference in intra-Arab relations; general political support for the Arab states and for the Palestine issue with simultaneous maintenance of ties with Israel; and the minimization of any tensions between its Middle Eastern and Western political relationships.[1] Two underlying characteristics emerge from this policy: the overwhelming desire to seek a balance based on an appearance of neutrality, and a similar desire to maintain a distance from the Middle East and most of its problems.

There were several reasons for Turkey's aversion to involvement in the Middle East. Historically, the Turkish Republic tended to associate the 'West' with modernization, while the 'East' stood for backwardness. The East was also considered a source of several evils, including security threats. For example, many Turks recalled the lack of Arab support in the late Ottoman era. Turkey was willing, therefore, to cut most of its physical and psychological ties with the Middle East. When a nationalist Ottoman parliament voted on 28 January 1920 for the National Pact (*Misak-I Milli*), which was essentially a geographical blueprint for the upcoming Turkish Republic, they accepted the loss of the Arab-populated portions of Ottoman territories. Most Turks were content to cut their connections with the Arabs, and the soon-to-be core of the modern Turkish state was uninterested in reprising its earlier role in the Middle East.[2]

Other, more pragmatic, reasons for wishing to remain distant from the Middle East were also present The perception grew in the 1950s that Turkey had erred in resembling a US agent in the Middle East, and thus the desire to eradicate this image was strong in subsequent decades.[3] Its reluctance to look like a proxy became even more acute as it came to feel that the West was a less-than-reliable ally, a mistrust which was fanned by such experiences as the Cuban Missile Crisis, the Cyprus issue, and the Johnson letter.[4] Moreover historical experiences had convinced many Turks that active reengagement in the Middle East could be downright harmful, possibly leading Turkey to become 'mired in a swamp.'[5] Thus, reticence in the form of non-interventionism became the crux of Turkish foreign policy towards the Middle East.[6] Any involvement with the countries of the Middle East was seen—both from military and ideological standpoints—as a potential source of insecurity.

Despite such basic ideological distancing and pragmatic concerns, it has nevertheless always been very difficult for Turkey to completely separate itself from the Middle East. First, it is undeniably a part of the geographical Middle East, attested to even by its inclusion in volumes such as this. Many of its demographic and historical characteristics (such as its Kurdish population) have also made Turkey fall into the historical Middle Eastern security complex.

International pressures have also served to keep Turkey bound to the Middle East. Starting in the 1950s and with the advance of the Cold War conflict, Turkey's participation in the Western alliance structure forced it to be a part of various Middle East formations. Turkey's major Western allies strongly promoted Turkey's participation in regional groupings, such as the Baghdad Pact, in order to help change the balance of power in the East-West conflict.

Various regional events also played their role. Starting in the late 1960s and throughout the 1970s, just as Turkey was learning how to cope with its 'torn-ness' through a carefully crafted and hesitant policy towards the Middle East, certain regional dynamics emerged to make this disengagement less possible. For example, the Soviet invasion of Afghanistan and the Iranian revolution drew the attention of major powers to the region, also presenting substantial challenges to Turkey's own security interests, and thereby drawing its attention, reluctantly, back to the East. Turkey nevertheless refused to make formal commitments, such as alliances, and tried to maintain balanced, or so-called 'multi-level'/'multi-dimensional' policies.[7]

In the early 1990s, with the end of the Cold War, Turkey felt a degree of excitement that it could now turn its attention more fully to the West, and thus made its formal application for European Union membership. However, two looming geopolitical challenges merged and succeeded in pulling Turkey back to the Middle East, reminding it of where it is located and of what it is a part: the Kurdish separatist movement, and political Islam. When these two issues—both emerging from Turkey's south and from the Middle East—were designated in the 1990s as the top two security challenges to Turkish national survival, it was clear that the Middle East had once again become a very much unwanted focus of the Turkish political psyche. Moreover, these challenges facilitated Turkish-Israeli cooperation, a clear deviation from Turkey's traditional attempts for a balanced foreign policy in the Middle East.

Even in fall 2003, the Iraqi crisis can be seen as another clear reflection of Turkey's continuing torn-ness between a desire to run away from the Middle East, and necessary involvement in its affairs. Perhaps the most graphic reflection of this torn-ness can be found in the words of the Turkish Islamist Prime Minister, Recep Tayyip Erdogan. After flying back and forth between Europe and Washington in late 2002, Erdogan complained that if the Europeans had given Turkey a firm date for EU membership (thereby clarifying Turkey's 'Western' position geographically and in terms of its identity), he would not have had to negotiate with the Americans over Turkish support for the US operation in Iraq.

Turkey's efforts to turn away from the Middle East and toward globalization (as represented by the EU in particular) do not constitute an isolated phenomenon in Turkish policy-making. Rather, they can be seen as a reflection of a larger structural pendulum in Turkish experience between the demands of security and the desire to globalize, the latter symbolized by the country's long-standing commitment to modernization and its general embrace of Western governance systems (i.e., political liberalization). Consequently, this chapter will next describe this structural pendulum's dynamics through a comparative survey of the roots of the Turkish elite's divided perceptions and strategies on integration with the EU. This is followed by a brief assessment of which side of the pendulum appears to be gaining further ground. This latter task is undertaken by examining Turkey's approval in August 2002 of a dramatic reform package meant to meet EU membership criteria.

Defining the Pendulum

A structural pendulum between globalization and security needs has long been present in Turkey due to certain characteristics of Ottoman/Turkish history and politics.[8] Never in Ottoman/Turkish history have liberalization attempts taken place in a vacuum. Rather, they have been carefully constructed and determined by the limiting borders of the systemic primacy of internal and external security concerns. Several characteristics emerged from, and subsequently contributed to, the persistence of a structural pendulum between security and liberalization. First, at a time when the Ottoman Empire was in a state of constant territorial contraction, those in favour of liberal reforms justified their liberalization agenda by claiming it would better protect the state from various threats. Security, in other words, was the end, while political liberalization was the means. Second, there was at the time (and arguably remains) a fear among the elite of an uncontrolled devolution of power. This security-based cautiousness towards liberalization was often connected to a concern that liberalization and political reform could empower ordinary citizens, of whom the elite held an inherent mistrust.[9] Third, the very ruling elite that assumed the mission of promoting liberalizing reforms was, ironically, the same group whose primary responsibility was to protect the country's national security. At times of immediate threat, when the two elements clashed, the elite's role as the professional security guardian of the state and the regime prevailed, therefore spelling at least a temporary end to liberal policies.

The resultant pendulum between liberalization and security continued through the Republican era. Having finally liberated the homeland, the leaders of the new Turkish Republic felt they had guaranteed the dominant side of the pendulum, namely, the security of the regime and country. This freed them to turn again to liberalization efforts.

The first political liberalization attempt came in 1924 with the formation of the first opposition political party, the Progressive and Republican Party (*Terakki-Perver Cumhuriyet Firkasi*). When the subsequent Kurdish-led Sheikh Said rebellion broke out in Turkey's southeast, the existing government's policies towards the rebellion were seen by Mustafa Atatürk and his friends to be overly soft. Tougher policies were prescribed, and more hawkish figures were sought to conduct them. The initiation of emergency laws and tribunals in a highly securitized environment cost the life of the new party and put an end to this first attempt at multi-party politics.[10]

The second multi-party attempt, beginning with the founding of the Free Party (*Serbest Firka*) in 1930, also fell victim to concerns over regime and state security. The ensuing massive societal support for the new party made it clear that potential anti-regime elements were both plentiful and ready to take advantage of multi-party politics in their struggle against the state, as represented by the ruling party. The ruling elite's fears of anarchy seemed to be materializing. Atatürk himself, despite having initiated this liberalization attempt, eventually concurred with concerns over security. He voiced his concerns in a talk with an opposition party leader: 'anarchy, there is anarchy everywhere. You [the opposition party leaders] are oblivious or blind to this fact...I can't be impartial under these circumstances.'[11] The new party was compelled to close itself down. A subsequent tragic incident, a religious rebellion referred to as the 'Menemen Case,'[12] in which an army officer was beheaded by rebellious Islamists, confirmed the primacy of national security. To the elite, any form of power relocation or diffusion to societal elements was determined to be fatal to the state and the regime owing to the fragmented nature of society. From that point on, all liberalization projects were destined to be filtered through their national security implications, a process that can be termed 'securitization.'

The Contemporary Debate

Philosophical Foundations and Strategies of the Sceptics

A perfect balance between security and liberalization has yet to be found, and the torn-ness between these two dynamics continues to haunt Turkish decision-making. Those Turkish state elements that prioritize security perceive globalization as a source of security challenges, and therefore remain sceptical of EU integration, the ultimate phase of Turkey's globalization process.

The underlying philosophies for the claims of those who, to various degrees, are sceptical about integration, seem to converge around three main points: the challenges that integration will present to Turkish identity, to Turkish sovereignty, and to Turkey's economic independence. What becomes visible in these arguments is that they are all linked ultimately to the survival of the Turkish nation-state. Clearly, then, national security is the underlying issue.

The presence of securitization in considerations of the EU accession issue is evident in the words of retired general Suat İlhan, who claims that his book, *Avrupa Birliğine Neden Hayır* (Why No to the European Union) provoked the first coordinated spark of anti-EU sentiments in Turkey. İlhan claims that EU membership and the accession process is 'basically the end of Turkey,' mainly because 'Turkey's distinct history, geopolitics, and mission do not and cannot tolerate the EU objectives and values.'[13]

He admits that soldiers do not know much about economics, and therefore, 'make realpolitik decisions based on history, geography, balance of power and historical rivalries.' This perspective has been observed when security establishment figures participate in meetings pertaining to the EU issue, with most of the debate and discussion boiling down to security factors and threat analyses, such as the Cyprus issue, the Greek conflict, and memories of Sèvres syndrome.[14] Indeed, İlhan argues that 'Eurasia is the land where all the major geopolitical rivalries have played out historically...the EU on the west has emerged as the island of stability, and China is emerging in the east as one. In between, there is instability and geopolitical rivalry. For this reason, they are trying to destroy us and our potential.'[15] What is striking in this analysis is that its starting point, framework, and context all revolve around traditional geopolitics and related major power/civilizational rivalries. He automatically assumes that everything, be it an international development or a transnational movement, should first fit with and make sense according to the parameters of geopolitical thinking, which itself is based on conflictual competition and zero-sum confrontations. Europe and its project of the European Union are therefore first considered along these lines and are seen as a European crusade against the East.

Along the same lines, Ümit Özdağ, head of Turkey's largest strategic think-tank, also defines the whole EU-Turkish adventure as part of the political rivalry that has been taking place between East and West ever since Attila the Hun's attacks against Europe. To Özdağ, Europe still sees Anatolia/Asia Minor as part of the old West—the former Roman Empire—and is trying to reconquer it now by way of the EU project.[16] This geopoliticization of the EU integration issue transforms any subsequent discussion into an evidence-seeking mission for geopolitical rivalry and enmity. Following this line of thought, for example, a document showing the overlap between the goals and demands of Kurdish insurgents (of the PKK) and the EU's pre-accession demands is presented as evidence of how what is naively thought of as integration or globalization is in fact a geopolitical issue. This same document has repeatedly been circulated among Turkish parliamentarians in order to present the 'other face' of the European agenda.[17] The language gets even blunter in some cases, as people warn that 'Turkey is to be raped while trying to become an EU member.'[18]

The first major set of arguments against integration revolve around the issue of identity, suggesting that since Turkey belongs to the East, traditional Turkish identity will be lost in the accession and membership process. Concerns over the loss of Turkish identity have been voiced by such diverse groups as radical Islamists and the Marxist Workers' Party. Özdağ takes this position and asks whether it is possible to be a Turkish nationalist while still supporting the EU process, since, in his view, the EU is aiming to federalize Turkey and the unitary Turkish nation-state.[19] Yet another sceptical scholar, Ali Özcan, draws on the former ideas and argues that promoting other cultural characteristics in Turkey, namely Kurdish nationalism, might lead to Turkish nationalism becoming part of an action-reaction process which could ultimately culminate in civil war.[20] Such a conclusion seems to take the securitization aspect of the culture- or identity-based arguments to their extreme.

A second set of argument focuses on a loss of Turkish sovereignty. Former general İlhan proposes that one cannot be a true 'Atatürkist' if one agrees with any future relinquishment of sovereignty to the EU, since Atatürkism is based on national sovereignty.[21] Moreover, the sovereignty argument goes on to express the concern that with any sharing or relinquishment of sovereignty, Turkey will also lose its historical potential of becoming a regional—or even 'world'—power. The logic behind this suggestion is that with EU membership, Turkey will lose its capacity to formulate and carry out an independent foreign policy. Furthermore, the EU is seen as instigating this weakening process in order to reduce the threat they feel from the 'other' that is Turkey. The sovereignty issue arises as well in relation to internal risks: one young scholar has warned that with EU integration Turkey may turn into a 'hell of ethnicity'[22] as it is populated by 47 different ethnic groups. Since integration is likely to draw attention to these sub-national groups, he foresees a fragmenting impact and a subsequent 'hell.'

The third main set of arguments combines economic with security issues. Erol Manisalı, another sceptic, warns that Turkey might become a colony of the West and the EU. He contends that the EU is bent on colonizing the economic energy of Turkey, while at the same time solving various security challenges in the region to its advantage (e.g., the Cyprus issue and the Turkish/Greek problems).[23] İlhan, meanwhile, links this economic argument to the geopolitical and cultural ones and notes that 'we are the first nation which fought against imperialism, and now we are changing sides. This does not fit with traditional Turkish identity and culture.'[24] His argument implies that Turks were one of the first peoples to fight a war of liberation against the West, and had therefore long ago built up an identity of being against imperialism. Also implicit in this argument is the idea that Turkey should not abandon its position among the exploited countries in order to join the ranks of the exploiters.

Ultimately, the underlying foundation of those sceptical about integration seems to be a threat-based geopoliticization of the agenda, which can be summed up best in General İlhan's words: '[we] have been waging war against Europeans for the last 1500 years...that is why all European Parliament decisions, e.g. Cyprus, Armenia, Kurdish, have all been against us—they are still waging a war against us.'[25] From this starting point, the integration sceptics apply various strategies to get their messages across. In line with their emphasis on security, their primary strategy is their discursive emphasis on the threat dimensions of EU integration. For example, they draw connections between EU demands and those of the Sèvres Treaty, which was to divide up the Ottoman lands after the First World War, and they emphasize the overlap between EU demands about minority rights and the demands of the PKK. Underlying such discourse are rhetorical efforts to fan societal nationalism and to remind the public of the historical enmity and suspicion that has long existed between Europe and Turkey. Another strategy has been the sceptics' alleged use of state intelligence organizations to gather information on pro-EU figures, with the presumed goal of discrediting them. One scandal erupted when the *Aydınlık* newspaper published the private email messages of EU representative Karen Fogg. It was later suggested by two prominent sceptics that these messages had been intercepted by military intelligence services. Though not exactly a strategy, a final rhetorical argument used by virtually all sceptics as a last defence against those in support of integration is to point to the futility of integration efforts since the Europeans will ultimately never accept Turkey anyway.

Philosophical Foundations and Strategies of the Integrationists

The primary arguments of the pro-EU integrationists can be broadly grouped under four main headings: modernization, economics/development, security, and democracy. The first of these arguments, and one particularly voiced by the business association TUSIAD and the centre-right Motherland Party, is that Turkey's historical modernization process has always been Westward. Western integration is dictated by Atatürkism, and is thus necessary.

The second main argument of the integrationists concerns economics and development. This is a very appealing and powerful argument used by virtually all integration supporters, and basically states that integration will bring about further wealth and development. Not only is integration presented as a path to such development and progress, it is often presented as the *only* path to reaching Turkey's dream of joining the ranks of the 'First World.'

Given the sceptics' reliance on security for their anti-integration positions, it is somewhat ironic that the third argument of the integrationists also relies on issues of security. Rather than viewing the West and its demands as sources of threat, the West and even the process of integration itself are presented as solutions for many of Turkey's longstanding internal and external security problems. Internally, chronic problems of both Kurdish separatism and radical Islam are seen as having a solution in EU integration. This argument is used both by politicians seeking a political solution to the Kurdish issue, such as former Prime Minister Mesut Yılmaz and former Chief of Parliament Hikmet Çetin, as well as by Kurdish groups, from the predominantly Kurdish HADEP party to more radical PKK-linked factions. Integration is also seen as a means of solving various external geopolitical security problems (e.g., the Cyprus issue, which former Foreign Minister İlter Türkmen argues may be resolved after EU integration by applying the Belgian model).

The final argument of the integrationists concerns issues of democracy and human rights. This argument is generally used by those groups who have experienced conflicts with the practices of the traditional state security apparatus, such as the Kurdish-dominated HADEP party, the various Islamist parties, Alevites, and some liberal groups/NGOs such as the Liberal Thought Association. The basic thrust of these groups' argument is that only through integration can Turkey hope to achieve true democracy and high human rights standards.

The primary overall strategy of the integrationists is, like that of the sceptics, also discursive in nature. Understandably very popular, the discourse of the integrationists provides constant support for the idea that integration will bring with it numerous benefits, from prosperity to human rights. In this spirit, EU accession has been described as a 'stepping stone' to the 'best of the world,'[26] an upbeat message widely broadcast by influential groups in the media.

A more concrete strategy has been the expansion of cooperation and alliances at the extra-governmental level. Turkish NGOs promoting EU integration overall or some aspect of the accession requirements often receive money from the West to fund their activities or educational exchange opportunities. The Liberal Thought Association, for example, receives money from the European Commission for publishing books and organizing conferences, and Germany's Konrad Adenauer Foundation provides financial support to many affiliated groups in Turkey. This type of cooperation has also been flourishing at the individual level, resulting in the building up of informal networks for cooperation, evidence of which can be seen in the high level of official and unofficial traffic between Europe and Turkey's Kurdish-populated Southeast Anatolia region. A classified document revealed that in 2001, the HADEP party mayor of Diyarbakir, a major city in Southeast Anatolia, spent more than half of his working days in Europe. Such 'informal networks' also appear to be expanding among journalists and intellectuals.

Yet another strategy could be labelled the 'boomerang' effect. In this case, pro-EU elements in Turkey, from NGOs to journalists to political figures, provide information to European parties so that those parties are able to pressure Turkey more effectively. The European Commission gathers information from many groups and individuals, and often pressures the Turkish state on the accession issue via EU member-state diplomatic representatives. Diplomatic notes, the annual European Commission progress reports, and European Parliament decisions all play a role in this process.

Coordination abilities of the two groups

Of the two groups, the integrationists currently appear more coordinated in their efforts. Their pro-EU activities are spearheaded by TUSIAD and the influential think-tank TESEV, and they appear to be better financed, to include in their membership greater numbers of professionals, and to have the support of public opinion. Their efforts are further helped by the fact that they are able to work freely and openly, since the state's official policy is pro-EU.

Nevertheless, the sceptics' voices have been gaining confidence and strength, garnering further support with each incidence of perceived EU hesitance in responding to Turkey's progressive moves. Perhaps most interesting of all is the convergence under the sceptical umbrella of many competing ideologies and figures: the arguments of the sceptics have brought nationalist MHP party members and the Marxist Workers' Party together, along with strange bedfellows Turan Yazgan (long time anti-Communist and pan-Turkist professor/activist), Anıl Çeçen (long-time left-wing professor and Atatürkist activist), and Şaban Karataş, who belongs to a philosophically conservative religious group.

Globalization Discourse on the Rise

The most recent sign of an apparent strengthening of the globalization/integration discourse came in August 2002, with the remarkable and largely unexpected approval by the Turkish parliament of a wide-ranging set of laws designed to meet some of the most sensitive political demands for EU accession.

Among these laws, the Turkish parliament abolished the death penalty (although, in line with Protocol Six of the European Convention on the Protection of Human Rights and Fundamental Freedoms [CPHRFF], it remains on the books to be used in times of war or when facing imminent threat thereof).[27] Notably, this means that PKK leader Abdullah Öcalan and other leading PKK militants will not be executed. The laws also amended Article 159 of the Turkish Penal Code, pertaining to crimes against the state, so that the Republic, the Turkish Parliament, the government, the ministers and the security forces (including the military) can now be criticized, provided such criticism does not contain insults.

As well, the non-Muslim minority communities established by the 1923 Lausanne Treaty (Greeks, Armenians, and Jews) will now be allowed greater rights over religious property, such as churches, and greater freedom to satisfy their cultural, religious, educational, social, and health needs through their own foundations, provided they first receive government permission.

In addition, the amendments introduce provisions that make retrial possible for civil and criminal law cases that receive approval from the European Court of

Human Rights (ECHR). Under the new law, a Turkish citizen subject to a conviction that the ECHR has found to contravene the CPHRFF can force the Turkish courts to review the original verdict. When the amendment was put into effect, former Kurdish ministers Leyla Zana, Hatip Dicle, Orhan Doğan and Selim Sadak, were granted a retrial in the State Security Court. The Court once again found them guilty. Nevertheless, European pressure has grown to such a degree that as of fall 2003 Turkish government officials have begun mentioning the possibility of finding a political solution for freeing them.

Finally, the new laws also allow Kurds and other ethnic groups in Turkey to make broadcasts in their mother tongues (provided they do not violate the 'national unity and the principles of the Republic'), and allow minorities to establish language courses. This measure does not, however, specifically provide for Kurdish and/or other minority language courses in state education, nor does it cover the use of these languages as a medium of instruction.

Taking all these points into consideration, arguably the most important aspect of the new package is the official recognition of a Kurdish presence as well as that of other ethnic groups, including Laz, Circassians, and Arabs. For the first time in the history of modern Turkey, the official state ideology, arguing that everyone living in Turkey is Turkish, has been radically altered. Given the state's fears of political reforms based on ethnicity and the challenges this could hold for national security (reflected historically in the pendulum), the question immediately arises as to how these laws (even with the conditions they include) were able to pass. How was such a swing in the pendulum possible? Two primary—but seemingly opposed—explanations are possible.

The first is that, after years of liberalization, its discourse has finally started gaining precedence over that of security. It could be argued that, in this case, the spokespeople of liberalization (such as the pro-EU NGOs) were able to make significant contributions to the ultimate passing of the controversial legislation. Furthermore, the understanding seems to have gained strength that the pro-EU discourse could not be matched by any other.

The acceptance of the bill in Parliament does seem at first to show the influence of the pro-EU civil forces, including the Turkish Industrialists' and Businessmen's Association (TUSIAD) and the Economic Development Foundation (IKV). Both of these groups utilized several tactics to create a strong pro-European climate among the Turkish public, deputies, and civil and military elite. This included the release of a declaration by 175 civil society organizations strongly urging the Turkish government and Parliament to comply with EU demands on democratization and respect for human rights, even minority rights. Another influential pro-EU civil initiative was the European Movement 2002, which (among other things) conceived of a simple yet effective tactic of mounting a digital clock opposite the entrance to the Parliament, counting down the days, hours, and minutes until the December 2002 summit in Copenhagen.

In terms of current discourse on the subject of integration, pro-EU elements clearly hold the upper hand on 'attractive' arguments. While the sceptics' arguments are mainly about concerns over sovereignty or the vaguely defined 'national security' of the country, EU proponents respond with an equally vague but far more seductive discourse promising democracy, a better life, and respect from the world. Perhaps because the issue of EU membership is treated as a magical key that will open the doors to all good things, or perhaps because there is an unquestioned association of EU integration with the high values that have long been cherished in the dreams of the Turkish elite (such as a functioning liberal democracy and a Western-style modernization), very few elements in Turkish public life seem able to reject outright the idea of EU integration. Even its harshest sceptics only seem able to take the position of agreeing with integration conditionally. By appealing to what might be seen as the public's long-time psychological inferiority complex in relation to the West, the issue of EU membership has become a ritualistic collective belief, against which, it appears, even a powerful entity like the military may not easily resist.

A second explanation is that the legislation passed because, for some reason, the guardians of security allowed it to. This could be because these spokespeople, and their core supporters in the Turkish military, are not without their own internal divisions on issues of liberalization versus security. Despite the sceptics' attempts to rely on security arguments, the military itself has remained conspicuously quiet throughout the membership debates. In fact, some of the fundamentals of EU membership and its discourse, such as modernization and Westernization, overlap with the basic long-standing philosophies of the Turkish military. Denying the EU discourse would therefore mean denying their own primary mission since the inception of the Republic, something they are obviously not willing to do.

The truth probably lies in a combination of the two explanations. The pro-EU discourse does seem to hold an irresistibly attractive message of welfare, democracy and becoming a part of the 'first-league' countries, leaving alternative discourse attempts basically marginalized and regressive. The strength of the discourse has even strengthened the actors who use it, allowing them to work more effectively to strengthen the discourse itself. It is understandable therefore, that the military would be unwilling to go against this popular front, opening itself up to unfamiliar criticism. Moreover, as discussed above, there are reasons to believe that the military is itself torn between its philosophy of modernization/liberalization, and its concerns over security. Nevertheless, at this point, it is difficult to believe that if the military had truly wanted to block particular liberalization attempts, such as the passage of these recent laws, it could not have done so.

The question then arises as to what the apparently torn military is likely to do in terms of future liberalization moves that will need to be made for EU accession. Presumably their preferred choice would be that the integration process continues to evolve, with the Europeans making substantive responses in recognition of Turkey's efforts, and with the security risks/prerogative cuts to the military remaining at a minimum. On the other hand, the military is likely holding on to a second possibility, which is that the current strength of the pro-EU discourse will be weakened by other developments. One such development could be the EU's failure to respond adequately to Turkey's reform efforts, leaving Turks feeling cheated. In addition, as the realities of integration become clearer, the current vague (but pleasant) characteristics of the pro-EU discourse could begin to ring hollow, with the integrated future looking far less idyllic. Similarly, this could be brought about by reconsiderations of the nature of some upcoming sensitive EU demands, such as the Cyprus issue. Ultimately, if the discourse began to lose its appeal, the military would no longer feel compelled to refrain from vocalizing traditional security-based understandings.

Conclusion

Recent geopolitical developments along Turkey's Middle Eastern borders have once again reminded it of the acuteness of the pendulum's security side. Turkey's security fears over the threat of Kurdish independence in northern Iraq and its possible implications for the citizens of Turkey's own southeastern region were among the many concerns behind Ankara's initial reluctance for international military action in Iraq. From the Turkish perspective, the status quo, no matter how imperfect, was highly preferable to the dangers of a post-Saddam Iraq. Yet with Turkish foot-dragging having failed to pre-empt the unwanted war, security perceptions continue to prevail in shaping Turkey's actions. With the same rationale that led Turkey to maintain a military presence in Northern Iraq since the middle 1990s, Turkey must now consider, in the period following Saddam's ouster, sending further troops alongside other international peacekeeping forces. Once again, involvement in the Middle East and its risky complexities is seen as the only way of protecting Turkey's own security. If Turkey agrees to send troops, it will be for the purpose of holding some degree of control over future developments along its south-eastern border. A main aspect of this control will require building up its relations with the United States, which, as the clear dominant power in the region, will hold considerable power over some of Turkey's most sensitive security threats, such as the future of the PKK.

Turkey will benefit by coming to accept the geographical reality of its position as a bridge between East and West. As Turkey continues on its globalization journey towards the West, it will no doubt have to do so with the inclusion of its Middle Eastern identity as well. Turkey needs, therefore, to convince both itself and the West that its Middle Eastern connections can be an asset (in ideational and geopolitical terms), not just a source of insecurity and backwardness. If Turkey succeeds at doing this, the historical pendulum between globalization and security, which has always appeared as a dichotomous phenomenon, may be transformed into a complementary one.

Notes

[1] Sefyi Taşhan, 'Contemporary Turkish Policies in the Middle East: Prospects and Constraints,' *Foreign Policy*, vol. 12, no. 1-2 (1985), pp. 7-21.
[2] William M. Hale, *Turkish Foreign Policy: 1774-2000* (London: Frank Cass, 2000), p. 47.

[3] Yasemin Çelik, *Contemporary Turkish Foreign Policy* (Westport: Praeger, 1999).

[4] The Cuban Missile Crisis produced an understanding that Turkey had been sold out, because the US negotiated secretly with the Soviets and agreed to remove Jupiter missiles from Turkish soil. The Johnson letter refers to an actual letter by President Lyndon Johnson, in which he warned Turkey that had they intervened in Cyprus in the 1960s, the US would not have defended them against any Soviet aggression. When Turkey finally did intervene in Cyprus, the US Congress promptly imposed an arms embargo. In later developments regarding the Cyprus issue, Turkey never saw its Western allies as taking its side.

[5] Ali M. Karaosmanoğlu, 'Turkey: Between the Middle East and Western Europe,' in Kemal H. Karpat, ed., *Turkish Foreign Policy: Recent Developments* (Madison: University of Wisconsin Press, 1996), p. 14.

[6] Philip Robins, 'Avoiding the Question,' in Henri J. Barkey, ed., *Reluctant Neighbor: Turkey's Role in the Middle East* (Washington, DC: United States Institute of Peace Press, 1996).

[7] Nur Bilge Criss and Pinar Bilgin, 'Turkish Foreign Policy towards the Middle East,' *Middle East Review of International Affairs* vol. 1, no. 1 (1997).

[8] This section draws on material presented in Ersel Aydinli, 'Decoding Turkey's Struggle with the PKK,' *Security Dialogue* vol. 33, no. 2 (2002), pp. 209-225.

[9] An historical example of this mistrust can be seen at the time of the dismissal of Sultan Abdulaziz by the modernizing Ottoman bureaucracy, and his replacement with Sultan Murat V. The following dialogue was recorded between a bureaucrat and the then prime minister, 'If we are not going to declare constitutional reform, why did we overthrow the Sultan, just to get a new one?' The response came, 'The state trusts you [bureaucrats]. Would you rather go ask the ignorant Turks of Anatolia about the destiny and security of our state?' Tevfik Çavdar, *Turkiye'nin Demokrasi Tarihi 1839-1950* [The History of Turkish Democracy 1839-1950] (Ankara: Imge-Ankara Kitabevi, 1999), p. 114.

[10] The new government, led by hawkish Ismet Inonu, introduced an emergency law called *Takrir-I Sukun* (Reconstruction of the Order), which gave every authority to the state in order to curb whatever it considered dangerous to its internal stability. The tribunals took advantage of this new law and shut down the party.

[11] Ahmet Agaoglu, *Servest Firka Hatiralari* [Free Party Memoirs] (Istanbul: Baha Matbaasi, 1969).

[12] The rebellion took place in a small town in Western Anatolia, where support for the Free Party was highly visible.

[13] Suat İlhan, personal interview by the author (Ankara, 20 April 2002).

[14] Personal observation by the author at a meeting at the Center for Eurasian Strategic Studies (ASAM). 'Sèvres syndrome' is a concept in Turkey, referring to the 1920 agreement that officially ended the Ottoman Empire and divided the Anatolian lands, creating an Armenian state and a Kurdish autonomous region with a possibility of independence in the future. The Turkish Independence War halted and made void the agreement. Nevertheless, since the Sèvres Agreement was imposed by Western powers, its goal to divide the country continues to weigh heavily in the common memories of the Turkish state and society.

[15] Suat İlhan, *Avrupa Birliğine Neden Hayır* [Why No to the European Union] (Istanbul: Ötüken Neşriyat A.Ş., 2000), p. 25.

[16] Ümit Özdağ, personal interview by the author (Ankara, Spring 2002).

[17] Unpublished document, obtained from former military commander.

[18] Former National Security Council member, personal interview by the author on customary condition of anonymity (Ankara, 4 May 2002).

[19] Ümit Özdağ, 'Avrupa Birliği ile Türkiye İlişkilerinin Jeopolitik Ekseni' [Geopolitical Dimensions of Turkey-EU Relations], unpublished paper (Ankara: 2002).

[20] Ali Özcan, interview with the author (Ankara, 2 April 2002).

[21] İlhan, personal interview by the author.

[22] Ali Resul Usul, personal interview by the author (April 2002). In addition, some of the ideas about the two groups' arguments and strategies stem from on on-going project with Usul.

[23] Erol Manisalı, *Yirmibirinci Yüzyılda Küresel Kıskaç: Küreselleşme, Ulus-devlet ve Türkiye* [Global Clamp in the 21st Century: Globalization, Nation-state, and Turkey] (Istanbul: Otopsi, 2001).

[24] İlhan, personal interview by the author.

[25] İlhan, personal interview by the author.

[26] Mehmet Ali İrtemçelik, personal interview by the author (Ankara, 10 May 2002).

[27] Council of Europe, *Protocol No. 6 to the Convention for the Protection of Human Rights and Fundamental Freedoms Concerning the Abolition of the Death Penalty*, European Treaty Series No. 114, Council of Europe, 13 August 2003 <http://conventions.coe.int/Treaty/en/Treaties/Word/114.doc>.

Chapter 9

American Hegemony and the Changing Terrain of Middle East International Politics

Michael C. Hudson

The occasion of Paul Noble's retirement provides an appropriate moment for us to reflect on the study of international relations and the Middle East. Specialists in these fields are indebted to 'the Montréal school' in general and to Paul Noble in particular for their contributions to the discipline. His classic analysis of 'the Arab system'[1] has been a cornerstone reading for many students for nearly two decades, and his more recent work[2] has helped us unravel the multiple, divergent effects of the post-Cold War environment on the prospects for inter-Arab cooperation in the new century. With his exemplary scholarly comprehensiveness, diligence and clarity to guide us, perhaps we will be inspired in our effort to interpret the extraordinary changes of recent decades in the region and the world.

    This chapter raises the question whether we need to reconsider our traditional understanding of the Middle East international system in light of the profound changes of recent years, and it asks whether the conventional theoretical approaches are adequate to the task. It is suggested that major transformations are occurring in five domains relating to culture, the economy, political structures, the nature of power, and finally the extension of America's hegemony over the region.

The Puzzle of the Modern Middle East International System

Looking back at the trajectory of Middle East international politics in the twentieth century, one begins to realize how difficult it is to understand it in terms of mainstream international relations theories, especially the dominant 'realist' approach in which the key concepts are states (as primary actors), power (and balances of power) and the insecurity of a relatively anarchic environment. Here was a region, as historian L. Carl Brown argued, penetrated yet never completely dominated by European imperialism; and despite that penetration it exhibited a kind of indigenous balance-of-power politics of constantly shifting alliances.[3] The arbitrary and 'illegitimate' birth of new states and regimes, especially in the Arab east, gave rise to a narrative of frustrated nationalism(s). Indeed, the *leitmotif* of Middle East international politics in the twentieth century was the apparently successful 'liberation' of often new and independent states from European imperialism. After the Second World War, with the emergence of the two superpowers, the region became a field of competition in the Cold War: one superpower or the other dominated certain states, but sometimes—as in the case of the United States and Israel—'the tail wagged the dog.' There was a debate over 'the Middle East as a subordinate international system'[4] as it seemed to be developing certain autonomous dynamics of its own. The newness of many of these states, and the praetorian-populist character of some regimes, led to a focus on the domestic determinants of foreign policy. Some of the best academic work in Middle East international relations, including that by members of the Montréal school, such as Bahgat Korany and Ali Dessouki's *The Foreign Policies of Arab States*,[5] focused on 'the foreign policy approach' to understanding regional dynamics. As transnational ideological projects faded and states became stronger (in terms of security and bureaucratic capacities at least) during the 1970s, most analysts believed that the regional system was 'maturing' and that structural-realism would become an increasingly satisfactory paradigm for understanding regional politics: interests and the balance of power (or, at least the 'balance of threat,' as Stephen Walt argued) would trump ideological projects.[6] Pragmatic balancing would prevail over ideological bandwagoning. The 'tense stability' (or 'stable tension'?) imposed on the region by Cold War competition gave way in the 1990s to a loose *'Pax Americana'* in which Washington, with the subordinate cooperation of Europe, exercised indirect domination. But the post-Cold war era quickly proved to be far less stable. By 2003 the US had become directly and simultaneously engaged in three regional wars—Afghanistan, Iraq (twice), and the 'war on terrorism,' with its Middle Eastern centre of gravity. In addition, it was engaged both diplomatically and (indirectly) militarily in the seemingly endless Palestinian-Israeli conflict.

Two main conflicts drew our attention. One of them, the question of Gulf security, seemed largely explainable in structural-realist terms. Indeed, it was marked by two 'classical' state-to-state wars, the Iraq-Iran war of 1980-88 and the Gulf war of 1990-91. But the metastasis of Gulf insecurity at the beginning of the new century into a theatre of the American 'war on terrorism'—in which Iraq and Iran were identified by Washington as part of an 'axis of evil'—seemed to stretch structural realism's definitions of conventional state-to-state contestation. The American invasion and occupation of Iraq in 2003 were opposed by the great majority of 'realist' international relations scholars, who simply did not believe the Bush administration's insistence that Saddam Hussein's regime was a threat to America's long-term security, owing to its weapons of mass destruction (WMD) capabilities, and the even less plausible argument that Iraq was implicated in al-Qa'ida's terrorist war against the US To be sure, American neoconservatives, raising 'realism' from an academic paradigm to an ideological mission, insisted, *à la* Thucydides, that the strong go as far as they can while the weak suffer what they must in those unruly parts of the world that have not yet been integrated into the Western liberal order of things. But one of the more thoughtful neoconservatives, Robert Kagan, insisted that America was acting, as it always had, to project its higher order of civilization to those places still in need of it.[7] Conventional realist theories of the balance of power would not explain such behaviour.

The other main conflict proved progressively less amenable to structural realist interpretation. For many years we tended mainly to view the Arab-Israeli struggle as a state-to-state affair, punctuated by wars in 1948, 1956, 1967, 1969 – 70, and 1973. The 1982 Israeli invasion of Lebanon was a little harder to fit into this conceptual box owing to the central role played by the Palestinian organizations—an emerging non-state actor—and the 1987 outbreak of the *intifada* 'war' was harder still to fit. Diplomatic initiatives over this period culminating in the Camp David Accords of 1978 were also structured—and studied—as state-to-state matters. But if structural-realism seemed to explain nicely the Egypt-Israel separate peace that emerged from Camp David, it had little to offer for understanding the failure of Camp David to solve the Palestinian problem, the 'heart of the issue.' Nor did it have much to contribute for enlightenment on the Oslo process (1993 – 2000), either for its initial success or its ultimate collapse. Assuming that 'the only remaining superpower' seriously intended to settle this problem, how could it possibly fail? The answer, perhaps, resides more in the nature of American domestic politics than in the global balance of power. And today, this festering conflict resonates transnationally throughout the Arab and Islamic world, linked to some extent to the new world war of our time, the 'war on terrorism,' a war that requires us to rethink the way we look at armed conflicts in the world today.

Rethinking the Middle East in World Politics

A central preoccupation of twentieth century international relations scholarship, framed as it generally was by structural-realist theory, was the 'stability of the state system,' and the debates revolved around power balances: bipolar vs. multipolar configurations; containment; arms races; nuclear deterrence; and the like. As we enter the twenty-first century, the terrain of international relations is different: not so much that we should totally abandon structural realism and a state-centred approach,[8] but enough that we do need to reconsider old approaches and pay more attention to newer ones. In general, we need to draw upon sociological and behavioural perspectives in order to get beneath the deductive abstractions of structural realism. We need to consider the growing importance of politico-economic factors in an increasingly globalized world. Oil and development issues clearly have particular resonance in explaining regional politics in the Middle East. And somehow we need to 'bring culture back in' to an area virtually marinated in utopian ideological movements and in which time-honoured norms of authority and community are challenged by new societal realities.

Indeed, the very term '*international* relations' seems increasingly quaint, especially in our region, since significant axis of conflict are no longer just between 'nations' (indeed many state actors today can hardly be considered 'nations' anyway), but between states and 'other things:' civil society, NGOs, international 'regimes,' movements, and networks. Even 'transnational' locutions can be misleading, as Peter Mandaville observes in his work on Islamist networks, inasmuch as they privilege a 'national' context that might better be replaced by the term 'translocal.'[9] There is a need somehow to bring culture back to the fore, to help us understand the growing influence of public opinion at all levels—subnational, national, transnational, supranational, and even translocal—and the information technologies that propel it. Conventional geographical categories too need rethinking, including that nineteenth-century term 'Middle East.' Constructivists may be too prone to reify transnational identities like 'pan-Arabism' and to exaggerate the speed and ease with which identities can be reimagined; nevertheless, if communities are to be defined through the density and significance of interactions of their putative members, then it is clear—especially since 11 September 2001—that the hoary terms 'Middle East,' 'North Africa,' and 'South Asia' no longer encompass the emerging regional, sub- and supra-national political conglomerates. Even from an American military-strategic perspective, these terms would seem to mean less and less, as the Pentagon grapples with battlefronts in the 'war on terrorism,' from the Philippines, Indonesia, and Malaysia, to Pakistan, Afghanistan and Kashmir, to Iran, Iraq, the Arabian Peninsula, Egypt and the Levant, to Chechnya, the Balkans, and western Europe, not to mention the American 'homeland' itself.

Five Domains of Transformation

Momentous changes—indeed, transformations—are occurring in the terrain of the Middle East in world politics. They should impel us to rethink our approaches to Middle East international relations. I contend that they are occurring across the following five domains:

The Cultural Domain: Communal identities are in flux as never before, fuelled by globalization trends and the new information technologies. Middle Easterners, and Arabs in particular, seem, if anything, increasingly polarized, or at least lacking in consensus, about principles of legitimate authority.

The Economic Domain: The triumph of liberal economic ideology worldwide, accompanied by the increase in commercial, financial, and technological flows centred on the advanced economies—in other words 'globalization'—relegates the Middle East region to deepened dependency.

The Structural Domain: States, less autonomous than before, now share the stage with a proliferation of non-state actors. These include not only the IGOs and NGOs discussed by writers on international regimes, but also dedicated transnational networks with the ideological will and the organizational capability to use force. The Middle Eastern state, in particular, while it has expanded its capabilities in many respects and remains strongly authoritarian, finds its legitimacy increasingly challenged by domestic societal forces and subject to powerful exogenous influences that can be supportive or subversive.

The Power Domain: Even more important than the proliferation of weapons of mass destruction, 'terrorism'—politically motivated organized violence against civilians—has become the great equalizer between the conventionally strong and weak. The suicide bomber is the 'smartest' weapon of the new century. It is necessary to retool analytically in order to understand balances of power, and the larger questions of stability and change, in the post-modern Middle East.

The American Domain: The United States stands astride this post-Cold War, post-modern globalized world, and the chief question for students of world politics or international relations is how stable this new order will turn out to be. Will America succeed, as hopeful conservatives such as Richard Haass and Robert Kagan have suggested, to 'integrate' the rest of the world to American preferences, or will the world degenerate, as pessimistic progressives such as Immanuel Wallerstein and Michael Hardt have warned, into a place of perpetual conflict rather than perpetual peace?[10]

The balance of this chapter unpacks these different domains in greater detail.

The Cultural Domain

An apparent feature of the globalized, high-tech, post-Cold War world is the accelerated molding and remolding of collective political identities across the traditional 'Middle East,' especially in the Arab world. This is a phenomenon whose larger effects remain to be seen. Nevertheless, it is not too early to speculate about the direction of things to come. Political scientists working on the Middle East have found the concept of political culture problematic at least in some of its early applications (ranging from Orientalist stereotyping to inadequate typologizing), and yet it seems indispensable (except perhaps to rational choice theorists) for any serious analysis of political legitimacy. Embedded cultural norms relating to authority and identity need to be studied, as do practices of communication. With the impact of new information technologies, questions need to be asked about the extent to which such norms and practices are being deconstructed, reconstructed, or replaced altogether.

We take as a starting point our rejection of the proposition that identities are permanently inscribed and 'primordial.' While some conservative Orientalists and historians may still hold this notion, most social scientists now accept that identity and community are to a significant degree constructed and subject to invention and reimagination. Anthropologists, for one, have shown these everywhere to be multiple and situational. Thus, for example, we must treat with scepticism assertions that sectarian identity in Lebanon is fixed and unmodifiable.

A snapshot of the identities 'map' of the Middle East today would reveal different domains of communal solidarity. It would reveal patriotic affiliations by citizens or subjects to their state, and even though most Arab states are problematic, we would be remiss not to recognize peoples' identities as Iraqi, Egyptian, or Jordanian, and so forth. If our camera had a fine lens, it would also reveal 'sub-national' (below the state level) communities of an ethnic or religious-sectarian character: Berbers, Maronites, Alawites, etc. And we would detect some 'sub-national' solidarity groupings like Kurds that are actually transnational, owing to the arbitrary drawing of 'lines in the sand' by imperialist powers. Were it equipped with a wide-angle lens, our camera would also capture 'supranational' communities defined by 'macro' linguistic and cultural-historical markers such as the community of Arabs in the geographically contiguous Arab countries and the significant geographically-disconnected diasporas. And the largest community of all would, of course, be the Islamic *umma*, noting the cleavage between the Sunni and Shi'a persuasions, and Muslim diasporas throughout the world.

At the risk of pushing our photographic metaphor too far, let us imagine that we have in hand three such snapshots: one from 1960, another from 1979, and a third from the 1990s and the present day. If our film could register the intensity of *'asabiyya* (group solidarity) at these various levels, our snapshot from 1960 might reveal a fairly intense pan-Arab identity, while state-level and sub-national solidarities would appear relatively pale. But by 1979 (the year of Egypt's separate peace treaty with Israel and the Islamic revolution in Iran), pan-Arabism would have faded, while state-level identifications would have become stronger. Also showing greater intensity would be some ethnic-sectarian 'minority' communities. Jumping ahead another twenty years, most dramatic perhaps would be the renewal—or, better, the reconstruction—of supranational Islamic solidarities. In the aftermath of the attacks of 11 September 2001 in New York and Washington, apparently by Islamist militants, one might expect the salience of transnational 'Islamism' to be greatly magnified, both within the Islamic world and outside it. For all concerned, the new information technologies have etched this particular construction of Islam on the global political consciousness, for better or for worse. Will the brutal symbolism of 9/11 intensify identification with a militant version of Islam, or will it on the contrary signify the moral bankruptcy of such a construction?

There was a time when political communities in the Middle East could be delineated essentially according to an ordinary map of the sovereign states of the region. Now we realize that communities are reconstructing themselves constantly and that they are not necessarily bounded by internationally recognized frontiers. Bedouin communities on the northern edge of the Sahara have more in common with each other than with loyalty to the North African countries with faraway capitals on the Mediterranean of which they are formally 'citizens.' Berber ethnic-national activism dominates areas within given countries and across borders. Thanks to American support, northern Iraq is being politically redefined as Kurdish, even as Turkey and the same American supporters seek to squelch Kurdish identity in eastern Turkey. Sudan remains formally a unified sovereign country, yet a Sudanese state patriotism, with loyalty to the government in Khartoum, is stubbornly contested by opposition groups in the south, with significant outside support. It may be an exaggeration to claim that there is a Shi'ite 'arc of crisis' including Iran, southern Iraq, eastern Arabia, northern Yemen, northern Syria and southern Lebanon, yet how integrated are the sovereign states that are bisected by the Sunni-Shi'a divide? Will post-Saddam Iraq, likely to be dominated by its Shi'a majority, develop a stable political order? Were the house of Saud to be overthrown, would Saudi Arabia remain in one piece? And how is it that many Arabs from Morocco to Kuwait are these days saying 'We are all Palestinians?' Should we consequently be studying a 'political community' of cosmopolitan upper-class businesspeople and/or technically trained professionals who are equally culturally 'at home' in London, Paris or Washington as they are where they actually live, in Casablanca, Cairo, or Dubai? The large diaspora communities of Turks in Germany, North African Arabs in France, and Levantine Arabs in Latin America, Canada and the United States used to be beyond the scope of 'Middle East international politics,' but how valid is this exclusion today? And, of course, what of an 'imagined' political community—an *umma*—of militant Islamist activists in some 60 countries, which supports organized and sometimes violent political action, even though its members may share neither land nor kinship nor common history?

No less important than the volatility of identities and the fluidity of their borders is the hotly contested negotiation over the bases of legitimate authority in the region. In its most visible manifestation, it pits Islamist challengers against relatively secularist authoritarian incumbents. But beneath this primary fault line lie other cleavages. Within Islam, the struggle over the 'correct' principles of governance continues to rage, as it has for much of the last two centuries, with the austere '*salafis*' contending with liberal reformers and with a clerical establishment subservient to particular regimes. And within the relatively secular camp we find liberal democrats contending with 'benevolent' authoritarian dictators. Hitherto, and instead of generating consensus, globalization has aggravated the differences over the proper bases of authority. Patrimonialism and kinship no longer carry the legitimating force they once did; the military may dominate many governments but its moral authority to do so has been tarnished. The hegemony of democracy as the globalized standard has yet to take hold across much of the Arab Middle East, in large part because it is tainted as an American product, even though America's material and cultural exports are avidly consumed. Indeed, America's claim to imperial moral authority is greeted with contempt, cynicism or weary acquiescence rather than genuine acceptance.

In short, the moral bases of governance and state behaviour which ideally should be anchored by fixed and stable consensuses on identity categories and authority principles are not; hence the ongoing crises of legitimation in this region, and the consequent challenges to regional stability. It remains to be seen whether the 'constructivist' tendency in international relations theory, which purports to accommodate identity factors and appreciate their malleability, is up to the task.

The Economic Domain

If, as Francis Fukuyama contended, the liberal model of the proper order of things in the world has triumphed over its competitors, in the economic realm this means that the neoclassical vision of competitive market economies integrated into the global economic order is today's 'gold standard.'[11] The United States utilizes its global hegemony to move recalcitrant regions toward this model. Ideology is harmoniously linked to a set of measurable commercial, financial and technological trends collectively known as 'globalization,' which has emerged as a conceptual anchor for our understanding of the post-Cold War world (the Arabs have now coined the term *'al-'awlama'* to designate it). The concept refers to 'increasing levels of interdependence over vast distances,' along economic, cultural, environmental, and political dimensions.[12] There is persuasive quantitative evidence for the robustness of this trend over the decade of the 1990s, although the very recent indications suggest a retreat, owing to the world economic slowdown and the attacks of 11 September 2001.[13] In the economic and environmental realms the 'global village' metaphor suggests both a generalized interdependence (and a subjective awareness of it) that at once links economic and societal actors in a region such as the Middle East to larger global communities, and also reduces the decisional latitude of sovereign governmental authorities in the face of international 'regimes,' which in turn are influenced by 'Empire.' In the cultural and political realms, the popular distinction between Benjamin Barber's 'Jihad vs. McWorld'[14] actually masks, as Mohammed A. Bamyah has pointed out, a peculiar symbiosis between 'traditionalist' establishments like the Saudi state and the instruments of modern technology: tradition is an instrument for achieving modernity.[15] Similarly, it has been noted by Jon Anderson, among others, that pan-Islamist organizations have seized upon globalizing technologies like the internet to advance (or should we say restore?) a mythical traditionalist order.[16]

But globalization can be a divisive as well as integrative force, and this seems especially the case in the Middle East. On the governmental level, certain heads of state may be more 'at home' in the cosmopolitan environment of major world capitals than they are in their own. Computerized intelligence sharing among Arab interior ministries (now, after 9/11, probably interconnected to a greater degree than ever with their American and other Western counterparts) illustrates lateral globalized integration on the level of governmental and security agencies. Yet many of these Middle Eastern leaders and the 'ruling circles' around them, globally 'wired' as they are, are perhaps more isolated from their people than they ever were. And while there may be a parallel lateral pattern of linkages from organizations in Middle Eastern civil society with 'global civil society,' the evidence of growing vertical participatory linkages with their own governments, while existent, is not particularly robust. The term 'digital divide' captures the likely growing distance between elites and masses inside established states, and it also appears to be widening, relatively, between regions such as Africa and the Middle East on the one hand, and the US and the industrialized, high-tech societies on the other. If it is true that the 'masses' in the Middle East are being increasingly left behind in global economic and social development, one might expect the level of discontent to be exploitable by some remarkably high-tech militant networks. An additional source of tension derives from the unevenness of globalization across the lower classes in the Middle East, where most have inadequate opportunity to partake in the global economy: they may be falling behind but they can also see that they are falling behind, as satellite TV is everywhere while internet connections are not. Fundamentally, however, globalization exacerbates the dependency of Middle Eastern political and economic elites on the West, above all the United States.

The Structural Domain

In the Arab political landscape from the Second World War unto almost the present day, the state steadily emerged as the dominant feature. It grew dramatically in terms of size, revenues, and coercive capacity. It also enjoyed, early on, a certain degree of legitimacy derived from the successful struggle against Western imperialism in its various forms.

One group of states embarked on a nationalist-reformist project, led mainly by military officers and a professional, reform-minded middle-class stratum. The authoritarian-populist regimes in these states framed the public priorities in terms of economic development through import-substitution-industrialization, egalitarianism through land reform and the emasculation of the very wealthy, and mobilization to unify the Arab nation, redress the grievous *nakba* (catastrophe) of Palestine, and prevent Western neo-imperialist designs on the Arab region. For them the Soviet Union became a balancer against Western encroachment and, to some extent, a model for political and economic development. Egypt, Algeria, Tunisia, Libya, Syria, Iraq, and the two Yemens pursued this course in their various ways.

A second group, while passively accepting much of the nationalist project, including the leading role of the state, featured regimes with an avowedly 'traditional' and 'patriarchal' character. These included Saudi Arabia, the other small Arabian states, Jordan, Lebanon, and Morocco. Unlike the 'nationalists,' and with the exception of Lebanon, these regimes celebrated their Islamic authenticity rather than relegating it to a lower priority. Many were rentier states: major oil exporters in which vast revenues accrued directly to the state or the dynastic regimes. Their well-to-do classes were co-opted rather than suppressed, and harnessed to non-'socialist' development plans; and their external orientation favoured the West as a bulwark against the challenges posed by the transnational ideological appeal of the 'progressive' states.

Both groups of states practiced, in varying degrees, a monolithic populist mobilization strategy. Political liberalization, let alone pluralistic democracy, was not on the agenda, except perhaps for Lebanon. The state led, framing the public agenda; society followed, deferentially and passively. The post-colonial Arab state, and state system, came to occupy a subordinate position in the post-Second World War, bipolar superpower-dominated global order. As pan-Arabism waned, following the defeat of Egypt's Jamal 'Abdel Nasser in the 1967 war with Israel, some Middle East specialists observed what they believed to be a 'maturing' of the Arab state system: individual states were becoming more autonomous, self-contained, self-interested, Weberian, and Westphalian. The states of the region were behaving as structural-realist international relations theory would have them behave: as rational self-help units, pragmatically sensitive to the global distribution of power. From the perspective of the two rival superpowers, the Middle East was a region of contestation in which each constructed client blocs that came to mimic their patrons, in what Middle East scholar Malcolm Kerr called 'the Arab Cold War.'

The terrain began to shift in the 1980s. Notwithstanding their bureaucratic 'overdevelopment,' states that seemed dominant over their societies began to falter, unable to continue to deliver on the socioeconomic promises that had tacitly fostered political passivity. Decades of considerable economic growth came to an end with the collapse of oil prices in the middle 1980s. The oil-rich rentier regimes experienced huge revenue declines. The nationalist-progressive ideological formulas of regimes began to fade. And the bipolar global order came to an end with the eclipse and demise of the Soviet Union, leaving the United States the hegemon of an increasingly integrated global economy and financial system, informed by an ascendant ideology of economic and political liberalism. International financial institutions, heavily influenced by the United States, came to intervene in the most sensitive of domestic policy issues in countries around the world, including most of those in the Islamic and Arab worlds. Westphalian sovereignty as a practical matter was being undermined everywhere. In the military sphere, where only the United States possessed a global reach, 'humanitarian interventions' (even failed ones) served notice on dictators that 'the international community' might intrude militarily against regimes whose internal policies egregiously violated international standards.

While states across the Arab world continued to expand their bureaucratic and *mukhabarat* (police and surveillance) capabilities, their authority was being increasingly challenged from both domestic and international sources. Arab societies began to display greater vitality than before, with associations and NGOs emerging during the 1980s to articulate alternative agendas and priorities, although rarely to participate in the policy-making process. Political scientists observed the new trend and produced a number of studies depicting the growth of what Richard Norton described as more 'vibrant' political societies, while also subjecting the once all-powerful, stable '*mukhabarat* state' to revisionist interpretations, of which perhaps the most cogent was Nazih Ayubi's book *Over-Stating the Arab State*.[17] But it was far from clear where the new societal energy would lead. While a stratum of intellectuals and business leaders sought to advance projects of political liberalization and democratization, it did not appear to be garnering a broad popular constituency. The far more rooted societal tendency belonged to the Islamists. And on the global level, as leader of a new global order, the United

States during the 1990s struggled to define its role, whether as 'umpire' during the Clinton administration, or perhaps as 'empire,' as the administration of George W. Bush seemed to be leaning during its first three years in office. Owing to America's overarching presence in the Middle East (particularly after the collapse of the Soviet Union) by virtue of its oil connection and its support for Israel, the direction of American policy could not but have a major impact both on states and societies. But by the same token, developments in the region could not be ignored for long in Washington, especially were they to spill over into the United States itself. Against this backdrop of (relatively) weakening states, societal ferment, and the new global order, the twin developments of transnational information technologies and political networking in the Arab world have the potential to accelerate sociopolitical change, contestation and uncertainty.

The Power Domain

Traditional 'realist' international relations literature conceived of power essentially in military terms, and even today defence ministries around the world calculate the balance of power in terms of the size of armies and the quality of weapons. Later, during the Second World War, economic size and growth rates were added to the equation. Today, in the age of global mass communications, culture—the ability, as American policy planners put it, 'to shape hearts and minds'—is recognized as still another dimension of power. Both sides on the American-Middle Eastern battle lines recognize the importance of the new cultural power: Americans launch popular culture 'missiles' over the radio and television, and radical Islamists and nationalists evoke powerful religious symbols to mobilize resistance.

Power in its more traditional meaning of instruments of violence has also undergone a transformation in two ways. On the American side, the historically unmatched resources being poured into the military establishment have created a defence establishment that is quantitatively and qualitatively unrivalled. In the international solar system America is the sun and all others are either planets or asteroids. But on the Middle Eastern side, there has also been a power revolution. It does not involve some quantum leap forward in the military power of states and conventional armies. Rather, it resides in the ability of networks to utilize low-tech violence in ingenious, hard-to-detect ways. 'Terrorism' is the generic name given to these techniques, which are exemplified by the threat of weapons of mass destruction (biological and chemical, mainly) and hard-to-detect, cleverly-delivered high explosives. The suicide bomber is the quintessential expression of Middle East terrorism. Given these new developments, calculating the 'balance of power' becomes a very complicated exercise and a challenge to international relations theorists.

Networks have become the most effective structural vehicle for Middle Eastern resistance. States and governments are too easily defeated, intimidated or co-opted. According to Manuel Castells, '[n]etworks constitute the new social morphology of our societies, and the diffusion of networking logic substantially modifies the operation and outcomes in processes of production, experience, power, and culture.' [18] Networks, he goes on to suggest, function most effectively as long as they share the same communications codes. Nationalist and Islamist symbols are particularly effective codes.

Islamist networks indeed seem to be particularly successful. There are four research questions that might help explain why this is the case; questions, however, that could be asked about network political organizations in general in the Arab east. First, how potent and socially pervasive is the symbolic content of the value agenda that their leaders frame? Second, how do they recruit, retain, and deepen the commitment of members of the network? Third, to what extent can they build upon and benefit from existing kinship, occupational, educational or financial networks? And fourth, does the information technology revolution allow political networks to extend their reach beyond face-to-face relationships; or to put it another way, can social capital (and trust) travel through cyberspace?

This is not the place to try and answers these questions exhaustively. But a casual survey of formal Islamist political networks like the Organization of the Islamic Conference, and less formal or even clandestine movements such as the Egyptian *gama'at*, the Shi'a networks of Lebanon, Iran and Iraq, the Palestinian Islamist groups, similar organizations in North Africa, and even the notorious al-Qa'ida, suggests that on all counts they can advance their agendas. First, with respect to the symbolic agenda, one does not have to go so far as some authors and claim that the whole discourse of contemporary Arab politics has become Islamicized to observe that the array of programs and projects encapsulated by the slogan 'Islam is the Solution' resonates deeply with individuals mired in the tensions and contradictions of contemporary Arab societies. Moreover, the pervasiveness of these symbols, especially when associated with longstanding nationalist concerns, extends throughout society and is not simply the concern of members. Thus an Islamist network like al-Qa'ida swims in a nutritious societal 'sea.' This is why it is incorrect to designate al-Qa'ida a cult, and why, despite its commission of morally atrocious acts, it enjoys at least passive support across social strata and also transnationally.

Second, as Carrie Wickham[19] observed in her study of Islamists in Egypt, drawing upon social movement theorists such as Douglas McAdam,[20] the network itself produces the social capital rewards for membership in addition to the instrumental agendas being put forth. Codes of dress and deportment are among the social cues, and pressures that attract and consolidate commitment to the cause. During the repressive periods in the regimes of Anwar Sadat and Husni Mubarak, the Islamists migrated into the subaltern and protected spaces in Egyptian society to find sanctuary and launch new initiatives to participate in high politics. Third, Islamist networks appear to be able to 'piggy-back' on pre-existing social and cultural networks. Al-Qa'ida, as noted above, may ride the *hawala* financial networks. Some say it free-rides on Arabian honey-trading networks. Did Usama bin Ladin's family and business networks indirectly enable the development of his political network? Islamist networks appear to originate in the 'old school ties' of schools and universities. The Taliban founders may have been alumni of the

Deobandi seminary. The Shi'a network organizers of Amal, Hizbullah and the Da'wa formed lasting bonds in the seminaries of Qom and Najaf. The Egyptian networkers may have first crossed paths at Al-Azhar. Shi'a American Muslim extremists networked in the storefront mosques of Jersey City and Brooklyn. Non-Islamist opposition networks also 'piggy-back.' Hanna Batatu's meticulous work on the Iraqi Communists and the Syrian Ba'thists reveals their sectarian and regional interconnections.[21] The founders of the Syrian Social National Party and the Arab Nationalists' Movement perhaps utilized alumni and student networks of the American University of Beirut as a platform for their own transnational political projects.

Finally, a case can be made that the internet and satellite television networks may vastly extend the global reach of transnational Islamist (and non-Islamist) networks. Whether it is Shaykh Qaradawi's call-in program on *al-Jazira* or the substantial communities constructed electronically around the *Islam On Line* internet portal, these communities in cyberspace, as Jon Anderson has described them, may constitute an enormous recruitment pool for future exploitation by the dedicated political networks.[22] Networks, then, are the sinews of a new kind of power in Middle East politics.

The American Domain

Since the Second World War, American influence throughout the Middle East has steadily expanded. It has come at the expense of other outside competitors, first France and Britain, then later the Soviet Union. It has also contained, if not eliminated, the main domestic challenges of nationalism and socialism. Its steadfast and increasingly generous support of Israel, in the face of universal Arab opposition, has allowed the Jewish state to consolidate its position as the most powerful state in the region. It has courted friendly ruling elites in virtually every Arab country with considerable success. The spate of anti-American violence in Lebanon following the Islamic revolution in Iran gradually dissipated and the Iranian regime moderated its activities following the death of Ayatollah Khomeini. The old anti-American coalitions, supported by the Soviet Union, dissipated with the collapse of the USSR. When Iraq invaded Kuwait in 1990, the US was able to forge an international coalition that included major Arab participants—Egypt, Syria, Saudi Arabia and others—in the campaign to drive Saddam Hussein back and punish his regime. At the same time Washington seized upon the Oslo negotiations between Israel and the Palestine Liberation Organization to shepherd a diplomatic process intended to settle the Arab-Israeli conflict once and for all. From the vantage point of the early 1990s, then, an analyst of Middle East international politics might have concluded that a 'normal' regional order was finally within reach, with the United States playing a fairly nuanced paternal role, its military involvements judicious and its diplomacy energetic.

But a decade later the picture was different. Militant Islamist networks were utilizing terror methods to attack American targets in Saudi Arabia, Yemen and elsewhere. The Washington-sponsored Arab-Israeli 'peace process' stalled and finally collapsed. American efforts to encourage a Middle East-North Africa economic community were derailed. American-led sanctions against the Iraqi regime angered Arab public opinion because of the collateral damage to Iraqi civilians. Then came the attacks of 11 September 2001 in New York and Washington. 11 September 2001 galvanized the US administration into formulating a new national security doctrine a year later to confront the dangerous post-Cold war world. Influenced by neoconservative perspectives, it laid a strategy of 'pre-emption,' whereby the United States would bring 'order' to a world in which transnational adversaries had been able to attack the very heartland of the United States and strike devastating blows to the most cherished symbols of its global economic and military power. The George W. Bush administration, strongly supported by American public opinion, unleashed American military power to depose the Taliban regime in Afghanistan and decimate the al-Qa'ida infrastructure there. It mobilized its intelligence and law-enforcement apparatus to uncover terrorist cells around the world and inside the United States. And in 2003, claiming that Iraq possessed weapons of mass destruction and was supporting Islamist terrorism, the Bush administration ordered the 'liberation' of Iraq: America's first invasion and occupation of an Arab country. American involvement, according to the neoconservatives, would not stop at mere geographical occupation: the larger goal was to induce Arab societies to reform themselves politically, economically, and culturally in order to 'drain the swamp' that nurtured anti-American terrorism. The United States henceforth would use its power and influence to promote liberal democracy, liberal economic restructuring, and reform of the educational and cultural systems to promote liberal values in place of alleged bigotry and hatred. As National Security Advisor Condoleeza Rice put it, '...America and our friends and allies must engage broadly throughout the region across many fronts, including diplomatic, economic and in helping to establish institutions of civil society.'[23]

The dramatic new assertiveness of the United States in the Middle East poses interesting questions for students of international relations. Is the Westphalian framework still applicable, when what the French call the American 'hyper-power' attempts to intervene in a state's domestic as well as external affairs? Or is it more akin to Rome's relations with its unruly Gallic and German frontier regions? Is the Middle East regional system now so subordinate to the United States that it has lost whatever independence it might have enjoyed in the earlier period of great power bipolarity? On the face of it, it seems plausible that classical realism still provides the best explanation: the strong do all that they can to dominate a hostile environment, and the weak must submit. Neoconservatives like to argue that it is such a dangerous world that extraordinary pre-emptive, indeed preventive, measures must be taken. But is the world really that dangerous? Most academic realist theorists would say no. And in any case, is security really the driving force behind American policy today, or is it just a mask for a profound 'national ideology' to spread American values to the entire world? As we have seen, neoconservative writer Robert Kagan admits that this may be the case. 'Realism,' then, is no longer a paradigm for understanding and predicting international behaviour; it becomes an ideology for a particular ruling circle.

Historically, successful empires owed their success to their ability to rule with peace and stability for long periods of time. They needed to do more than simply win wars. The '*Pax Romana*' brought a degree of order and capability to subdue far-flung 'barbarian' societies in Europe, many of which later merged into (and finally conquered) the empire. The Ottoman empire ruled much of this region for a very long time under a '*Pax Islamica*'—a combination of religious authority and bureaucratic capacity. Britain dominated much of it with a '*Pax Britannica*'—with the moral authority of 'Western civilization' combined with judicious colonial administration. In the 21st century can the United States construct a '*Pax Americana*' through its instruments of military pre-emption and political-diplomatic 'integration'? Can it provide '*pax*'? Can it provide development and good government? The American occupation of Iraq, in its initial stages at least, does not appear promising. And what kind of moral authority does America possess to accomplish these tasks in a region where sovereignty and independence, though frayed, are still widely cherished, and some of America's policies are so abhorred?

Conclusion

I suggest that we need to rethink our approaches to Middle East international relations because the terrain of Middle East in world politics is changing in each of the following five domains: (1) The Cultural Domain, where communal identities are in flux as never before, fuelled by globalization trends and new information technology; (2) The Economic Domain, in which globalization—the commercial, financial, and technological flows centred on the advanced economies—relegates the Middle East region to deepened dependency, while neoclassical development strategies deepen inequalities and social tensions; (3) The Structural Domain, in which the pre-eminence of states is challenged by societal and transnational structures; (4) The Power Domain, where 'terrorism' and the proliferation of certain weapons of mass destruction dramatically alter the traditional conceptions of 'balance of power'; and (5) above all, The American Domain. This last domain predominates because America's global hegemony appears to be beyond challenge by any state or combination of states, because 'Realism' as an ideology has—for the time being at least—captured America's power centres, and because the principal security problem for the United States lies in the greater Middle East and Islamic world: not in the Middle East state system but in its larger societal and transnational domains.

Will the United States eventually subdue and transform its adversaries in the greater Middle East, so that this region *in toto*—not just its leaders and governments, already compliant in the face of American requirements—will be fully integrated into the larger *Pax Americana* which already extends to such a great portion of the globe? An adequate international relations theory must be able to provide the intellectual traction to deal with this question. It follows, then, that such a theory must illuminate the domestic politics of American foreign and security policymaking. It must cast analytical light on the neoconservative network that currently molds US policy, while explaining American perceptions of the Middle East and Islam, comparing and contrasting the influence of key lobbies and interest groups, and conversely, leading us to a better understanding of how political forces in the region—and not just governments—perceive and behave toward America.

This is not to suggest that intra-regional politics—one of the principal focuses of this volume—are unimportant. Indeed, if only in light of the region's 'problematic' status in the eyes of American neoconservatives, there is a need to try and comprehend the new forces at work. It is a complex picture. Inter-state relations are changing in the face of American and global pressures, political and economic. What is the future of the League of Arab States or the Gulf Cooperation Council when the United States and its allies are trying to erect a 'new security architecture' for the region, in which Israel and Turkey will play ever larger roles? Can Arab regional alliances and organizations be relevant when the US prefers bilateral relationships? Certainly, non-state actors need to be accorded greater attention, especially transnational networks, 'terrorist' or otherwise; and in the same vein, it is important to calculate the effects of the new media and information technologies in reshaping political identities and commitments across borders.

For international relations theorists of the Middle East, classical realism clearly is not enough, despite the fact that some American neoconservatives believe they are walking in the footsteps of Thucydides and Machiavelli. Nor is a simple 'second image' approach, which holds that the independent variables are essentially domestic. A 'clash of civilizations' model is reductionist. Culture and economics increasingly matter. Middle East international relations in the twenty-first century will not be adequately explained by paradigmatic chauvinism; rather, disciplinary eclecticism offers a more promising path.

Notes

This chapter is a revision of a paper presented at the Conference in Honour of Professor Paul Noble, Montréal, 19-20 June 2002.

[1] Paul C. Noble, 'The Arab System: Pressures, Constraints and Opportunities,' in Bahgat Korany and Ali E. Hillal Dessouki, eds., *The Foreign Policies of Arab States*, 2nd ed. (Boulder: Westview Press, 1991).
[2] Noble, 'Prospects for Arab Cooperation in a Changing Regional and Global System,' in Michael C. Hudson, ed., *Middle East Dilemma: The Politics and Economics of Arab Integration* (New York: Columbia University Press, 1999).
[3] L. Carl Brown, *International Politics and the Middle East: Old Rules, Dangerous Game* (Princeton: Princeton University Press, 1984).
[4] Leonard Binder, 'The Middle East as a Subordinate International System,' in Binder, *The Ideological Revolution in the Middle East* (New York: Wiley, 1964).

[5] Korany and Dessouki, eds., *The Foreign Policies of Arab States: The Challenge of Change*, 2nd ed. (Boulder: Westview Press, 1991).

[6] See Stephen M. Walt, *The Origins of Alliances* (Ithaca: Cornell University Press, 1987).

[7] Robert Kagan, *Of Paradise and Power* (New York: Knopf, 2003), pp. 85-87.

[8] Stephen D. Krasner, 'Sovereignty,' *Foreign Policy* no. 122 (January-February 2001), pp. 20-29.

[9] Peter Mandaville, 'Reimagining the Ummah: Transnationalism and the Changing Boundaries of Muslim Political Discourse,' paper delivered to the Conference on Globalization, State Capacity, and Islamic Movements, University of California at Santa Cruz (Santa Cruz, CA, 7 – 10 March 2002).

[10] See Richard N. Haass, 'Foreign Policy in a Post-Post-Cold War World,' the 2002 Arthur Ross Lecture, Foreign Policy Association (New York, 22 April 2002); Kagan, *Of Paradise and Power*; Immanuel Wallerstein, 'America and the World: The Twin Towers as Metaphor,' in Craig Calhoun, Paul Price and Ashley Timmer, eds., *Understanding September 11* (New York: Social Science Research Council and New Press, 2002); Michael Hardt, 'War and Empire,' lecture at the conference in honour of Professor Hisham Sharabi, Georgetown University (Washington, DC, 26 – 27 April 2002); and Hardt and Antonio Negri, *Empire* (Cambridge: Harvard University Press, 2000).

[11] Francis Fukuyama, *The End of History and the Last Man* (New York: Free Press, 1992).

[12] 'Measuring Globalization,' *Foreign Policy* no. 122 (January-February 2001), p. 56.

[13] 'Globalization's Last Hurrah?' *Foreign Policy* no. 128 (January-February 2002).

[14] Benjamin Barber, 'Jihad vs. McWorld,' *The Atlantic Monthly* vol. 269, no. 3 (March 1992), pp. 53-65.

[15] Mohammed A. Bamyeh, *The Ends of Globalization* (Minneapolis: University of Minnesota Press, 2000), pp. 80-81.

[16] Jon W. Anderson, 'The Internet and Islam's New Interpreters,' in Dale F. Eickelman and Jon W. Anderson, eds., *New Media in the Muslim World* (Bloomington, IN: Indiana University Press, 1999).

[17] Augustus Richard Norton, 'The Future of Civil Society in the Middle East,' *Middle East Journal* vol. 47, no. 2 (Spring 1993), pp. 206-16.

[18] Manuel Castells, *The Rise of the Network Society*, 2nd ed. (Oxford: Blackwell, 1996, 2000), p. 500.

[19] Carrie Wickham, 'Constructing Incentives for Opposition Activism: Islamist Outreach and Social Movement Theory,' paper presented at the Annual Conference of the Middle East Studies Association (Chicago, 5 December 1998).

[20] Gary T. Marks and Douglas McAdam, *Collective Behavior and Social Movements* (New York: Prentice-Hall, 1994).

[21] Hanna Batatu, *The Old Social Classes and the Revolutionary Movements of Iraq* (Princeton: Princeton University Press, 1978); and Batatu, *Syria's Peasantry, the Descendants of Its Lesser Rural Notables, and Their Politics* (Princeton: Princeton University Press, 1999).

[22] Anderson, 'Cybarites, Knowledge Workers and New Creoles of the Information Superhighway,' *Anthropology Today*, vol. 11, no. 4 (August 1995), pp. 13-15.

[23] Condoleeza Rice, 'Remarks at the National Association of Black Journalists Convention,' 7 August 2003, *WashingtonPost.com*, 7 August 2003 <http://www.washingtonpost.com /ac2/wp-dyn/A30602-2003Aug7>.

Index

Abdullah, Crown Prince of Saudi Arabia
 (Abdullah bin Abdulaziz), 5, 7, 130-1
Abdullah II, King of Jordan (Abdullah
 bin Al Hussein), 129-30
Abu Musa (Persian Gulf), 72, 77
Abu Sayyaf, 6
accommodation, 3, 34, 65-7, 69, 88
 and conflict, 66
 and cooperation, 65-7, 76-7
 Iran-Saudi Arabia, 71-2
 procedural, 67
 substantive, 67
Afghanistan, 1, 5-6, 112, 126, 134, 150,
 164, 166, 176
Africa, 37-8, 53-6, 135-6, 170
 North, 37-9, 51, 53-6, 132, 135, 166,
 174, 176
Al-Azhar (Egypt), 175
Alawites, 168
Alevites, 156
Alexandria (Egypt), 128
Algeria, 45, 92, 171
al-Jama'a al-Islamiyya, 6
al-Jazira, 44, 132-4, 175
al-Qa'ida, 6, 9, 164, 174, 176
Amal, 175
American University of Beirut, 175
anarchy, 16-17, 30-1, 34-5, 41, 47, 84,
 88, 152
Anderson, Jon, 170, 175
anti-Americanism, 70, 76-7
Aqazadeh, Gholam, 76
Arab-Israeli conflict, 1, 10, 17, 19-20,
 24, 39, 41, 51, 75, 86, 94, 125, 164-5
 al-Aqsa intifada (2001-Present), 51,
 125-9, 133, 144-5
 Camp David Accords (1978), 71, 165
 Camp David II negotiations (2000),
 135
 first intifada (1987-91), 19, 95, 125-
 6, 165
 Israeli invasion of Lebanon (1982),
 19, 85 126, 131, 165

Israeli War of Independence (1948),
 85-6, 165
Madrid process (1991), 7-8
October War (1973), 19, 41, 71, 167
Oslo process (1993-2001), 7, 165,
 175
Palestine-Jordan 'Black September'
 conflict (1970), 85
Quartet, 10
Roadmap to Peace (2003), 10
Sinai War (1956), 165
Six Day War (1967), 4, 50, 71, 85-6,
 126, 165, 172
War of Attrition (1969-70), 165
Arafat, Yasser, 135
Aras River, 110
Armenia, 110, 155
Aron, Raymond, 19
Asad, al-, Bashar, 95
Asad, al-, Hafiz, 83, 86-7, 95-6
Asia, 36-8, 40, 43, 46, 51, 54-5, 92, 144
 East, 37, 54-6, 135-6
 South, 37, 53-6, 132, 135-7
 Southeast, 37, 53-6
Atatürk, Mustafa Kemal, 152
Australia, 56
'axis of evil', 164
Aydinli, Ersel, 6
Aydınlık, 155
Ayubi, Nazih, 92, 172
Azerbaijan, 107, 110, 114-15

Baghdad (Iraq), 9, 11, 131
Baghdad Pact (1955), 22, 86, 150
balance of power, 23, 68, 74, 84, 95-6,
 153, 163, 165, 167, 173, 177
 'balance of weakness', 42
 bipolar, 16, 20, 22-3, 34, 48, 50, 165
 impact on regional conflicts, 65
 multipolar, 2, 16, 18, 20-1, 23, 34,
 41-2, 51, 165
 unipolar, 6, 11, 18, 20, 21-3, 51, 68
Bamyah. Mohammed A., 170

Barber, Benjamin, 139, 170
Barnett, Michael, 86-7, 144
Batatu, Hanna, 175
Bedouins, 94, 168
Beirut Declaration (2002), 130
Beqa' (Lebanon), 9
Berbers, 168
Bianchi, Robert, 92
Binder, Leonard, 36
Brecher, Michael, 36, 83
Brown, L. Carl, 36, 163
Brynen, Rex, 4-7
Bush, George W., 130-1, 134, 142, 144,
    164, 173, 176
Buzan, Barry, 31, 36

Cairo (Egypt), 128
Canada, 142, 169
Cantori, Louis, 36
Caribbean, 37-8, 53-6
Castells, Manuel, 173
causality
    efficient, 35, 47, 50-1, 58-9
    motivating, 35, 42-3, 47-8, 59, 68,
        70, 76, 78
    permissive, 35, 42, 47-8, 50-2, 58-9,
        68-9, 78
    stimulus, 35, 58-9, 68-9, 78
Çeçen, Anıl, 157
Central America, 37-8, 53-6
Chechnya, 166
China, People's Republic of, 36-8, 49,
    53, 56, 117, 153
Clinton, Bill, 173
Cold War, 34, 48-51, 65, 71, 139, 150,
    163-4
    Egypt, 22
    unipolarity after, 4, 6, 22, 49, 68, 167
colonialism, 1, 16-17, 137, 171, 177
Convention on the Protection of Human
    Rights and Fundamental Freedoms
    (1950), 157-8
Convention Relating to the Status of
    Refugees (1951), 112
Copts, 139
corporatism, 83, 87, 91-5
Cuban Missile Crisis, 150
Cyprus, 150, 153-6, 160

Damascus Declaration (1991), 71-2
David, Stephen R., 84, 87

Da'wa, 175
Dawisha, Adeed, 83
democracy, 11, 22, 31, 46, 74, 84, 141,
    155-6, 159, 169, 171-2, 176
Deobandi seminary (Pakistan), 175
Devine, James, 3, 6
Dessouki, Ali, 21, 36, 164
diasporas, 73, 168-9
Dicle, Hatip, 161
Diyarbakir (Turkey), 156
Dura, al-, Muhammad, 128

Egypt, 2, 4, 8, 18, 20, 22, 36-8, 40-1, 45,
    49-50, 53-4, 56, 71, 75-6, 86-7, 92,
    117, 128, 130-2, 134, 137, 139, 142,
    165-6, 168, 171-2, 174-5
    accommodation of Israel, 71
El-Meehy, Asya, 3-4
environment
    operating, 68
    policy-making, 68-9
Erdogan, Recep Tayyip, 8, 151
Europe, 6, 55, 73, 149, 151, 153, 155-6,
    164, 166, 177
    Eastern, 51
European Court of Human Rights, 158
European Movement 2002, 158
European Union, 6, 9-10, 36, 38, 51-2,
    149-51, 153-60
    European Commission, 156-7
    European Parliament, 155, 157

foreign policy, 32, 34, 59, 66, 69, 77
Fogg, Karen, 155
France, 36-7, 89-90, 143-4, 169, 175-6
Friedberg, Aaron, 34
Front Islamique du Salut, 75
Fukuyama, Francis, 170

Gause, F. Gregory, III, 2-3, 36, 86
Gaza (Palestine), 126, 128, 133, 137
Germany, 36, 89-90, 169
Ghayth, Sulayman Abu, 10
globalization, 1, 6-7, 10, 78, 127, 141,
    149, 151, 153-4, 157, 164-7, 169-70,
    177
    economic integration, 2, 6, 11, 21, 31,
        40, 46, 52, 56, 58, 77, 166, 172,
        177
    impact on regional conflicts, 65, 77
Gramsci, Antonio, 85

great powers, 16, 19, 21-2, 36, 50
Gulf Cooperation Council (GCC), 40,
    42, 71-2, 77, 178
  'Six-plus-two agreement', 71
Gulf War (1990-91), 5, 7-8, 19, 24, 39,
    70-1, 73, 75, 95-6, 125, 133, 164
Gulf War (2003), 1, 5, 7-10, 41, 50, 75,
    126, 151, 160, 164

Haass, Richard, 167
HADEP (People's Democracy Party),
    156
Hajj, the, 73
Hamas, 75
Harakat Ansar al-Islam, 6
Haram al-Sharif (Jerusalem), 127
Hardt, Michael, 167
Hebron (Palestine), 134
Herman, Charles, 66
Hitti, Nassif, 87
Hizbullah, 9, 41, 75-6, 175
Honduras, 117
Hosseini, Ahmed, 117
Hourani, Albert, 4
Hudson, Michael C., 10
Human Rights Watch, 112
Huntington, Samuel, 43, 139, 178
Hussein, Saddam, 5, 9, 11, 20, 49, 125,
    131, 160, 164, 169, 175
Hussein I, King of Jordan (Hussein bin
    Talal), 86

İlhan, Suat, 153-5
Imishli (Azerbaijan), 110, 112
Indonesia, 132, 145, 166
information and communications
    technology (ICT), 1, 5, 6, 10, 43, 45,
    52, 56, 127, 132, 135, 137, 139, 166-
    8, 170, 173-4, 177-8
  direct broadcast satellite TV, 127,
    132-3, 137, 139, 171, 175
    al-Jazira. See entry above
  Arab Radio and Television
    Network, 132
  CNN, 133
  MED-TV, 139
  Middle East Broadcasting Centre,
    132, 139
  Orbit, 133
  internet, 132, 135-9, 141, 170-1, 175
  telephone use, 135-6

Innenpolitik, 81, 88-9
inter-governmental organizations, 166
Iran, 2-3, 6, 9, 11, 19-22, 24, 36-43, 49,
    52-4, 56, 65, 70-8, 87, 96, 105-18,
    141-2, 164, 166, 169, 174
  and Europe, 73
  and Saudi Arabia, 70, 72, 77
  and United States, 70
  Article 48, 112
  Bureau of Aliens and Foreign
    Immigrant Affairs, 111-13, 115-
    18
  conservative movement, 74, 76-7
  Islamic Revolution (1979), 20, 39,
    70, 76, 108, 131, 150, 168, 175
  Khorasan, 107-8
  Ministry of Interior, 109, 111-12, 115
  minorities
    Azeri, 107, 110
    Hazara, 111
    Sunni, 107
  Parliamentary Commission for
    National Security and Foreign
    Affairs, 107
  reform movement, 70, 73, 76, 78
  war with Iraq (1980-1988), 19-20, 39,
    73, 96, 111, 118, 164
Iraq, 5-9, 11, 18, 20, 22, 39, 41-2, 44-6,
    49, 72-5, 77-8, 86, 92, 94-6, 125-6,
    130, 132-4, 137, 143, 151, 160, 164,
    166, 168, 171, 174-7
  invasion of Kuwait (1990-91), 18
  Iraqi Governing Council, 9
  war with Iran (1980-1988), 19-20, 39,
    73, 96, 111, 118, 164
Islam, 1, 9, 20, 39-40, 43-4, 46, 78, 126,
    131, 133-4, 140-4, 151, 156, 168-9,
    172, 174-5, 178
  militant, 5, 7, 11, 20, 41, 46, 75, 77,
    137, 141, 152, 154, 166, 170-1,
    175-6, 178
  Shi'a, 9, 20, 39-40, 111, 168-9, 174-5
  status of women, 11
  Sunni, 40, 107, 168-9
  umma, 168-9
Islamic Jihad, 9, 75
Israel, 2, 4, 8-10, 19-22, 36-43, 45, 50,
    53-4, 56, 65, 71, 86, 96, 125-35, 137,
    144-5, 149-51, 164-5, 168, 172-3,
    175, 178
  Likud party, 126

Jacobsen, Karen, 109
Japan, 36-8, 51-4, 56
Jerusalem, 87, 127, 144
Johnson, Lyndon B., 150
Jordan, 4, 20, 22, 40, 42, 45, 82, 86, 92,
    94-5, 129-31, 133, 135, 139-42, 168,
    171
jus sanguinis, 108
jus soli, 108

Kagan, Robert, 164, 167, 176
Kaplan, Morton, 30, 34
Karataş, Şaban, 157
Kashmir, 6, 166
Kerr, Malcolm, 36, 172
Khamenei, Ayatollah (Ali Khameini), 76
Khatami, Mohammad, 70, 73-4, 117
    détente with US, 70
Khomeini, Ayatollah (Ruhollah
    Khomeini), 75, 175
Kirkuk (Iraq), 8-9
Konrad Adenauer Foundation, 156
Korany, Baghat, 21, 83, 164
Kurds, 6, 8-9, 39-40, 139, 150-2, 154-6,
    158, 160, 168
    Sheikh Said rebellion, 152
Kuwait, 5, 8, 39, 42, 91, 132-3, 135, 137,
    139, 140-2, 169, 175

Ladin, bin, Sa'd, 9
Ladin, bin, Usama, 5, 6, 9, 131, 174
Latin America, 42-3, 46, 92, 132, 135-6,
    144, 169
Lausanne Treaty (1923), 157
Lawson, Fred, 85
League of Arab States, 7-8, 17, 19, 130,
    178
Lebanon, 6, 20, 40, 42, 45-6, 50, 83, 86-
    7, 91, 94, 96, 131-3, 135-7, 139-42,
    167, 169, 171, 175
    civil war (1975-76), 83, 85, 96
Lebow, Richard, 69-71, 73, 76
Liberal Thought Association, 156
Libya, 92, 171

Machiavelli, Niccolò, 178
Makiki refugee camp (Afghanistan), 112
Malaysia, 166
Mandaville, Peter, 166
Manisalı, Erol, 154
Maronite Christians, 83, 168

Marxist Workers' Party, 154, 157
Mashad (Iran), 112
Mattar, Gamil, 36
McAdam, Douglas, 174
Mecca (Saudi Arabia), 5, 139
Medina (Saudi Arabia), 5
Menemen Case, 152
Mexico, 52
MHP (Nationalist Movement Party), 157
Miller, Benjamin, 23, 50
Misak-I Milli (Nationalist Pact), 150
Mojahedin-e Khalq, 10
'Montréal school', 81, 163-4
Morgenthau, Hans, 20
Morocco, 45, 94, 128, 130, 133, 135,
    137, 139-42, 169, 171
Mousa, 'Amr, 7
Muasher, Marwan, 130
Mubarak, Husni, 8, 131, 174
Muslim Brotherhood, 95

Nagorno Karabakh, conflict in (1993),
    105, 110
Najaf (Iraq), 175
Nasser, Jamal 'Abdel, 4, 6, 19-20, 22,
    24, 86-7, 172
nationalism, 72, 154-5
neopatrimonialism, 1, 92-4
New York (USA), 126
New Zealand, 56
Noble, Paul, 2-3, 6, 15-21, 23-4, 78, 81,
    125, 163, 165
non-governmental organizations, 106,
    109, 115-18, 156, 158, 165-6, 172
North America, 55
North Atlantic Treaty Organisation, 9
Northern Alliance, 112
Norton, Richard, 172
Nye, Joseph, 31

Öcalan, Abdullah, 157
Oceania, 38, 55-6
oil, 1, 8, 18, 21-2, 24, 39-40, 46, 51-2,
    72, 75, 77, 131, 165, 171-3
omnibalancing theory, 84
Organization for Economic Co-operation
    and Development, 136
Organization of the Islamic Conference,
    174
Organization of the Petroleum Exporting
    Countries, 70-2, 76

embargo (1973-74), 22, 46
Ottoman Empire, 1, 149-51, 155
   Pax Islamica, 177
Özcan, Ali, 154
Özdağ, Ümit, 153-4

Pahlavi, Reza, 70, 107
Pakistan, 110, 166
Palestine, 4-6, 8, 10, 18-20, 22, 40-4, 50,
   75, 83, 86, 94-6, 125-31, 133-7, 142,
   143-4, 149, 164-5, 169, 171, 174-5
   accommodation of Israel, 65
pan-Arabism, 1, 4, 17-18, 20, 24, 42-3,
   86-7, 105, 125, 137-8, 166, 168, 172
pan-Islamism, 4, 20, 75, 105, 168, 170
paradigms
   bureaucratic theory, 69-70, 83, 109,
      115, 118
   constructivism, 3, 31, 35, 43, 45, 82,
      85-7, 106, 166-9
   democratic peace theory, 45, 74, 89
   dependency theory, 10, 21, 23, 31,
      34, 47-9, 52, 166, 171, 177
      asymmetric interdependence, 21-3
   idiosyncratic theory, 3, 82-4, 87, 89
   institutionalism, 91, 106, 166
      international refugee regime, 3,
         106
   liberalism, 31, 35, 43, 45-7, 172
   Marxism, 31, 35, 85
   neo-liberalism, 69, 71
   neo-realism, 3, 6, 16, 18, 82-5, 87-90,
      93, 95
   prospect theory, 69, 71, 74, 76
   realism, 3-4, 6, 16, 18, 20, 30, 35, 69,
      71-2, 82-3, 87-8, 96, 126, 145,
      153, 163-5, 172-3, 176-7
   world system theory, 31
patrimonialism, 169
Philippines, 166
PKK (Kurdistan Workers' Party), 157-
   60, 163
political liberalization, 6, 22, 46, 70-1,
   73-4, 151-3, 158-9, 171-2, 176
Przeworski, Adam, 93

Qadafi, al-, Mu'ammar, 7, 131
Qaradawi, Shaykh, 175
Qatar, 133, 135
Qom (Iran), 177

Rabat (Morocco), 128
Rafsanjani, Hashemi, 70-4, 76, 110
   'Good Neighbour' policy, 70-1, 73
Ramazani, Rouholla K., 36, 74
Ramezanzadeh, Abdollah, 108
realpolitik, 10, 130, 156
refugees
   Afghan, 3, 105-17
   Azerbaijani, 3, 105-7, 109-12, 114,
      118
   increase in crime due to, 107-8
   Iraqi, 105
   Palestinian, 129, 137
   permissive state policy towards, 110,
      114, 118
   preventive state policy towards, 106,
      110, 112, 114, 118
   refugee warriors, 106
regime autonomy, 3, 69, 81-5, 87-8, 91,
   93-4, 96
regime security, 69, 73, 75-8, 107, 126,
   130, 151-2, 160
regional challengers, 65-7, 70
regional economic integration, 23-4, 31,
   34, 77
   Israel, 24
Rice, Condoleeza, 176
Ripsman, Norrin, 89-94
Rizvi, Gowher, 36
Roman Empire, 153, 176
   Pax Romana, 177
Romano, David, 139
Rose, Gideon, 88
Rowe, Paul, 139
Ruggie, John, 23, 31
Russia, 10, 37-8, 49, 52-3

Sadak, Selim, 161
Sadat, Anwar, 71, 86-7, 174
Salloukh, Bassel F., 3
Saudi Arabia, 3, 5-8, 18, 20, 22, 39-40,
   42, 45, 50, 54, 65, 70-5, 77-8, 130-5,
   139-42, 144-5, 169-71, 175
   and United States, 72
Schmitter, Philippe, 91-2
Second World War, 19-21, 89-90, 164,
   171-3, 175
separatism, 68
September 11th attacks, 1, 5, 77, 126,
   131, 137, 166, 168, 170, 176

Serbest Firka (Free Party), 152
Sèvres, Treaty of (1920), 153, 155
Shah, the, *See* Reza Pahlavi
Sharm el-Shaykh summit, 7
Sharon, Ariel, 10, 126-7
Singer, David, 30
social movements, 1, 7, 81, 84, 92-5,
    107, 165, 167, 170, 176
South America, 37-8, 53-6
sovereignty, 2, 4, 16-18, 20-1, 75, 109,
    153-4, 158
Spiegel, Steven, 36
state capacity, 3, 16, 18, 21, 69, 106,
    109-10, 114-16, 118-19, 125-7, 137,
    164
state-society relations, 3, 16, 46, 81-7,
    89, 91-4, 96, 125
Stein, Janet, 70-1, 76
Sudan, 40, 46, 75, 92, 136, 144, 168
Syria, 3, 8-9, 22, 39-42, 45, 71, 82-3, 85-
    6, 92, 94-6, 128, 133, 169, 171, 175
    accommodation of Israel, 65
    Ba'th Party, 83, 85, 94-5, 175
    intervention in Lebanon (1976), 83,
        85, 96
Syrian Social National Party, 175
systems
    dominant, 2, 16, 29-30, 32, 35-6, 48-52
        intrusive, 6, 21, 23, 36, 39, 49, 58
    global, 2, 21-3, 29, 35-6, 52, 68
    regional, 16, 20-1, 23, 32, 34-6, 39,
        50, 68
        Arab, 2, 4-5, 7-8, 16, 18-20, 40,
            125, 163
        Middle Eastern, 1, 8, 21, 23, 29,
            36, 40
    sub-regional, 2-3, 32
        Persian Gulf, 10, 71-2, 74-5, 78
    international, 31, 47
    global, 69
    regional, 69

Taliban, 75, 110-12, 115, 174, 176
Telhami, Shibley, 134, 144
Temple Mount (Jerusalem), 127
Terakki-Perver Cumhuriyet Firkasi
    (Progressive and Republican Party),
    152
terrorism, 5, 7, 9-10, 44, 126, 131, 164,
    167, 173, 176-8
Thucydides, 164, 178

Tunbs, Greater and Lesser (Persian
    Gulf), 72
Tunisia, 45, 92, 130, 171
Turkey, 2, 6-9, 11, 24, 36-41, 43, 45, 53-
    4, 56, 85, 139, 142, 149-60, 168, 178
    Atatürkism, 154-5, 157
    minorities, 157-8
    relations with Greece, 153-4
    Republic (1920-Present), 152, 159
Turkish Economic and Social Studies
    Foundation (TESEV), 157
Turkish Industrialists' and
    Businessmen's Association, 155,
    157-8

Union of Soviet Socialist Republics, 71,
    171-3, 175
    accommodation of US, 71
    invasion of Afghanistan (1979-89), 150
United Arab Emirates, 72, 132, 136, 142
United Arab Republic, 86
United Kingdom, 36-7, 39, 89-90, 95-6,
    142-3, 177, 179
    Pax Britannica, 177
United Nations, 9-10, 22, 106, 125
    High Commission for Refugees, 106,
        118, 111-19
United States of America, 1, 5, 7-10, 22,
    36-8, 41, 49-52, 65, 67, 69-70, 72-8,
    91-2, 98, 126-31 133-7, 140-5, 150,
    160, 164-73, 175-8
    accommodation with USSR, 71
    and Israel, 22, 50
    Commission on Refugees (USCR),
        105, 111, 113-14
    Pax Americana, 166, 179-80
    protection of GCC, 71
    'war on terrorism', 1, 5, 7, 126, 164-6
'Usbat al-Ansar, 6

variables
    distributional, 31, 42, 45, 58
    domestic, 3, 10, 16, 30-2, 34, 46-7,
        50, 57, 68-9, 73, 75, 77, 82, 84,
        88-9, 178
    economic, 1, 18, 22-4, 68-9, 72, 84,
        167-8, 166, 177
    ideological/identitive, 10, 17-18, 20-
        1, 31, 43, 58, 69, 73, 84-5, 105-6,
        108, 125, 127, 144-5, 150, 154,
        159, 164-6, 177

interactional, 30-1
positional, 2, 21, 23, 30, 34, 47, 57,
    59, 66, 68-9, 71-2, 77, 82, 96,
    106, 126, 152, 154
structural, 10, 23, 30-31, 42, 45, 58,
    84, 115, 177
textural, 31, 58
unit-level, 16, 88

Wallerstein, Immanuel, 31, 167
Walt, Stephen M., 84, 164
Waltz, Kenneth, 16-21, 30-2, 34, 57
Washington, DC (USA), 126
Washington Consensus, 22
weapons of mass destruction, 9, 41, 75,
    164, 167, 173, 176-7

Weinstein, Franklin, 87
Wendt, Alex, 31
West Bank (Palestine), 10, 128-9, 133-4,
    137
Western Sahara, 144
Wickham, Carrie, 174
World Food Programme, 117

Yazgan, Turan, 157
Yemen, 42, 46, 54, 169, 171

Zahedan (Iran), 108, 112
Zakaria, Fareed, 88-9, 91
Zana, Leyla, 161
Zartman, William, 66
Zetter, Roger, 111